Small-Town Restaurants in Virginia

Dip Dog in Marion

Kelsick Gardens in Gloucester

Napoleon's in Warrenton

JOHN F. BLAIR, PUBLISHER

Winston-Salem, North Carolina

L'Italia in Staunton

*The Lafayette in
Stanardsville*

Small-Town Restaurants in Virginia

Joanne M. Anderson

DESIGN BY DEBRA LONG HAMPTON
PRINTED AND BOUND BY R. R. DONNELLEY & SONS
PHOTOGRAPHS BY THE AUTHOR

Cover photographs clockwise from top left:
*Betty's Kitchen, Altavista; Old Chickahominy House, Williamsburg; The Home Place, Dinwiddie;
The Trellis Cafe, Restaurant & Grill, Williamsburg*

Library of Congress Cataloging-in-Publication Data
Anderson, Joanne M. 1949–
Small-town restaurants in Virginia / Joanne M. Anderson.
p.   cm.
Includes index.
ISBN 0-89587-211-0 (alk. paper)
1. Restaurants—Virginia—Guidebooks.   2. Virginia-Guidebooks.
I. Title.
TX907.3.V8A53   1998
641.59755—dc21   98–15963

Contents

Try Both next time in Skylz

Region 4
Northern Virginia

Region 5
Tidewater and Eastern Shore

Acknowledgments

This book came to fruition with the help of many special people. My parents, Bob and Betty Brown of Abingdon, have encouraged me throughout my life. I am particularly grateful to them for gathering restaurant information in southwestern Virginia and for their offers to travel around the state.

The support, love and tireless restaurant-hopping of my husband, John, made the whole adventure more exciting and fun.

My friends Lisa White and Sandy Bosworth also took to the back roads of Virginia with me.

Thanks go to Bea and Ted Ake for reading the book and offering constructive comments and to Jack and Jo Chamberlain for their advice on eating out in their home turf—the Northern Neck and the Eastern Shore.

I am grateful to Beth Obenshain, editor at the *Roanoke Times*, for publishing my first restaurant stories. I am also grateful to my friend and fellow author Allison Blake for her support and counsel.

I owe thanks to many of my guests at Clay Corner Inn—the Monks, the Reaveses, the Tauls, the Vicks and others—for offering suggestions and drawing maps on scraps of paper.

A hearty thank-you is in order for the restaurant owners, managers and servers who spent time answering my questions during unannounced visits or telephone calls and who gave me menus, tours and interesting tidbits about their lives, restaurants and towns.

A final thanks goes to my publisher for patience, guidance and professional assistance all along the way.

Introduction

This book is the result of my interest in, curiosity about and love affair with small towns and restaurants. Small towns because they're, well, small. People there look you in the eye and have a sense of community spirit. Restaurants because they have evolved from mere places to satisfy hunger to centers of social activity and entertainment. The people who run restaurants work hard, make sacrifices and strive to please every person who enters their doors. They are often as interesting as the restaurants themselves.

The establishments included in these pages run the gamut from no-diamond diners to five-diamond gourmet restaurants. The major criteria for inclusion were that a restaurant be clean, the staff be friendly and the food be good enough to eat.

I offer no critiques. What I found too greasy, too rare, too salty—too whatever—you might love. And what I consumed with delight you might consider unappetizing. I mention many dishes that I found to be delicious, but do so merely as someone expressing her personal taste, not as a food critic.

For the same reason I don't critique cuisine, I don't rate the restaurants with a system of stars, forks, crowns or anything else. I may think the service is slow on the same night you're enjoying a special anniversary dinner and wish to dine for the entire evening. I appreciate linens, candlelight and classical music, but I can also enjoy twirling on a stool at an old-time diner listening to local folks chat about whose milk froze on the stoop the previous night. You might not like the former, or you might squirm at the latter. Running a restaurant is not a simple job. In fairness to owners and managers, you should eat in a restaurant several times before drawing conclusions about food and service.

For the purposes of *Small-Town Restaurants in*

Virginia, a "small town" is an incorporated town, an independent city or a spot in the road with a United States Post Office and a population under 30,000. Of course, there's an exception to every rule, and I've made one for Charlottesville, which has a population of slightly more than 40,000. Restaurants not within corporate limits are listed under the closest town or under the town to which their mail is addressed. The restaurants on the Blue Ridge Parkway that I've included are listed under the parkway as if it were a town.

My original goal was to include 210 restaurants. I chose that number because the Commonwealth of Virginia turns 210 years old in 1998, the year of this book's publication. As it turned out, there were so many restaurants of interest that I easily exceeded that number.

I visited each of the restaurants included in this book. And I paid for all of my meals.

Some restaurants were recommended to me by patrons and townspeople. I found others thanks to information received from chambers of commerce and visitor centers. I discovered others by just driving around. A few restaurants you might expect to find are not included here. This may be because the restaurant was closed the day I was in the area. Or perhaps because I never got the word about it. Or perhaps because I'd already met my self-imposed limit of three restaurants per town. (In a few cases where restaurants listed with a particular town are actually outside the town boundaries, I've included more than three.)

I made every effort right up to the printing date to assure that the information presented here is accurate and current. However, restaurants change hands, serving schedules are adjusted and menu items disappear. You should call ahead to verify hours of operation whenever you're planning to visit a particular restaurant.

Whatever your taste in dining, I hope you'll find some restaurants here that you didn't know about before and that you'll find just plain interesting.

How to Use This Book

Small-Town Restaurants in Virginia is divided into five geographical regions—roughly the same ones used by the *Virginia Is for Lovers* travel guide and the Bed and Breakfast Association of Virginia. The only difference is that I've combined the Tidewater/Hampton Roads area with the Eastern Shore in a section I call "Tidewater and Eastern Shore." Region 1 covers the Southwest Blue Ridge Highlands; Region 2 features the Shenandoah Valley; Region 3 highlights Central Virginia; Region 4 covers Northern Virginia; and Region 5 features the Tidewater and Eastern Shore.

The towns are arranged geographically within each region, and the restaurants are covered in alphabetical order within each town. The towns are noted on regional maps at the beginning of each section. Indexes of towns and restaurants are at the end of the book.

For each restaurant, I provide basic information like

address, telephone number, meals served and price range. *Inexpensive* generally denotes breakfast under $5, lunch under $8 or dinner under $10. *Moderate* is used for restaurants where breakfast is $4 to $8, lunch is $6 to $12 or dinner is $10 to $20. *Expensive* restaurants are those where breakfast costs more than $8, lunch costs more than $10 or dinner costs more than $20.

Seasonal schedules are given for those establishments not open year-round. Reservations are mentioned only if they are required or recommended. In citing each restaurant's "style," I've tried to make the designations self-explanatory: "fine dining" is just that; "casual nice" means that a restaurant is upscale but informal; "resort" indicates that the establishment combines dining, lodging, entertainment and activities; "home-style" suggests that the restaurant is very casual; "family-style" indicates that it's appropriate for everyone; "diner" means that it has counter stools (perhaps in addition to booths and tables); "drive-in" means you can have food delivered to your car. "Full bar" means that all alcoholic beverages are served; it doesn't necessarily mean there's a bar with stools. I also provide a brief list of "superlatives." These may be outstanding features, dishes I observed or things for which the restaurant is widely known.

After the basic information for each restaurant, there's a brief write-up touching on things like the history of the town and the restaurant, the restaurant's atmosphere and decor and the variety of foods served throughout the day.

Your Comments and Suggestions, Please

Of course, one author can't know everything about Virginia's restaurant business. Let me hear from you — what you like about the book, what you don't like, what restaurants you'd like to see included in future editions. Your comments and suggestions might help keep this book accurate and ensure that it fairly represents those who work so hard at bringing good food to clean tables in small towns throughout the Commonwealth.

Please mail your letters to me in care of the publisher or send e-mail to jmawriter@aol.com.

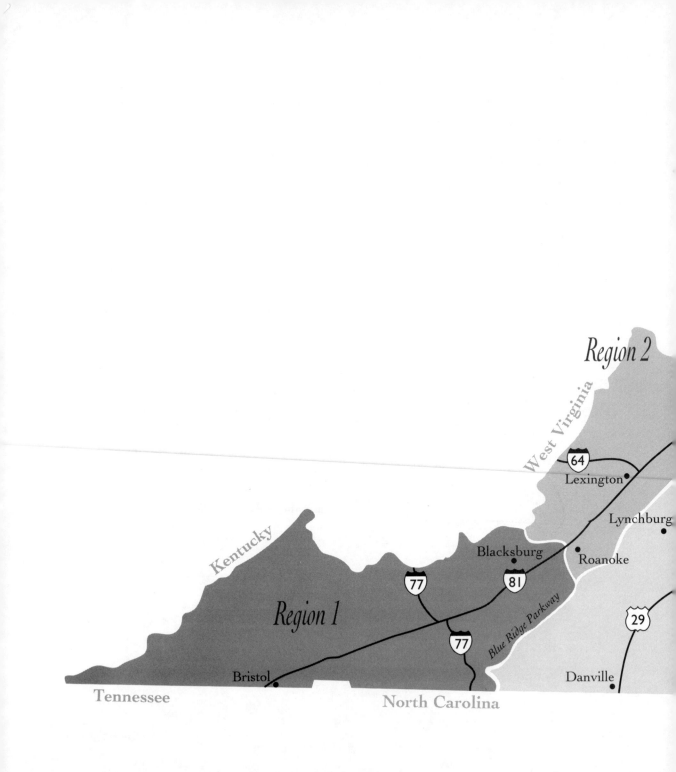

Region 2

West Virginia

64
Lexington

Lynchburg

Kentucky

Blacksburg

77

81

Roanoke

Region 1

Blue Ridge Parkway

29

77

Bristol

Danville

Tennessee

North Carolina

Winchester

Maryland

Arlington

Alexandria

Small-Town Restaurants in Virginia

Region 4

81

66

Harrisonburg

Fredericksburg

Blue Ridge Parkway

95

64

Charlottesville

Region 5

RICHMOND

64

Chesapeake Bay

Atlantic Ocean

Region 3

95

85

Norfolk

Virginia Beach

South Hill

17

Region 1

Region 1

Southwest Blue Ridge Highlands

Kentucky

Tennessee

North Carolina

Bluefield

Narrows
Pearisburg
Mountain Lake
Blacksburg
Ironto
Radford
Dublin
Christiansburg
Pulaski
Floyd

Tazewell

Lebanon
Saltville
Marion
Wytheville
Hillsville

Glade Spring
Abingdon

Gate City
Galax
Fancy Gap

Blue Ridge Parkway

77

81

77

Southwestern Virginia was shaped by pioneers, farmers, miners and rugged individuals like Daniel Boone, who blazed the Wilderness Trail through the New River Valley.

Half a million acres of national forest in this region offer wilderness for hiking, camping, exploring, hunting and fishing. The area is also home to the highest mountain in the state, Mount Rogers, which rises more than 5,700 feet above sea level. And several miles of the 2,000-plus mile Appalachian Trail are located here.

Many of the small towns in the western part of the region owe their existence to the coal-mining industry, and small museums and markers pay tribute to this heritage. Other towns developed as trading posts or train depots. Some have flourished while others floundered, but each has a unique story to tell.

Campus Drive-In

Campus Drive-In

U.S. 23 BUSINESS / GATE CITY, VA 24251
(540) 386-3702

Style	Drive-in
Meals	Breakfast, lunch and dinner, Monday through Saturday
Price Range	Inexpensive
Superlatives	A colorful sign outside reads, "Great old-fashioned hamburgers and hot dogs fixed to your liking."

*G*ate City is the gateway to the Smoky Mountains. It's been the county seat since 1815, when it was called Winfield for General Winfield Scott. It was later renamed Gate City for its location in Moccasin Gap, through which the Wilderness Road went west. It's a nice town—not fancy but friendly.

Walking into the Campus Drive-In is like stepping into an old friend's place. People look your way. Some of them smile or nod as if to say, "Glad you walked in. Take a load off your feet."

If the customers aren't running the jukebox, the waitresses probably are, and they're not stingy with their quarters. I approached to see what they stocked for music, and a server who had just dropped in her money but not made a selection asked, "What do you want to hear?"

Of course, you don't have to come in. You can stay in your car and sound your horn for curb service.

The restaurant was built by Darrell Dougherty in 1955. It's named the Campus Drive-In because it's right down the street from the high school. The walls are slate-blue. Fluorescent fixtures and ceiling fans with lights illuminate the place when the sun isn't pouring in the front windows.

Seven swivel stools, eight booths and half a dozen or so tables provide seating. Behind the counter is an open window to the kitchen with a wire strung across it. The orders are clipped up here with wooden clothespins. The system reminded me a little of the restaurant in *Frankie and Johnnie*, with Michelle Pfeiffer and Al Pacino.

In addition to the country ham so popular in Virginia, the Campus Drive-In has city ham at breakfast. According to Debra Dougherty, who owns the restaurant with her husband, Allen (son of founder Darrell), city ham is regular smoked ham, while country ham—which they sell a lot more of—is the salt-cured version.

The hamburgers are good, and the chicken tenders are the least greasy fried chicken pieces I've had. The breading is peppery but not too hot. French fries, onion rings, tater tots, fried mushrooms, cheese sticks—all that stuff is here, too.

Dinners like pork barbecue, flounder, popcorn shrimp, catfish and chicken tenderloins come with french fries, slaw and rolls. You can finish any meal with pie, cake (if there's any left), a banana split, a sundae or hot fudge cake.

Then you can leave, and nod to the others on your way out.

Hob-Nob Drive-In

DANIEL BOONE HIGHWAY (OLD U.S. 23)
GATE CITY, VA 24251
(540) 452-4538

Style	Drive-in
Meals	Lunch and dinner, Tuesday through Saturday
Price Range	Inexpensive
Superlatives	Ostrich burgers, milk shakes

Someone told me to bear left in town and "just drive for a while." Once I passed the new highway about a mile out, I wondered if there could be a real place to eat out here.

Then I spotted it on the right, a small, low, reddish building with a sign that seemed extremely short—at least in these days of 50- to 70-foot highway posts. It was packed when I drove in at 5:30. The cars included a new Jeep Cherokee, a Lexus, a Ford Explorer, a mix of mid-size Buicks and Oldsmobiles and a few pickup trucks and small imports.

The Hob-Nob is basically red, black and cream with fluorescent lighting. The bright, clean windows have miniblinds, and there's an aura of friendly banter among the tables.

Ten booths and three or four tables with dark red vinyl chairs make up the inside eating area. Of course, it's a drive-in, so you can take your meal out or eat in your car—just honk and wait and you'll be tended to.

Built in 1953, this small restaurant got its name because it quickly became a popular place to eat and chat with neighbors or folks passing through.

In the 1970s, the new, improved, four-lane U.S. 23 replaced the old road, putting the Hob-Nob out of sight from travelers. A young couple who met while working here as kids took over the restaurant for several years before moving on to open their own. Once again, the Hob-Nob's demise seemed imminent. But

Hob-Nob Drive-In

along came a grandson of the original owner, who purchased it and continues to operate it.

Biscuits are served anytime. You can order them with gravy "while it lasts." Pancakes are around 60 cents each—just order however many you want. Eggs, ham and breaded steak are also available.

The sandwiches and burgers are run-of-the-mill—except for the ostrich burger, which isn't on the menu but is available some of the time. Ostrich farming is gaining popularity. Only time will tell if it's fad or fortune.

Besides the popular Neapolitan flavors for milk shakes, you can get cherry, raspberry and peanut butter. Dinners include potato, slaw and roll. And for 99 cents, you can make a trip to the salad bar. Country ham, chicken, flounder, oysters, shrimp and catfish are among the entree choices.

If you can find a parking place, the Hob-Nob deserves your business if for no other reason than to honor its defiance in the face of progress.

Alison's

Alison's

Style	Family-style
Meals	Lunch and dinner, Monday through Saturday
Price Range	Moderate
Superlatives	Ribs, baked potato soup
Extras	Wine and beer

*E*very small town likes to find something unique about itself to promote. Abingdon's claim lies in being the oldest incorporated town on a stream that flows to the Mississippi River. It's also the home of the State Theatre of Virginia—the Barter Theatre—and the site of the popular Virginia Highlands Festival, held each August. Three centuries of well-maintained buildings are featured in its charming, 20-block historic district.

Many Abingdon visitors make their way to Alison's. If you get here early, you might get a covered parking place. There used to be a drive-in restaurant in the back, and the carport-style roof is still in place. But the key word here is *early*. Alison's is very popular, and it's just a mile north of Exit 13 off I-81.

Alison Gill and her husband, Marvin, opened the restaurant in October 1994. They know lots of their customers by name. And to their credit, staff turnover is very low.

The interior is blue and white across the front and yellow and white in the little room at the back. The little room has flowers and vines painted on the walls, and some of the chairs have a motley mix of paints. Some flower prints and pepper and tomato posters hang on the walls. The floors are classic white and black tiles. The place is bright, simple, artistic.

Before you even order lunch, a small basket of bread with an herb cream cheese is delivered to your table. Around 10 entree salads, a variety of burgers, more than a dozen sandwiches and eight or nine lunch platters are offered. The daily specials might be grilled trout on vegetables topped with Creole sauce and served with fries, or it might be Cajun barbecued chicken breast, bacon and cheese on a bun. There's always a quiche and a soup.

The dinner menu includes appetizers, burgers, sandwiches, pasta, stir-fry, grilled specialties and seafood. The "Triple Delight Stir-Fry" has lobster, beef, scallops, broccoli, water chestnuts, peppers and scallions. The seafood entrees include a fresh catch, fried shrimp, crab legs and a mixed seafood platter. Filet mignon, New York strip, teriyaki chicken and a half or full rack of ribs are some of the other choices. Follow any of this with homemade peach or blackberry cobbler and you'll have one fine meal.

The second key word at Alison's is *value*. The portions are generous, the food delicious and the price reasonable.

A couple of years after Alison's was created, the Gills and chef Jack Barrow opened The Peppermill Restaurant, located across the street closer to town. It's a bit more upscale and pricey but is still comfortably affordable. The Peppermill serves lunch Monday through Saturday and dinner Tuesday through Saturday. On Sunday, the staff takes a well-earned day off.

The Starving Artist

134 WALL STREET / ABINGDON, VA 24212
(540) 628-8445

Style	Cafe
Meals	Lunch, Monday through Saturday; dinner, Tuesday through Saturday
Price Range	Moderate/Expensive
Superlatives	Vegetarian entrees, steak, pasta dishes
Extras	Wine and beer

When artist Shawn Crookshank finished college, he found there wasn't much work for art majors in his hometown of Abingdon. So he and his wife, Kim, bought a little restaurant in 1985, renovated it and opened The Starving Artist. The name honors all the artists who make a living doing restaurant work.

The art exhibit in the restaurant is changed monthly and often showcases unknown artists. The walls are white on the top with old pine boards on the bottom. Dark green vinyl tablecloths are dressed up with white linen napkins and fresh flowers. The carpeting and chair pads are also dark green.

Lunch appetizers range from shrimp cocktail and smoked Norwegian salmon to nachos and Cajun fries. Hot croissants, French onion soup and a soup du jour are also offered. The salads can go with a sandwich or constitute a light lunch by themselves. The chicken, tuna and shrimp salad may fit the latter category.

The 20 or so sandwiches are named for artists. The Salvador Dali is billed as a surrealist tuna melt. The Jackson Pollock is piled high with thinly sliced roast beef dripping with Monterey Jack cheese. Auguste Renoir, Henri Matisse, Georgia O'Keeffe, James Joyce, Andy Warhol, Ansel Adams—they're all represented. The "Expressionist Sandwich" is yours to create from a list of meats, cheeses and breads.

Dinner appetizers include sea scallops pesto, oysters Rockefeller and escargots. Pasta lovers and vegetarians will find salmon fettuccine, pasta primavera, vegetable stir-fry and other entrees. Maryland-style crab cakes, scallops au gratin, filet Oscar, Cajun prime rib, Cajun shrimp, Delmonico steak, filet mignon, lemon chicken and other seafood and beef choices are also offered.

Desserts like raspberry walnut torte, Kentucky Derby pie, coconut cream pie and banana cream pie are homemade at The Starving Artist.

ABINGDON

The Tavern

222 EAST MAIN STREET / ABINGDON, VA 24210
(540) 628-1118

Style	Casual nice
Meals	Lunch, Monday through Saturday; dinner, seven days a week
Price Range	Moderate/Expensive

Superlatives	Historic atmosphere, stuffed filet mignon
Extras	Full bar

A few years before the first of earth's fellow planets was discovered, and almost a century before Alexander Graham Bell patented his telephone, The Tavern was open for business.

There's no record that George Washington slept here, but Henry Clay, King Louis Philippe and Andrew Jackson reportedly did. And not a lot has changed in the interior since their visits.

Sure, there are some new support beams, and the fireplaces have been converted to gas, but as soon as you set foot on the brick floor behind the old wooden door, you'll be enveloped in the historical spirit of the place. Take the arm of a friend on your way upstairs if you're predisposed to vertigo. There's quite a pitch to floors this old. But the tilt only adds to the restaurant's authenticity and warm intimacy.

The building has a colorful past. If only these walls could talk! The first post office west of the Blue Ridge was housed in the east wing; the original mail slot is still visible from the street. The building has served as a bank, a bakery, a general store, a cabinet shop, a barbershop, a private residence and an antique shop.

Today, The Tavern operates under the watchful eyes of Max and Kathy Hermann, both United States Air Force veterans. Max is a native of Germany, and his influence can be found in the menu's continental touches. Kathy is a native of Damascus—the one in Virginia.

The lunch fare ranges from simple to special. *Simple* includes a veggie-cheese melt, smoked turkey club, and the "Tavern Burger." *Special* encompasses things like spinach, bacon, shrimp and provolone salad and a mini quiche plate with three delightful varieties.

The wine list spans the globe, with selections from Virginia, California, Washington, France, Germany and Australia. There's a selection of imported beers, including a dessert beer served in a chilled wineglass. You can also purchase port or a cigar. And you may smoke the cigar in the smoking section.

Dinners with a German bent include Wiener schnitzel and "Kasseler Rippchen." From Cajun country, there's jambalaya. From our own waters, there's trout. Other tempting entrees showcase lamb, steak, shrimp, chicken and salmon.

So many patrons requested to purchase the food and beverages at The Tavern for home use that Max and Kathy opened an international grocery store in town near the entrance to the Creeper Trail. More than 200 imported beers, wine, cheese, chocolate, prime meats and exotic seasonings are among the inventory.

So if good weather beckons and you can't stand staying indoors, rent a couple of bikes at the gourmet shop, carry out some sandwiches and treats and head for one of life's greatest simple pleasures, a picnic.

The Old Mill

118 MILL STREET / LEBANON, VA 24266
(540) 889-4310

Style	Family-style
Meals	Lunch and dinner, Monday through Saturday
Price Range	Moderate
Superlatives	Prime rib, pork barbecue sandwich, meatloaf
Extras	Wine and beer

Solomon's temple in ancient Jerusalem was built from the cedars of Lebanon. When this Virginia town was settled, it was named for the biblical event brought to mind by the wild cedar trees growing here. Lebanon is the county seat of Russell County. When the courthouse burned in 1872, thrifty local residents salvaged much of the rubble and used it to build a new one.

One of the town's old mills, constructed around 1918, was a ramshackle building with a rickety porch and a tin roof at the time it was purchased and turned into a restaurant. Touches from the old days remain. Some of the beams in the upstairs dining room continue right through the walls and across the whole building. Inside the front door is a staircase that starts into the air, then goes nowhere. Bands once played on the platform at the top of the steps. When the owners stopped having live music and remodeled the downstairs, they removed the bottom steps but saw no reason to take away the middle. Anyway, it's a conversation piece.

The lunch features "Old Mill Barbecue," the "Old Mill Burger," a Reuben, a turkey club, a BLT, a Monte Cristo and other popular stuff.

The Old Mill's steaks are a big draw. New York strip, rib-eye and filet mignon are charbroiled to your liking, with or without Cajun spices. Prime rib is offered on Friday and Saturday evenings. And there's always a wide range of seafood entrees, as well as pork tenderloin and ground steak.

You can finish your meal with a hot fudge brownie or with strawberry shortcake in the summer. Or you can try a "Butterscotch Wonder," a five-layer dessert you won't find anywhere else.

GLADE SPRING

The Swiss Inn
33361 LEE HIGHWAY (EXIT 29 OFF I-81)
GLADE SPRING, VA 24340
(540) 429-5191

Style	Fine dining
Meals	Dinner, Monday through Saturday. Reservations are recommended.
Price Range	Moderate/Expensive
Superlatives	Schnitzel, pastries
Extras	Full bar

*I*n this country house built around 1835, Emil and Angela Waldis have created an upscale atmosphere that is surpassed only by their restaurant's classic cuisine and luscious pastries.

He is Swiss and she is Italian. Back in 1961, they agreed that a two-year adventure in North America would be exciting and headed for Canada. Emil had apprenticed to be a chef at some of the finest European restaurants, so finding work wasn't difficult.

After two years, they went to see New York, where Emil spent six years as pastry chef at the Four Seasons. Next, he helped open a restaurant in Roanoke. Then he started Emil's in Lynchburg in 1971. Though he retired in 1984, the couple's adventurous spirit just wouldn't go away. They started another restaurant— this one in Georgia—and then another one. And Emil retired again.

Along the way, they purchased a restaurant in Glade Spring, Virginia—a restaurant that five managers in a row hadn't been able to make successful. So guess who's out of retirement again?

And—as if a gourmet restaurant isn't enough—Emil and Angela added a 32-room motel in 1993.

The dining rooms—all five of them—are an inviting blend of rustic comfort and casual elegance. The linens, the candlelight and the soft music quiet your mind, and the complimentary spiral cheese sticks tease your palate for what's to come.

The menu offers abundant choices. A Swiss specialty, available as an appetizer for two or an entree for two, is cheese fondue. Sauerbraten, roast tenderloin of pork and veal Zurich are on the "Old World Favorites" list. Among the fowl entrees are mesquite-smoked duckling and Jamaican chicken. A variety of seafood comes blackened, broiled or baked. The pecan-crusted mountain trout is delicious.

Emil's pastries are exquisite both to look at and to savor. Everything is made from scratch and melts in your mouth. Save room for the chocolate velvet, the Black Forest cake, the lemon curd torte or the walnut tart.

Since Glade Spring isn't close to much of anything, you might as well book a night here and enjoy the alpine atmosphere and the continental breakfast. Emil and Angela are the warmest of hosts and the kindest of people. And, as you can tell, their adventure in North America hasn't ended.

Brenda's Hub

89 SOUTH MAIN STREET / GALAX, VA 24333
(540) 236-6701

Style	Home-style
Meals	Breakfast, lunch and dinner, seven days a week
Price Range	Inexpensive
Superlatives	Chicken and dumplings, chicken livers, homemade cobblers

*K*nown as the "Home of Mountain Music," Galax has hosted the annual Old Fiddler's Convention since 1935. The town's name comes from a plant common on local mountainsides. The galax plant's waxy, heart-shaped leaves are a rich, deep green in summer and bronze in winter. Used by florists all over the country in fresh and dried arrangements, they're an integral part of the town's economy.

Speaking of names, the word *hub* once referred solely to the center of a wheel. Nowadays, it's taken on the broader meaning of a center of activity. This restaurant has been an unofficial hub since it opened as a drive-in restaurant for teens in the 1950s. Since August 1996, it's been Brenda's Hub.

Helen Smith has seen the changes. She waitressed the first night the original restaurant opened—just that one night to help out the owner. About 40 years later, she returned to waitressing and has been back about four years now.

Brenda's is a simple place with a few Indian prints for sale. The big front windows have burgundy tab curtains with a gold fleur-de-lis print. The back room has wood paneling with a contemporary pastel border. The whole place can probably hold around 60 to 70 people.

Breakfast starts early. You can get just about any combination of eggs, ham, sausage, Canadian bacon, biscuits, grits, omelets and hot cakes you want.

Brenda's Hub

The "Hub Club" is a popular lunch sandwich. Burgers, chicken, baked ham, barbecue, tuna salad, chicken salad, and roast beef and turkey sandwiches are also served, as are assorted soups and salads.

Roast beef, turkey, rib-eye steak, veal cutlets, chicken, pork chops, flounder, shrimp, oysters and a seafood plate are among the choices at dinner.

It's reasonable, it's folksy and it's a true hub in this town. And according to Helen, Brenda's serves "real" food—"what the folks are raised on around here."

FANCY GAP

Mountain Top Restaurant

U.S. 52 / FANCY GAP, VA 24328
(540) 728-9196

Style	Home-style
Meals	Breakfast, lunch and dinner, seven days a week
Price Range	Inexpensive
Superlatives	Breakfast and dinner buffets, home made fruit cobblers and cakes

The Mountain Top is not only reminiscent of 1950s roadside restaurants with a motel, it really is one. Run by Tommy Phillips and his daughter Teresa, the 23-unit motel was built by Tommy's dad in 1953. The restaurant followed in 1959. Tommy's grandparents Ezra and Nora Phillips built and operated a restaurant with cabins a couple miles down the mountain.

Breakfast was given a good review by a couple from Charlotte, North Carolina, I met in the parking lot. They said they often stop in the morning on their way to visit their daughter in Virginia. Hot cakes and eggs are the breakfast mainstays, served with salt-cured country ham, tenderized cured ham, sausage or bacon.

At lunch, sandwiches—the names of which all end with *deluxe*—come with french fries, tater tots or hash browns. Chicken, barbecue, BLTs and hamburgers are among the choices. Spaghetti and some side orders are also available.

Dinner comes with potatoes and rolls. The Mountain Top offers the usual home-style meals—fried chicken, liver and onions, breaded veal, country ham and chicken Parmesan. Seafood platters and steaks are available, as is a buffet featuring meats, vegetables and salad.

Country ham is a special item here. You can get it at any meal and even buy a whole one to take home.

Speaking of buying things, there's a bookcase in the center of the right-hand dining area with an eclectic collection of items for sale—plastic Corvettes, local crafts, jams, jellies, some little dolls and a covered wagon perhaps a foot long. For the practical-minded, there are thermal socks, flashlight batteries and sweatshirts.

One thing you really should buy, however, is a slice of homemade cake or a dish of fruit cobbler.

The Burgundy House

HICKORY HILLS SHOPPING CENTER / U.S. 58
HILLSVILLE, VA 24343
(540) 728-2923

Style	Family-style
Meals	Lunch, Thursday through Tuesday; dinner, Thursday, Friday, Saturday, Monday and Tuesday
Price Range	Inexpensive/Moderate
Superlatives	Baked goods, soups, steaks, sauces
Extras	Wine and beer

*T*his town of around 2,000 became the county seat shortly after Carroll County was formed in 1842. Charles Carroll was the only surviving signer of the Declaration of Independence when the county was named for him. The name Hillsville might well have come from the area's rolling hills.

Located in the corner of a strip shopping center two miles from Exit 14 off I-77, The Burgundy House is a pleasant surprise in a part of the state not particularly noted for its dining experiences. It was established in 1993 by Bill and Kathy Quesenberry, who moved to Hillsville after finding the restaurant business in Patrick County to be too seasonal.

The Burgundy House

The warm, inviting interior is mostly brown and burgundy. One dining room has booths on the edge and tables in the middle; some of the breads and cookies made at the in-house bakery are showcased in the center of the room. A second dining room is a bit classier, with burgundy linen tablecloths, white napkins, Appalachian art and exquisite furniture pieces designed and built by Kathy's mother, Susie Shelor.

The restaurant offers burgers, sandwiches, salads, plate lunches and special plate lunches. In the plate lunch category are fried chicken, barbecued chicken, country ham and hamburger steak and gravy. Special plate lunches include spaghetti with meat sauce or marinara and rib-eye steak.

Dinner starts just the way I like it to—with a small, complimentary appetizer of home-baked bread, fruit and cheese. Entrees come with a garden salad and either a baked potato, rice or steak fries. You may choose from mesquite-grilled chicken, chopped steak, rib-eye steak, filet mignon, pork chops, eggplant Parmesan, shrimp scampi and yellowfin tuna steak.

The wine list includes a German white, a Virginia Riesling, a Cabernet Sauvignon, a Gamay Beaujolais and a few others. Beers include Beck's, Moosehead and Coors. Alcohol is not served on Sundays, and there's a limit of three per person.

Like the breads, the desserts are made in the bakery. The fruit cobblers, brownies, cookies and cheesecake are great.

The Burgundy House is a down-home kind of place with a touch of fine dining, some great baking and good value.

Peking Palace

Peking Palace

U.S. 58 / HILLSVILLE, VA 24343
(540) 728-5539

Style	Chinese
Meals	Lunch, seven days a week; dinner, Friday through Sunday
Price Range	Inexpensive
Superlatives	House combination, moo goo gai pan
Extras	Wine and beer

Jimmy Hsu, owner of the Peking Palace, came to the United States from Taiwan in 1971. He worked in Roanoke for two decades before opening his restaurant in 1991.

The space had previously been a restaurant, and Jimmy has done a wonderful job of refurbishing the interior. It's bright, light, clean and comfortable. Track lights and Oriental-style lamps provide illumination. There are double linens under glass at the tables and booths. About 120 guests can be seated in three dining rooms.

There's a lunch buffet every day. All the lunch specials come with soup and fried rice. Some of the options—such as curry chicken and spicy hot chicken—include an egg roll, too. Pepper steak, Chinese-fried shrimp, sweet and sour pork and beef chop suey are some of the other options.

Among the hot-and-spicy dinner entrees are orange-flavored chicken, twice-cooked pork or shrimp and chicken sauteed with bamboo shoots, water chestnuts and vegetables in hot sauce. Milder alternatives include the house shrimp special, crispy beef and Hong Kong chicken. The popular house combination includes beef tenderloin, sliced chicken and fresh shrimp sauteed with Chinese vegetables in a special sauce. The moo goo gai pan is another favorite among patrons. The family dinners feature a variety of Chinese foods for a set price and can be ordered for two, three, four, five or six people. There are also Southern attractions like ham steak, fried chicken and pork chops, as well as a cheeseburger and a roast beef sandwich.

Some Chinese items—figurines, plates, porcelain Buddhas and carvings—are offered for sale at the counter.

It's a credit to Jimmy that his restaurant was recommended for inclusion in this book by the owner of The Burgundy House up the road.

Dip Dog

Dip Dog
U.S. 11 WEST / MARION, VA 24354
(540) 783-2698

Style	Drive-in
Meals	Lunch and dinner, seven days a week
Price Range	Inexpensive
Superlatives	Dip dogs, homemade onion rings, frozen custard

*M*arion is named for Francis Marion, the "Swamp Fox" of Revolutionary War fame. It's a pleasant small town with some good antique shops on Main Street.

The Dip Dog is a very small place with an old sign and enough cars in the middle of a weekday afternoon to pique one's curiosity. The building looks much newer than the sign and isn't much bigger than a two-car garage. Inside, there's a standing area a few feet deep and two order windows. All the food is listed on signs behind the person at the window.

According to James Brown, a retired government worker who loafs at the Dip Dog and volunteers as maintenance man on occasion, "everyone knew about this place" when he was covering his territory from Dublin south to the Tennessee line.

There are four picnic tables outside, but it was a cold day when I visited, so most people were eating in their cars or standing and talking to occupants eating in other cars.

Started in 1957 by Lester Brown, the Dip Dog was acquired by Grant Hall, Sr., in 1965. Hall's son Grant Jr. bought it in 1980 and constructed a new building five years later. The old sign was on the roof of the original building and had neon lights on it. Hall plans to renovate the sign with neon again.

Dip dogs—what the restaurant is famous for, at least locally—are 75 cents. It's a hot dog on a stick dipped in a special batter, then quickly deep-fried to a golden brown and served with mustard. "It looks like a corn dog, but it's not," stated Hall emphatically.

If a dip dog isn't your style, you have plenty of options—hamburgers, plain hot dogs, fresh onion rings, and sandwiches like steak, pork barbecue, ham and egg, grilled cheese and chicken breast. If you're really hungry, you can order a complete dinner of shrimp, oysters, flounder or chicken and follow that with frozen custard, a banana split or an ice cream sundae.

Despite working in such a small place, my order taker didn't seem to understand the concept of "not too big." I ordered a small frozen custard—"not too big, please." What I got measured nearly a foot from top to bottom, and less than a third of it was cone.

From what I heard when I mentioned this place to anyone within 30 miles, this was where you either had your first job or took your first date. Or both.

It's a good thing I pulled in when I did. By the time I left, the number of cars and pickup trucks outside had about doubled, and the parking area was close to full. In the middle of a weekday afternoon.

Main Street Gifts & Eatery

138 EAST MAIN STREET / MARION, VA 24354
(540) 783-9244

Style	Cafe
Meals	Lunch, Monday through Friday
Price Range	Inexpensive
Superlatives	Cute place, great bagel sandwiches and homemade soups, gourmet coffees and teas

*T*ucked in the back of a large frame shop, this little eatery is part of a three-generation enterprise. The frame shop is owned by Tricia Spencer, who is in her 13th year in the business. The Travel Center—the travel agency on your right as you enter the store—is owned by her mother, Pat Purser. And the delightful cafe is operated by her grandmother, Ann Haulsee.

Credit Spencer with this innovative idea. Years ago, she told her grandmother that she wanted to go into business but needed some help.

"I sold real estate and worked at a hospital most of my working life, but I'd done a little framing and a lot of cooking along the way," said Haulsee.

Framing Unlimited by Tricia became a reality. A dozen years later, she expanded and moved into this big space on Main Street. Her mother moved the travel agency from across the street, and her grandmother started the cafe.

Haulsee laughs when asked about recipes. "Recipes? I learned to cook with a little bit of this, little bit of that, tasting as you go along." And her approach certainly works. This popular spot needs no advertising.

Most sandwiches are served on an onion, poppyseed, plain, sesame or wheat bagel, but you can get anything on whole-wheat or sourdough bread, too.

The soups are very popular. They include chicken and pasta, cream of broccoli, cream of potato and ham and bean made the old-fashioned way, with a real ham bone. Haulsee tried some fancy soups but they didn't sell well, so now she sticks to basics that customers like and come back to have again.

The biggest dessert hit is the coconut cream pie, which Haulsee is often out of toward the end of the lunch crunch each day. Other desserts include Kentucky Derby pie, German chocolate cake and "Oreo Cheesecake."

With your lunch, you should try the raspberry, peach or mint julep iced teas. Gourmet coffee and the Arizona line of drinks are also offered.

A gourmet kitchen shop next to the cafe stocks fine utensils, cookbooks, Virginia wines, baskets and a variety of kitchen paraphernalia.

Saltbox Cafe & Grill

151 WEST MAIN STREET / SALTVILLE, VA 24370
(540) 496-5999

Saltbox Cafe & Grill

Style	Cafe
Meals	Breakfast, lunch and dinner, seven days a week
Price Range	Inexpensive
Superlatives	Vegetables, char-grilled hamburgers

Salt was so important in meat preservation in the days before refrigeration that it was the object of a battle during the Civil War. Saltville was the major supplier of salt for the South. The clash took place right in town on October 2, 1864. The fortifications that Confederate soldiers used in their successful defense can still be seen today. Modern residents celebrate their heritage the week before Labor Day, when they heat up the old salt kettles, boil down brine to make salt, then enjoy four days of laughter, good food, music and camaraderie.

When Pete Smith opened the Saltbox, he had a good idea what to expect in the restaurant business. His parents owned a local motel and restaurant for 17 years. They and his grandparents also built and operated other motels and restaurants in Southwest Virginia.

The Saltbox has a cream-and-turquoise interior with seating for 140, including a separate banquet room. It's spacious, bright and clean.

Smith's sister Joey is responsible for the name. "We wanted something in keeping with the town's history and thought this would work well," said Smith. And yes, Northerners, he knows it's also a style of home architecture.

Breakfast here is basic—eggs, omelets, pancakes, French toast, biscuits with various fillings and the typical morning meats.

Smith believes his restaurant makes one of the best hamburgers east of the Mississippi. "This is a hamburger and beans and cornbread joint," he stated. Many people come in for the vegetables, too.

The "Macho Fries" come topped with a homemade sauce and cheddar cheese. The pork barbecue is hickory-smoked, and there's a rib-eye steak hoagie for lunch.

You can dress up dinner with a shrimp cocktail to start and "Rocky Road Fudge Cake" to finish. The oysters are hand-breaded, the shrimp come jumbo or baby-size and the steaks are T-bone, New York strip or rib-eye. All the entrees come with slaw, grilled French bread and french fries or a baked potato. Strawberry shortcake, a cream pie of the day, Dutch apple pie and pecan pie (Southern or chocolate chip) are usually available for dessert.

If you have time, wander next door to Madam Russell's 1778 house. This log cabin was home to a lady who was a Methodist missionary and the sister of the Virginia son who said, "Give me liberty or give me death."

BLUE RIDGE PARKWAY

Château Morrisette

MILEPOST 171.5, BLUE RIDGE PARKWAY
MEADOWS OF DAN, VA 24120
(540) 593-2865

Style	Casual nice
Meals	Lunch, Wednesday through Sunday; dinner, Friday and Saturday. The restaurant is open year-round, but call ahead if the weather is questionable. Reservations are suggested for dinner.
Price Range	Moderate
Superlatives	Wine, setting, view, creative cuisine
Extras	A winery tour and tasting is offered for $1.00 per person. A full bar is available.

Set against the backdrop of the Blue Ridge Mountains, this is one of only two full-service restaurants at wineries in Virginia. The state boasts 43 wineries. This one has soared to third-largest in terms of production in less than 20 years.

The business was started in 1978 as Woolwine Winery by William Morrisette. Four years later, his son David, then just 22, became company president. David took the small vineyard to a full-scale winery with a 120-seat restaurant and retail and wholesale operations.

Château Morrisette's wines are distributed in Virginia and North Carolina. Wine Club members number 3,000, and the mailing list for the *Grapevine* newsletter tops 26,000. The winery attributes its popularity to "good wines, increased awareness of our product, repeat and word-of-mouth business."

Keep a sharp eye for Milepost 171.5, as the turnoff is easy to miss; it's 7.5 miles south of the junction with Va. 8. Turn off the parkway, then immediately left on Winery Road.

Winery tours take about 20 minutes and are followed by a tasting. The operation is surprisingly small, considering that Château Morrisette produces 25,000 cases of wine annually.

The owners have long had a love affair with the black Labrador. Nicholas, the current mascot, will probably meet you near the front. The restaurant is called Le Chien Noir—"The Black Dog." There are Black Dog Jazz Concerts in summer. There's also a Black Dog red wine and a Black Dog Blanc. Our Dog Blue, a semisweet wine with floral aromas, was introduced in 1996.

The food is innovatively prepared and presented, and the menu is changed to capitalize on seasonal game and produce. For lunch, you might find a portobello mushroom and tomato sandwich with honey mustard, grilled onion, sprouts and spinach. Or sauteed pork loin with shiitake mushrooms and green peppercorn sauce. Or baked catfish with tropical fruit and mild goat cheese.

Two of the more interesting appetizers on the dinner menu are hand-rolled sushi with smoked salmon and buffalo brochette with smoked onion chutney and wild mushroom ketchup.

Entrees include a variety of game, like sauteed loin of rabbit, grilled buffalo flank steak, roasted venison loin and quail with Boursin and walnut stuffing. Common things like chicken and beef tenderloin are dressed up—the former with candied ginger and Asian vegetables, the latter with a wild mushroom risotto cake, smoked tomato-corn salsa and cilantro pesto crème fraîche.

Before leaving, check out the gift shop. In addition to wines by the bottle and case, you'll find Château Morrisette glasses and clothing, books and Virginia gifts.

Log House 1776

520 EAST MAIN STREET / WYTHEVILLE, VA 24382
(540) 228-4139

Style	Home-style
Meals	Lunch and dinner, Monday through Saturday
Price Range	Moderate
Superlatives	Old log buildings, gift shop, pork tenderloin
Extras	Full bar

Originally called Abbeville, then Evansham, Wytheville received its present name when it was incorporated in 1839. The name honors George Wythe, a signer of the Declaration of Independence, America's first law professor and the designer of the Seal of Virginia. Wytheville is the hometown of Edith Boling Wilson, wife of Woodrow Wilson, the 28th president of the United States and a native Virginian himself.

Log House 1776 is well worth a five-minute drive off the interstate. Get off I-81 at Exit 73 and head toward town. In about three miles, you'll reach a log house built by a Revolutionary War soldier. Other log structures on the property were built in 1804.

During the Civil War, Joseph Chadwell, the owner, and Benjamin Steptoe, a freed slave who lived in the cabin that now houses the deli, went together to fight for the Confederacy.

The restaurant was opened by James and Pat Green during our nation's bicentennial year. They had moved their bakery into the building a couple of years earlier but weren't crazy about the early-morning hours a bakery demands.

The log walls create a nostalgic warmth. Lace under glass adorns most tables downstairs; upstairs, there's a mix of tablecloths and lace. The large, round table downstairs rests on a barrel pedestal. Kerosene lamps sit on some tables, and a beautiful old lamp hangs in the center of one room. The fireplaces have been converted to gas without destroying the warm ambiance.

At lunch, guests can use the sandwich menu or select from the dinner menu at $1.50 less than dinner prices. The "Sunshine Sandwich" is one of the most popular items. It's toasted French bread with aspara-gus, ham or turkey, provolone and bleu cheese. You can also get burgers, sandwiches, salads, soup and a variety of appetizers, such as a grape cheese cluster, egg rolls, cheese sticks and corn fritters with honey.

The chef's specialties are two varieties of pork ten-derloin. The "Log House" version features pork filled with apples, celery, onions, breadcrumbs, spices and a special sauce. The "South of the Border" pork ten-derloin is filled with cheese, mildly hot peppers and special sauce. The "Confederate Beef Stew"—as pre-pared for General Robert E. Lee and his troops—in-cludes apples and herb potatoes. Two vegetables come with dinner. The house specialty is stuffed yellow crookneck squash filled with onions and crackers and topped with cheese.

The triple-layer cheesecake has chocolate, praline pecan and white almond layers covered in a hard chocolate shell. Raspberry cheesecake, bread pudding and coconut cream pie are some of the other desserts.

Before you leave, don't forget to go out back and see the birds, rabbits, gardens and gift shops. Among the birds is a type of partridge that, with training, can talk. Pat is working on teaching them to say, "Hi there, you're pretty."

Pat has a simple explanation for keeping the birds and rabbits: "Children get restless riding around."

But you don't have to have kids to enjoy this place.

Scrooge's

HOLSTON ROAD (EXIT 70 OFF I-81)
WYTHEVILLE, VA 24382
(540) 228-6622

Style	Casual nice
Meals	Dinner, seven days a week
Price Range	Moderate
Superlatives	"Pig and Pepper Soup," beef
Extras	Full bar

Scrooge's is a cut above most restaurants you'll find in its setting—next to a national chain motel.

The interior is tastefully done in deep green and burgundy. The wallpaper border has pheasants on it, and the walls display a few hunt prints. There's a fire-place on the far wall, oil lamps at the booths and tall plants with little white lights on them in the corners.

The specialties of the house include Scrooge's sig-nature "Pig and Pepper Soup" and the beef entrees. My filet mignon had a light touch of cracked pepper and was done to a perfect medium rare. The prime rib is also an excellent cut of beef. Accompanied by a fresh salad, a small loaf of soft white bread and a baked potato, either makes a superb meal.

The seafood selections include snow crab legs, flounder Florentine, grilled swordfish and lobster tail. Cajun chicken, "Cordon Bob," "Tiny Tim's Chicken" and "Ebenezer's Chicken" are alternative preparations of the popular bird. Such items as stuffed shells, sea-food ravioli, pesto primavera and shrimp Alfredo are also available.

All this comes from a kitchen under the watchful

eye of chef Mark Wagner, who trained at the Green-brier. That just might explain the superior cuisine.

The pub on the premises is bright and classy. There are meeting rooms on the second floor of the building, and a fine gift and furniture shop is located next door.

If you're a Dickens fan, you can shop right at the restaurant for mugs, polo shirts, sweatshirts and other items bearing caricatures of Ebenezer Scrooge.

FLOYD

Pine Tavern

U.S. 221 / FLOYD, VA 24091
(540) 745-4482

Style	Family-style
Meals	Lunch, Friday; dinner, Wednesday through Sunday
Price Range	Moderate
Superlatives	Seafood, "Chef's Choice"
Extras	Wine and beer

*T*here's a lot of pine in this neck of the woods, so that's probably how Pine Tavern came by its name in 1927. It later became a lodge with a mess hall. In the mid-1930s, the taproom was added. The restaurant followed a few years later. It's all located a few miles north of Floyd on the west side of the highway.

The pine walls are original. There's also a pine floor and beam ceilings. Add to this some locally handcrafted ash, walnut and cherry furniture and a solitary candle flame on each table and you have that wonderful, rustic warmth that wood evokes.

Michael Gucciardo, a native of Brooklyn, has been the chef here for nearly a decade. He's now part-owner, too. He's a creative kind of guy, and his "Chef's Choices" are fast becoming popular—although guests may not know what they'll be eating until it's served. It's the ultimate compliment to have customers display such confidence—sort of like going to your hairdresser and saying, "Cut it any way you want," and trusting that the outcome will be satisfying.

The Pine Tavern's appetizers might include shrimp and smoked salmon in a special sauce, roasted peppers with artichoke hearts or a creamy seafood chowder. The chowder is great.

The entrees range from plain, all-American cuisine to innovative dishes—sea scallops over fettuccine, chicken Madeira, "Rigatoni Madechiara," Szechuan-style tofu, spicy red beans over polenta and rib-eye steak. The Sunday menu is all-Italian. At 8:30, it's open mike for the evening.

The homemade desserts vary according to availability of fresh local produce. Michael tries to have one fruit, one nut and one cheesecake dessert. The peach shortcake features peaches that Michael picks on the way to work. The dark chocolate torte with raspberry sauce features fresh berries, as does the blackberry spice cake.

The Pine Tavern is a neat spot perhaps 20 minutes off the Blue Ridge Parkway, less than an hour from Roanoke and just a couple miles outside the quiet, little town of Floyd.

Piggy Bank Cafe

106½ EAST MAIN STREET / TAZEWELL, VA 24651
(540) 988-2560

Style	Cafe
Meals	Lunch, Monday through Friday
Price Range	Inexpensive
Superlatives	Sourdough bread, pork barbecue

*K*nown as Jeffersonville from 1799 to 1891, this town was chosen by means of a fistfight to be the county seat. When officials couldn't decide which of two towns would be the county seat, a fighter was selected from each place, and they fought it out for the honor of their towns.

The Bank of Clinch Valley—number 17 among the 52 buildings on Tazewell's historic walking tour—now serves as the Piggy Bank Cafe. An original tin ceiling and turn-of-the-century bank documents under glass on the tables provide a nostalgic setting for this restaurant, a novel endeavor sponsored by the Cumberland Mountain Community Services agency.

The agency provides comprehensive mental-health and substance-abuse services to three mountain communities in western Virginia. The cafe was envisioned as a way to offer meaningful work and skills development to folks who needed a steppingstone to employment. The restaurant became a reality in 1992.

The building dates from around 1904. Large windows containing their original glass and off-white curtains allow natural light. An original teller's cage was reassembled for the cashier's station. Light rock music plays in the background.

Program manager Babs Hoops and supervisor Wanda Angles oversee all facets of the restaurant operation. Both of them exude friendliness, warmth, and kindness.

The barbecue is homemade. Enjoy it here, because you can't make it at home—the recipe is a secret. And the Piggy Bank might just have the best sourdough bread east of the Mississippi, sourdough having been the bread of choice among the pioneers who settled the West. The bread is made on the premises, and you can get any of the sandwiches on it. The BLT here stands for "bank loan transaction," but rest assured that it includes all the expected stuff. Club sandwiches, the "Prime Rate Burger," salads, platters and grilled sandwiches are available.

The homemade desserts might include coconut pie or yellow cake with peanut butter frosting.

Whatever you order, you can bet that it'll be made fresh and with care, that it'll be tasty, that it'll be reasonably priced and that your patronage will enhance the lives of those working through the cafe to achieve greater things. The jobs here are temporary. The workers are expected to move along and take with them the skills and experience the restaurant provides.

You may leave your tip at the cashier's station or on the table—or in the piggy bank. There's one on every table.

Le Café

246 NORTH WASHINGTON STREET
PULASKI, VA 24301
(540) 980-9110

Style	Family-style
Meals	Breakfast and lunch, Monday through Saturday; dinner, Friday and Saturday. Reservations are requested for dinner.
Price Range	Inexpensive
Superlatives	"Seafood Supreme," homemade desserts

*P*ulaski is one of only two towns in Virginia with a Polish name, the other being Warsaw. Revolutionary War hero Casimir Pulaski, the man for whom the town was named (after being called Martin's Tank), was killed in the siege of Savannah, Georgia, in 1779.

You've got to wonder about someone who found her way here from Montana—someone who quit her job as cook at a restaurant because it was "too stressful," then opened her own place, where she not only cooks but orders, bakes, plans, handles the finances and manages the operation. "I get to make all the decisions," states owner Judy Osborne. And that makes all the difference to her.

Le Café originally opened on the second floor of a historic building in downtown Pulaski, then moved around the corner to occupy the lower level of a larger structure.

Osborne has done a nice job of creating intimacy in what was a department store. Lattice walls separate diners along one wall and form a barrier between the restaurant and the other half of this huge space.

The chairs with needlepoint cushions come from Italy. Osborne bought a damaged shipment and used a couple of chairs for parts to repair the others. They're downright elegant.

You'll note the eclectic selection of china Osborne bought at garage sales and thrift stores. Antiques and crafts are for sale on consignment.

Osborne has been collecting recipes for decades. She'll try anything she sees in magazines and newspapers. Her cornbread recipe came off an Albers cornmeal package she bought years ago out west. She serves it with black beans—one of her efforts to appeal to the Southern palate.

Her breakfasts are fancied-up versions of popular fare. Scrambled eggs come with cheese and are served on a croissant, for example. The sweet rolls and muffins are homemade.

The coffee and tea selections number a couple dozen. French vanilla cappuccino and the "flavor of the day" top the list in popularity.

Homemade soups are a big hit with the lunch crowd, but the "Seafood Supreme" is the item ordered most often. It features seafood salad piled high on a toasted English muffin and topped with melted cheese.

Make sure you save room for dessert. Osborne's personal favorite is the "Apple Carrot Cake." But if you're counting calories, order the fat-free cheesecake. Or if you long for an old-fashioned favorite, try the homemade black raspberry ice cream.

Dinner is served Friday and Saturday, and reservations are preferred. The menu changes weekly.

There are three entrees from which to choose, like teriyaki steak, honey-mustard pork cutlets and Swiss chicken with lemon pilaf.

Osborne is not a chatterbox, and her business philosophy reflects her character and *modus operandi*: "Work hard and do your best."

Graffiti's Cafe
793 BROAD STREET (U.S. 11) / DUBLIN, VA 24084
(540) 674-4861

Style	Cafe
Meals	Lunch and dinner, seven days a week
Price Range	Inexpensive
Superlatives	Healthy food preparation, 1950s atmosphere

*I*f you like Chubby Checker, "Rock Around the Clock" and "The Monster Mash," you'll be right at home here. Painted aqua on one side and pink on the other, with black trim all around, Graffiti's doesn't have graffiti on the walls, contrary to what you might expect. It's got James Dean and Marilyn Monroe posters and scores of black-and-white high-school photos. It's bright and clean and reminiscent of the days when baby boomers were pre-teens.

The building was originally a convenience store, then a fabric store. Late in 1995, Graffiti's owners, brothers-in-law Ricky Morris and David Mauck, signed a lease and renovated the building in order to move their three-year-old ice cream shop here. According to Morris, the bankers wanted more than ice cream to go along with the financing, so the brothers-in-law were forced to expand their repertoire.

"We wanted to serve hamburgers and tater tots and french fries, all that stuff, but we also wanted to be health-conscious," stated Morris. So they looked into an "instant burger" machine that uses fresh meat, takes 50 percent of the fat out of it and retains the juices and flavor. Graffiti's can make six quarter-pound hamburgers at once. The machine is used for tater tots and french fries, too. "The health department loves it," Morris continued. "It's a whole lot easier to keep the place clean when you have no grease."

Morris is a Dublin native and a member of the class of 1974, the last class to graduate from the now-non-existent Dublin High School. His sister Connie married David Mauck. The whole operation has become a family affair. Connie is a schoolteacher who helps in the summers. Morris's wife, Regina, does whatever needs to be done. And all of their kids have worked at the restaurant at one time or another.

Besides hamburgers, tater tots and french fries, Graffiti's serves fish sandwiches, foot-long hot dogs, grilled chicken, barbecue sandwiches and a variety of subs, salads and side orders.

Graffiti's offers 40 flavors of Hershey's ice cream, available in a dish, a float, a malt, a milk shake or a banana split or with hot fudge cake.

It's the kind of place where people sit and talk awhile and nod to one another—a place where you can get a healthy burger and groove to 1950s tunes.

The Farmhouse Restaurant

CAMBRIA STREET / CHRISTIANSBURG, VA 24073
(540) 382-4253

Style	Casual nice
Meals	Dinner, seven days a week
Price Range	Moderate
Superlatives	Rustic charm, steaks, onion rings
Extras	Full bar

*N*amed for Indian fighter William Christian, the town of Christiansburgh was incorporated three years after George Washington took office. Somewhere along the way, the last letter of the town's name fell off. On May 9, 1808, the first rifle duel known to have occurred in Virginia took place here, on a hill near Sunset Cemetery. The site proved prophetic, as both participants died. Today, Christiansburg is the site of the Wilderness Trail Festival. On the third Saturday in September, Main Street—the former Wilderness Road—is closed to automobiles during this celebration of local history.

The Farmhouse Restaurant opened in 1963. Fourteen years later, 26-year-old David Leinwand bought it. Although he had no restaurant experience, Leinwand had business acumen. Once a 100-seat restaurant with 11 employees, The Farmhouse now has 625 dining seats, 110 lounge seats and 100 employees. The banquet facility added in the early 1990s accounts for much of the growth.

A few years back, the *Roanoke Times* conducted a survey in the New River Valley, southwest of Roanoke. The word respondents most often associated with The Farmhouse was *consistent*. According to Blacksburg resident Arnold Mink, The Farmhouse serves "the best prime rib and homemade onion rings in the valley." Another local fan, John Moody, said it was one of the few places where grilled pork chops are available.

The house is part of a farm built in the 1800s. In the early 1970s, a train caboose was incorporated into the dining area; you'll note some narrow passageways with wooden, cratelike booths on each side. An eclectic collection of art, antique tools and old photos hangs on the walls.

Among the appetizers served here are oysters Rockefeller and scallops wrapped in bacon.

The Farmhouse is well known for its steaks. Just about every cut is on the menu, including specialties like beef Wellington and Châteaubriand. Other house specialties are Szechuan salmon and seafood Newburg. Ribs, chops, chicken, seafood and pasta dishes are also served. Entrees with less than 30 percent of their calories from fat and fewer than 500 calories total are marked with a heart.

For those who enjoy wine but aren't sure what's what, there's a helpful description of more than 10 wines sold by the glass.

In 1996, Kevin Murphy, a restaurant consultant who was teaching at Virginia Tech, came to The Farmhouse as full-time general manager with a five-year lease and an option to buy the place. One of his first changes was creating a nicely bound, attractively printed menu. Some of the regulars, however, were attached to the paper place mat menus that had been on the tables for decades. A conciliatory Murphy left those in place. And that's why The Farmhouse has two styles of menus—at least for a while.

Giovanni's Gourmet

9 RADFORD ROAD / CHRISTIANSBURG, VA 24073
(540) 382-7218

Style	Casual nice
Meals	Dinner, seven days a week
Price Range	Moderate
Superlatives	Seafood, vegetarian dishes
Extras	Wine and beer

*P*ort Said is located where Egypt meets the Sinai Peninsula, on the southeastern coast of the Mediterranean Sea and the northern end of the Suez Canal. Traffic passes through Port Said from all over the world.

It was in this multicultural environment that Giovanni's owner and chef, Abdul Hameed Hassan, was raised. Trained as a lawyer and judge in his native land, Abdul is just as comfortable in a kitchen as he is in a courtroom. As a teenager, he worked in a restaurant in Italy. When he came to the United States in 1991, he worked at the famed Mama Leone's in the Big Apple.

In 1994, he purchased Sal's Pizza in Christiansburg and took over what he understood was more of a fine restaurant than it turned out to be. Not discouraged but challenged, Abdul began the tedious process of renovating not only a building but also a reputation.

The language barrier was a challenge he tackled by connecting with Literacy Volunteers of America. There, he met Robin Laing, who helped him learn English while increasing her own knowledge of Arabic. In June 1995, they were married. Today, both of them devote their full-time energy to Giovanni's Gourmet.

Their plans are great. While they strive toward creating an elegant interior and a setting for fine dining, Abdul is making culinary innovations that appeal so much to local patrons that he's been asked to offer international dinners and special events.

Their restaurant seats 50 or 60. Robin explained that a complete dining experience—not what she calls "warehousing people, getting them in and out the door to turn the tables again"—is their top priority.

The emphasis is on quality food in a refined atmosphere. The menu varies daily. The appetizers may include seafood-stuffed mushrooms and sauteed calamari. Fresh cream of mushroom might be the soup of the day.

Abdul's vegetarian dishes are very popular, as are his seafood and veal entrees. The crab cakes are made from scratch.

Desserts are changed often, too, although Italian cheesecake and the "Italian Feather" are stable menu items. The latter is mascarpone cheese with a touch of vanilla and amaretto served over homemade chocolate sponge cake.

Hunan House

U.S. 460 / CHRISTIANSBURG, VA 24073
(540) 382-8999

Style	Chinese
Meals	Lunch and dinner, seven days a week
Price Range	Inexpensive/Moderate
Superlatives	Flower garnishes, prawns Szechuan-style
Extras	Full bar

Hunan House

*K*nowing your market is rule number one of any business. Hunan House owners Ping Zhao and Teddy Yang show that they have a good grip on this concept in the way they've decorated their restaurant and structured their menu to appeal to their American customers.

The dining rooms are more contemporary than in most Chinese restaurants. Everything is bright with natural light and colorful in shades of pink, mauve and purple. "People often ask who our decorator is," said Ping. It was Ping herself and Teddy's wife, Tracy Chen, who selected the paint, wallpaper and fabric.

And then there's the salad bar. Because most customers love salad, Hunan House has an extensive selection of fresh lettuce, peppers, onions, carrots, radishes, broccoli, fruits, seeds, bacon bits and cherry tomatoes.

Not counting the lunch menu or the 55 choices under appetizers, soups, desserts and American dishes, there are 90 Chinese dinner entrees. Among them are the popular sweet-and-sour versions of fish, pork, shrimp and chicken, along with orange beef, lemon chicken and pineapple duck. A third of the selections are marked as hot and spicy, but spices can be altered according to personal preference.

Ping and Teddy have not overlooked Americans' love affair with steak. According to Ping, one of the most popular dishes is the house steak, which comes sizzling on a hot plate with vegetables and special sauce. Americans who like to stick to their native cuisine can dine on fried shrimp, rib-eye steak, flounder fillet, ham steak or other entrees.

Hunan House is less than a quarter-mile off I-81 at Exit 118. Go west on U.S. 460. You'll see the restaurant on your right on a slight rise. It's a brick building with a large yellow sign with red letters.

The garnishes are exquisite at Hunan House.

Alleghany Inn

Alleghany Inn

1123 GROVE STREET / RADFORD, VA 24141

(540) 731-4466

Style	Fine dining
Meals	Lunch, Tuesday through Sunday; dinner, Tuesday through Saturday. Reservations are recommended.
Price Range	Moderate/Expensive
Superlatives	Presentation and service, crab cakes, salmon
Extras	Full bar

*T*he railroad town once called Central or Central Depot was renamed Radford in 1892 to honor John B. Radford, a local resident and medical doctor. An absent-minded fellow, Radford once came to a fence, took all the rails off, walked his horse through, then put the rails back, only to realize he and the horse were on opposite sides of the fence. Today, Radford looks and feels like a college town. Radford University was established in 1910 and has approximately 8,000 students in its five colleges.

Southwest Virginia native Margaret Springer always wanted a bed and breakfast inn. Her brother Jeff Jarvis had been dabbling in real estate and the restaurant business in Radford for years. So when he discovered that the big white building on Grove Street—once a fine residence and a restaurant—was in foreclosure, he called his sister, and they took a look.

Pipes had burst inside, soaked carpeting was lying over hardwood floors, ceilings were falling down in places. They loved it. They bought it.

During several months of renovation in 1995, four guest rooms with new bathrooms were carved out on the second floor and a small apartment was built in the back of the first floor.

The rest of the first floor of the 1905 house is occupied by the gourmet restaurant Jarvis had long envisioned. His plan was to bring to the New River Valley a dining experience unlike anything around. And he has. French service, beautiful china, soft music, candlelight, opulent culinary presentations and fine, fresh food are hallmarks of the Alleghany Inn.

"When we had some guests here from France who were reminded of their favorite restaurant in Paris, we knew we were doing something right," recalled Jarvis.

About half the menu is changed seasonally to take advantage of fresh produce and game. Chef's specials are prepared nightly.

Soups include asparagus and crabmeat bisque and

beef consommé. Appetizers include baked Brie en croûte and melon with Virginia ham.

Entrees are planned with nutrition, freshness and attractive presentation in mind. All meals come with vegetables, one starch and a salad. Among the stable entrees are filet mignon, prime rib, smoked pork loin, grilled marinated tuna steak and herb-crusted baked salmon. In season, you're likely to find a venison dish, live lobster, Cornish hens and crab cakes. Executive chef Robert Lowe believes the crab cakes are popular because they're 95 percent real crab.

One aspect of the Alleghany Inn's desserts that sets them apart is the sauces. The caramel, melba and chocolate sauces—all homemade—are used for plate garnish and presentation as well as for topping sweets. The Alleghany's chocolate mousse is wonderfully light, thanks to the addition of whipped egg whites. Peach cobbler, blackberry cobbler, grasshopper pie and New York cheesecake are also presented in picture-perfect style.

BT's

218 TYLER AVENUE / RADFORD, VA 24141
(540) 639-1282

Style	Pub
Meals	Lunch and dinner, seven days a week
Price Range	Inexpensive/Moderate
Superlatives	Friendly atmosphere, sirloin steak
Extras	Full bar

As a college hangout, this ranks pretty high—a bar,

pool tables, dartboards, televisions, booths and tables on two levels. As a place to eat a meal, it holds its own very nicely.

Wooden booths line the walls of the small dining area downstairs. There are a couple of tables in the middle of the room. Around a corner from the dining area are the bar, more booths and a dartboard area. Behind the bar is the game room. More tables are located on the second level. There are big windows upstairs, and it's always fun to watch what's happening outside on the streets below.

The surprise was a midafternoon snack of steamed shrimp and an apple. A healthy portion of shrimp came on a large plate, garnished with red and green peppers artfully arranged around the edge. And just a few minutes after it was ordered, the apple arrived in the shape of a bird. It was photo-worthy.

The service, typical in college towns, was very friendly. Manager Ken Day was cooking that day, and he stopped at my table to see if everything was okay. Perhaps at 2:30 in the afternoon, there's time for that.

The name comes from the two men who started the restaurant in 1983. The *B* has since bowed out, but

BT's

the *T*—Tom Whitehead—still oversees every facet of the business.

The menu is pretty common young-people stuff—"appeteasers," sandwiches, burgers. There's a special every day of the week. On Friday, it's seafood; on Tuesday, it's "South of the Border"; on Sunday, it's all-you-can-eat spaghetti.

A popular entree is the one-pound sirloin steak. It's called the "Governor's Choice," but no one knows if a governor has ever eaten here. The "Governor's Choice" and its half-pound cousin, the "Dalton Hall," come with a baked potato, salad and bread. Other house favorites are lasagna, St. Louis–style ribs (another one-pound entree), jambalaya and the "Radford Rio"—a spicy taco salad. And there's a vegetarian section on the menu.

Dozens of drinks are printed on the back of the menu, as is one of my favorite sayings. It's been modified, the word *food* replaced by *libations*: "If you have enjoyed our libations, tell a friend. If not, tell us."

Four Seasons

BLUEFIELD
Four Seasons
WAL-MART PLAZA / BLUEFIELD, VA 24605
(540) 322-4121

Style	Family-style
Meals	Breakfast, Saturday and Sunday; lunch and dinner, seven days a week
Price Range	Inexpensive/Moderate
Superlatives	Steaks, seafood, homemade cookies

*B*luefield straddles the border of Virginia and West Virginia. It was named for its fields of wild chicory and their pretty blue flowers. Bluefield was a small farming community until trains began to transport its coal to energy markets elsewhere. Around here, when people speak of the Battle of Matewan and the Battle of Blair Mountain, they aren't talking about the Revolutionary War or the Civil War. These were battles of armed miners against their bosses.

The restaurant known as Four Seasons might just as well be called "Three Brothers." The owners are Pakistani siblings—a physician, an architect and a restaurateur. Sohail Bhatti's brothers urged him to leave his restaurants in Pakistan to oversee this new one on its June 21, 1996, opening. And when I spoke with him a year later, he still hadn't taken a day off.

The brick restaurant can seat about 300 people on two floors. It's bright and open, with lots of large windows. Though Four Seasons was designed for cafeteria-style dining, table service soon became the standard.

Breakfast, served only on weekends, offers the basics—eggs, bacon, sausage, country ham, omelets, pancakes, French toast, biscuits and gravy.

Appetizers like the "Flowering Onion," beans and cornbread and potato skins are available at lunch and dinner, as is a soup du jour.

At midday, you'll find sandwiches, salads and pasta dishes, served with a vegetable of the day. Fettuccine Alfredo, shrimp fettuccine, pasta primavera, warm salmon salad and shrimp vermicelli salad are among the offerings.

The most popular dinner entrees here are rainbow trout—deep-fried or grilled—blackened snapper and rib-eye steak. There are more seafood entrees—a pound of crab legs and shrimp Creole among them—than beef and chicken entrees. Sohail says that his native cuisine is too hot and spicy for the American palate, so he sticks with what we eat—things like grilled salmon steak, filet mignon, prime rib, barbecued chicken and pecan chicken.

The desserts may include peanut butter pie, strawberry pie and carrot cake. Four Seasons sometimes gives away homemade cookies after lunch and dinner. They're reason enough to come here at any season.

To reach the restaurant, exit U.S. 460 at the sign for Bluefield College, Virginia. Turn left at the traffic light, still following the signs. Four Seasons is on your left in the Wal-Mart plaza.

The Last Fountain

BLUEFIELD
The Last Fountain

566 VIRGINIA AVENUE / BLUEFIELD, VA 24605
(540) 326-1166

Style	Home-style
Meals	Breakfast and lunch, Monday through Saturday
Price Range	Inexpensive
Superlatives	Chocolate ice cream soda, hot dogs, homemade chili

*T*he day was sunny, but I was feeling listless. It was a long drive from Covington, Virginia, to Beckley, West Virginia, and down to Bluefield. I cruised into the Virginia side of this two-state town and popped into the bank for suggestions for lunch. The Last Fountain is about the only place right downtown, so I headed across the street.

For someone who needed her day brightened, this was the place to come. I entered on the gift shop side of the store—and stayed there for the better part of half an hour. I bought a gift book, a battery-operated computer keyboard vacuum about the diameter of a pencil, some cards, some bookmarks. There were also gifts for men, for the kitchen, for brides, for babies — for every occasion, and in all price ranges.

Bluefield native Linda Garrison and her husband, Bruce, originally from Richmond, have owned this combination gift shop, pharmacy, sundry store and restaurant since buying it from Linda's father in 1967. He opened it in 1935.

The Last Fountain, located on the other side of the store, made the day doubly bright. It's an old soda fountain with 10 stools and about 40 seats. There was one vacant table — a round oak table nestled in the corner by the windows on the far side. It proved to be the best spot in the place. Lively conversations, happy waitresses and a nostalgic atmosphere obliterated the morning's woes.

A Western omelet, various egg sandwiches, French toast and eggs with bacon, sausage or country ham are offered at breakfast.

There are 18 sandwiches, along with about a dozen hamburger and hot dog variations. Side orders include peaches with cottage cheese, onion rings and a scoop of salad on lettuce with tomato and crackers.

At the next table, the waitress delivered two fountain items that looked like something right out of a magazine. I had to ask. "Chocolate ice cream soda" was the answer from my fellow diners, who then proceeded to offer accolades about their choice. This wasn't their first visit — and it certainly wasn't their first chocolate ice cream soda.

This whole place was very refreshing. I'd go out of my way to stop in again for gifts and one of those old-fashioned fountain delights.

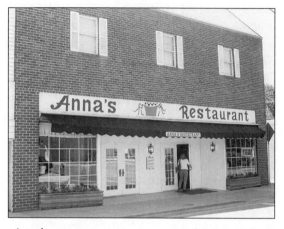

Anna's

NARROWS

Anna's

100 NORTH MONROE STREET
NARROWS, VA 24124
(540) 726-3545

Style	Home-style
Meals	Lunch and dinner, seven days a week
Price Range	Inexpensive/Moderate
Superlatives	Country-fried steak, meatloaf, apple dumplings
Extras	Wine and beer

*T*his town's name comes from its location on a narrow section of the New River, which is really a very old river. Narrows — called "The Narrows" in its early days — was occupied by Confederate troops in 1864 when Union general George Crook was forced to evacuate Blacksburg.

After its days as a five-and-dime in the early 1950s, the building that now houses Anna's went through stints as a sewing factory, a mini-mall, a co-op store and a storage facility. The Fraziers—Jerry and Anna—started the restaurant in 1984. "I always said I'd put your name in lights," Jerry reportedly told Anna after naming the place for her.

The decor is country—old ice skates, ice tongs, antiques, two ladders suspended horizontally from the ceiling with assorted baskets and tinware hanging from them. One side of the restaurant is paneled. The opposite wall is painted white and decorated with hand-stenciling. The tables have blue-and-white-checked tablecloths under glass.

Everything that can be made from scratch is—pork barbecue, slaw, meatloaf, mashed potatoes, gravy, rolls, cream pies, apple dumplings and bread pudding with butter rum sauce.

Anna's buffet is very popular on Friday and Saturday nights and Sundays. Four or five meats are offered—always fried chicken and fried fish, sometimes peel-and-eat shrimp or roast beef. Mashed potatoes and gravy and macaroni and cheese are two of the favorite sides.

This is a country kind of place with a country kind of cooking and all different kinds of folks coming in to eat and catch up on local news.

Friends & Family
100 WOODLAND DRIVE / PEARISBURG, VA 24134
(540) 921-4717

Style	Home-style
Meals	Breakfast, lunch and dinner, seven days a week
Price Range	Inexpensive/Moderate
Superlatives	Homemade pies, pinto beans with cornbread
Extras	Wine and beer

*T*here's been a settlement on the site of Pearisburg for a long time. The name appears as Pearsburg on a map printed in 1755, but the spelling is incorrect, as the town was named for either Captain Richard Pearis or Captain George Pearis, depending on which history book you consult. Pearisburg is the county seat of Giles County, located in a beautiful, mountainous section of the state near the West Virginia line. A portion of the Appalachian Trail passes nearby.

Becky Young opened Friends & Family in a former flower shop and landscaping store in the spring of 1996. The interior is predominantly white, with green and burgundy highlights. Bay windows in the front let in lots of light. With small people in mind, the restaurant offers not only a couple of booster chairs and highchairs, but also a little table with small chairs.

The menu is written with real country flair. Breakfast features the "Cock-a-Doodle-Do Special"—pancakes, that is. Items like eggs, country ham, omelets and homemade sausage gravy and biscuits are referred to by names like "Hungry Farmer," "Porky's Delight," "Henhouse Special" and "Old Faithful."

The "Beginners" (for country folks) or "Appetizers" (for city folks) include breaded kosher pickles, french-fried potato chips and homemade chili beans. The sandwiches also have creative names. The "Big Bird Dog" is a foot-long hot dog with chili and fixin's, while the "Pup" is just a regular hot dog with chili. The "Yard Bird" is a chicken breast sandwich. "New River Minnow" is cod on a bun.

Dinner reads in the same vein. The pork entrees are listed under the heading, "Suey—That Pig Is Good," while the chicken entrees follow the heading, "Pluck Dem Chickens Clean. We Got Guests Comin'." Beef, fish and combination plates are also offered. Everyone should be able to find something they like among the 30 entrees.

The cream pies—coconut, butterscotch and chocolate, to name just a few—are homemade, as are the fruit pies. If you're trying to give up pie, then try some homemade cake.

MOUNTAIN LAKE

Mountain Lake Hotel

VA 700 / MOUNTAIN LAKE, VA 24136
(800) 346-3334 OR (540) 626-7121

Style	Resort
Meals	Breakfast and lunch, Monday through Saturday; dinner, seven days a week; Sunday brunch. The resort is open from May to October.

Price Range	Moderate/Expensive
Superlatives	Setting, "Scallops Amaretto," "Lemon Berry Jazz"
Extras	Full bar

*P*atrick Swayze and Jennifer Grey danced here while filming *Dirty Dancing*. Rutherford B. Hayes, Reba McIntyre and Sam Shepard have dined here.

Mountain Lake Hotel is a 2,600-acre resort with 90 guest rooms, boats, swimming, table games, hiking trails, outdoor activities and a few nice little shops. Built in 1936 from stones on the Mountain Lake property, it replaced a wooden structure that had housed overnight guests as far back as 1857. The cottages date to the early 1900s. Individuals built and furnished them and held a 15-year lease. When the lease expired, ownership was transferred to the resort.

The 50-acre lake is one of only two natural freshwater lakes in Virginia, the other being Lake Drummond in the Dismal Swamp. It is fed from underground springs that keep the water at a temperature of less than 73 degrees.

The seven-mile drive up from U.S. 460 is pleasant, as long as you keep your eyes on the road. Actually, it's coming down that can test your nerves.

Breakfast and dinner are one price plus tax and tip. Breakfast consists of an appetizer, juice, a full breakfast platter, coffee and tea. When more than 100 people are expected, a breakfast buffet with waffle and omelet stations is set up.

Sunday brunch is an extravaganza worth attending. Custom-ordered omelets, top-your-own waffles, freshly carved meat and a plethora of brunch fare like potatoes, casseroles, fresh fruit, breads and fantastic desserts are offered.

The focus at lunch is on salads, sandwiches and burgers.

Dinner can be an enchanting experience. Candles and linens accent each table. Despite the large size of the dining room, there's an intimate ambiance. The menu lists five or six entrees that are changed nightly but always include one beef, one chicken, one fish and one vegetarian dinner. You then have a choice of desserts—usually light ones that complement the meal perfectly. My personal favorite is the "Lemon Berry Jazz," a lemon chiffon pie with thin layers of berries in the middle and drizzled on top.

You don't have to be an overnight guest to dine here. And don't let the weather spoil your plans to go to Mountain Lake, as it's charming regardless of mother nature's mood.

BLACKSBURG

Anchy's

1600 NORTH MAIN STREET
BLACKSBURG, VA 24060
(540) 951-2828

Style	Casual nice
Meals	Lunch, Tuesday through Friday; dinner, Tuesday through Sunday; Sunday brunch. Reservations are recommended on weekends.
Price Range	Moderate

Superlatives	Norwegian salmon, chicken cordon bleu, steaks
Extras	Full bar

*F*ounded in 1798 on 38 acres donated by William Black, Blacksburg is best known today as the home of Virginia Tech, the largest university in the state. Blacksburg has been called "the most wired village in the country" for being among the first places to have a computer network linking the town and the World Wide Web. Though the student population of around 25,000 is close to twice that of permanent residents, Blacksburg ranks as one of the top retirement communities in the United States.

The restaurant known as Anchy's opened in 1989 in a former gun shop and indoor shooting range. The exterior is stucco with pastel colors on the trim and sign for a California- or Florida-style touch. The interior was designed under the direction of general manager Osmund Chan, who majored in communication and design at the University of Toronto and worked in Canada for several years in food-service management.

Chan's meticulous attention to detail is visible throughout Anchy's. Superior on the cleanliness scale, this restaurant was designed for both operating efficiency and dining comfort. The miniblinds, for example, are between two sheets of glass, so dust is unable to collect on them. The executive room, a glassed-in area at one side of the dining room, doubles as a smoking section and has its own air-conditioning system. Extrawide aisles in the kitchen were designed for employees' protection.

Anchy's

Deli sandwiches, salads and daily specials are offered at lunch, along with à la carte items like chicken tenders, clam strips and deviled crab.

Dinner may begin with an appetizer, a soup or a salad featuring feta cheese, smoked salmon or shrimp. The angel hair pasta dishes include primavera with Alfredo sauce and sea scallops with a choice of sauces. Norwegian salmon fillet broiled and served with dill sauce is a house specialty. The breaded shellfish medley includes deviled crab, shrimp, oysters, scallops and clam strips. Baked chicken cordon bleu is a popular item, as is the "Peking Steak," which comes with a sweet oyster sauce. Most of the seafood and steaks can be prepared blackened upon request.

Chocolate mousse and "Chocolate Raspberry Bash" are my favorite desserts, but you could have pecan pie instead.

Guests are invited to relax over coffee, tea, an after-dinner drink or cappuccino. Anchy's is a good place to kick back in a college town that can reel with activity at times.

Boudreaux's

205 NORTH MAIN STREET
BLACKSBURG, VA 24060
(540) 961-2330

Style	Cajun
Meals	Lunch, Tuesday through Saturday; dinner, Tuesday through Sunday; Sunday brunch
Price Range	Inexpensive
Superlatives	Jambalaya, étouffée, shrimp bisque
Extras	Full bar

*B*rothers Jeff and Greg Ames, both Virginia Tech graduates, traveled through the Cajun country of Louisiana and Mississippi in search of recipes for their Blacksburg eatery. "Chefs came out of their kitchens with pages of recipes," said Jeff. Others gave ideas, names of suppliers, posters. In September 1995, Boudreaux's opened to rave reviews that continue to this day.

In a simple spot smack in the center of downtown, you'll see a small neon alligator over a single door. When you walk through the door, you'll find a casual dining room with wooden tables and chairs and a small bar in the back corner. Original art hangs on one wall. Posters with Cajun themes are on the others. The ceiling fans turn slowly. In fact, the only things moving fast are the hosts and servers. Everything else is comfortably slowed down.

If you haven't been to Cajun country, here's a place to expand your eating experience—with "Gator Bites," for example. If you have been, then just relive your travels with some Louisiana alligator tail or seafood gumbo.

Pronunciation assistance is offered right on the menu for two of the three most popular entrees. Jambalaya is a colorful mix of shrimp, crawfish, chicken and sausage in a mildly spicy tomato Creole sauce. The étouffée contains chicken, shrimp or crawfish sauteed with peppers, onions and celery. It's served in a thick Cajun sauce. The pecan chicken is an unusually moist breast of chicken finished with a smooth rum sauce. The blackened stuff is here, too — catfish or Delmonico steak. Most everything comes with a square of cornbread and your choice of dirty rice, new potatoes or pasta salad. All the food is made to order, so you can specify something a little hotter or milder to suit your taste.

The desserts are Cajun, too — bourbon pecan pie and chocolate walnut chess pie, along with occasional specials.

During Sunday brunch, Boudreaux's offers omelets, eggs Benedict, croissants and other items in addition to the Cajun menu. It's not buffet-style, so your order is freshly prepared and served.

If you're wondering who or what Boudreaux is, wonder no more. It comes from Cajun fairy tales and is the equivalent of the Southern "Bubba."

Ipanema
107 ELLETT ROAD
BLACKSBURG, VA 24060
(540) 951-4501

Style	Brazilian
Meals	Lunch, Tuesday through Friday; dinner, Monday through Saturday
Price Range	Moderate
Superlatives	Delicate sauces, fried bananas
Extras	Full bar

Reinaldo Monnerat Fonseca was fascinated with United States history while growing up in Brazil. In the early 1980s, however, after a decade in New York and Boston, he returned to his native land.

Disillusioned with what he had found in our country, Fonseca was hesitant when friends invited him to Virginia and told him that the people were friendly there. Someone offered him a job in Roanoke. Not convinced but still adventurous, he came.

"It *is* different here," he now says. "The people really are nice, and they treat foreigners with respect."

Early in 1992, Fonseca started Ipanema with some borrowed money, a flair for the good things, a helping of hope and a splash of confidence. His two brothers helped him renovate a run-down building. He paid them half of what they were due, promising them the other half when business turned profitable.

Well, they've been paid off. These days at Ipanema, the linens are in place, the candles are lit and there's a fresh flower or two on each table.

Fonseca serves up lots of fried bananas with his

Brazilian entrees. "Galinha Tropicana" is a sauteed chicken breast with fried bananas, pineapple and grapes in a pineapple brandy sauce. The jumbo shrimp, fresh clams and mussels will satisfy seafood lovers, and a selection of beef and pork entrees is there for the carnivores. Linguine, angel hair pasta and fettuccine are among the light entrees. There are also four "Chef's Suggestions"—medleys of meats and fish. The light, tasty sauces here truly accent—never overwhelm—the food.

There are bananas, naturally, in a couple of the desserts, but you can also get a chocolate roll with ice cream and Grand Marnier if you want.

After eating at Ipanema, you'll feel satisfied without the heaviness often associated with dining out. The meals here are carefully prepared and nicely presented without rich or greasy additions.

IRONTO

Mountain View Italian Kitchen

3199 NORTH FORK ROAD / ELLISTON, VA 24087
(800) 396-2512 OR (540) 268-2512

Style	Italian
Meals	Lunch and dinner, Tuesday through Sunday. Reservations are recommended, especially on weekends.
Price Range	Moderate
Superlatives	Funky atmosphere, taste, quality and quantity of food
Extras	Wine and beer

You can mail a letter to Ironto, but it won't go through the Ironto post office, because there isn't one. There isn't a town either, though there's an exit off I-81 named Ironto. Mail is handled by the Elliston post office on the other side of the interstate. According to the postmaster there, Ironto is just a nickname for the small area around the Mountain View Italian Kitchen.

This restaurant is the kind of place any marketing consultant would look at with skepticism. But the Mountain View defies conventional reasoning. It succeeds despite being in an old building, being off the beaten path, running no formal advertising and having an odd atmosphere.

Atmosphere is an interesting concept. Though no place lacks it, some places definitely have more than others. The atmosphere is surely different here—*funky* might be the best description.

Late in 1996, the entrance was moved. Guests once stepped into the kitchen, then took a deep step to the left into the dining room. Now, you walk right into the linoleum-floored, concrete-block eating area. Inexpensive bright blue vinyl chairs, big, thick benches you're bound to trip over if you get up without paying attention and functional tables make up the furnishings. Two large windows frame a field sliced by a railroad track backed by a hillside.

Not much has changed in this 1959 building, originally a convenience store and post office. Owner Richard Hamilton and his late wife, Linda, bought the place at auction in 1990. She ran a small deli, and he ran the convenience store. She had the brainstorm of selling pizza by the slice and putting in three tables. On the second day, the restaurant outgrew its space.

As Paul Harvey would say, now you know—or can figure out—the rest of the story.

The Mountain View isn't spiffy or classy, but you don't come here for spiffy and classy. You come here for the food. It's tasty, fresh, generous and delicious every time. And guess what. You'd better make a reservation. The last time I stopped without one, the wait was about three hours.

The restaurant offers both standard and gourmet pizzas: steak and cheese, sauteed spinach, primavera, veggie and a stuffed one with ham, pepperoni, sausage and salami inside. There are around five dinner variations for chicken, veal and seafood. Pasta dishes are what the Mountain View is known for. The baked ziti is a fabulous, filling and flavorful casserole.

For those who like variety, there are more than a half-dozen combination entrees. The one called "Little Bit of Everything" includes a broccoli-stuffed shell, Italian sausage, lasagna and eggplant rollatini.

If you're going up or down I-81 and have an appetite, take exit 128 and head west on County Road 603 for about four miles. Mountain View is the building on your left with old Coca-Cola signs on it. But the restaurant serves only Pepsi. That probably makes as much sense as anything here.

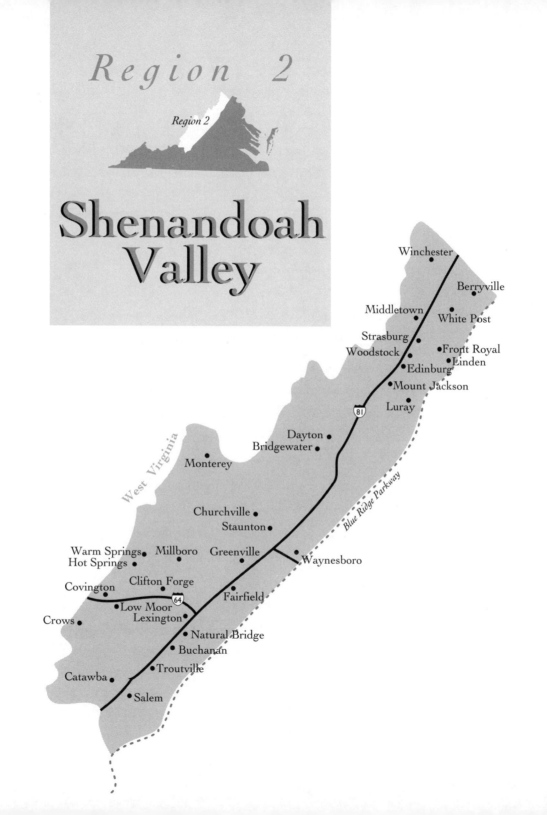

Region 2

Region 2

Shenandoah Valley

Winchester
Berryville
Middletown
White Post
Strasburg
Woodstock
Front Royal
Linden
Edinburg
Mount Jackson
Luray
Dayton
Bridgewater
Monterey
West Virginia
Churchville
Staunton
Warm Springs
Millboro
Greenville
Hot Springs
Waynesboro
Covington
Clifton Forge
Low Moor
Fairfield
Crows
Lexington
Catawba
Natural Bridge
Buchanan
Troutville
Salem
Blue Ridge Parkway
81
64

One of the prettiest words in the English language also happens to be the name of one of the prettiest valleys anywhere—*Shenandoah*. Some say the word means "daughter of the stars," while others claim it means "river of high mountains." But there's no dispute that it connotes natural tranquility.

The valley is around 200 miles long and is bordered by the Blue Ridge Mountains on the east and the Allegheny Mountains on the west. You'll find a scenic panorama from the valley to the mountains—and even inside the mountains. The limestone caverns, underground streams and unusual rock formations here are world famous.

West of the valley are towns like Hot Springs, Warm Springs, Healing Spring and Falling Spring, all named for mineral springs reputed to have therapeutic value for a variety of ailments.

The natural beauty of the valley and the surrounding mountains has made this region a popular tourist destination for travelers from all over the world.

Claudia's Blues Cafe

Claudia's Blues Cafe

300 EAST MAIN STREET / SALEM, VA 24153
(540) 387-2523

Style	Cafe
Meals	Dinner, Tuesday through Saturday
Price Range	Moderate
Superlatives	"Bayou Dip," jambalaya, Key lime pie
Extras	Full bar

Some 230 miles southwest of Washington, D.C., and 60 miles north of the North Carolina line lies Salem, a city of close to 25,000 residents. Salem was settled in 1768 and was chartered as a city exactly two centuries later, in 1968.

An exciting new attraction on Salem's pedestrian-friendly Main Street is Claudia's Blues Cafe. As far as restaurant sizes go, this is one of the smallest. But as far as restaurant popularity goes—well, let's just say it's a very popular spot, and for good reason.

Claudia Lambruscati, a bartender for many years and the wife of Steve Lambruscati, a fireman for the city of Roanoke, opened her tiny blues cafe in May 1996. Her husband, a former high-school industrial arts teacher, made all the tables and shelves and the bar.

The place can't be much more than 15 feet by 25 feet. It has eight barstools, one table for four and three tables for two. The walls are decorated with prints, posters and photos of blues artists. Many people stop in because of the blue neon light in the window, the symbol of "the Hook"—John Lee Hooker. Claudia had it made for her cafe. Blues music plays continuously here. Some of Claudia's glasses are even blue. The plates don't match at all; it's an eclectic collection she's accumulated.

From a kitchen about the size of a walk-in closet comes some great Cajun food. Dinner can start with "Bayou Dip," mozzarella sticks, buffalo wings or fried mushrooms. Burgers, a Cajun chicken sandwich and the "Blues-B-Que" are some of the sandwich options. The entrees range from hearty salads, chicken pasta and jambalaya to blackened chicken, blackened catfish and blackened rib-eye steak. If *blackened* isn't your thing, that's okay, as items like steamed shrimp, beans and rice and a "Bayou Spud Platter" are also on the menu. The pies are homemade.

Claudia herself has an eclectic personality—charming and smart, with a homespun touch. She definitely knows her bar, her music and her business. She doesn't have room to store Diet Coke, so I ordered "any light beer." She told me of a Mexican beer that goes well with spicy food, saying I was "guaranteed to like it." And indeed I did.

Jägerheim

121 EAST MAIN STREET / SALEM, VA 24153
(540) 389-5082

Style	German
Meals	Lunch and dinner, Monday through Saturday
Price Range	Inexpensive/Moderate
Superlatives	Jäger schnitzel, Wiener schnitzel
Extras	Full bar

*T*ranslated literally, *Jägerheim* means "hunter's house." You might guess that right away at this res-

Jägerheim

taurant from the floor-to-ceiling beer cans and bottles on the left wall, the trophies of raccoon, opossum, turkey, duck and deer and the long wooden bar.

If you wander on back past the old brick wall behind the bar, you can find a booth or table in the dining room there. The walls have dark wood trim and a high shelf with beer steins and carved animals on it. Flowered vinyl tablecloths cover the tables, and the booths have red vinyl seats. There are little white lights all around the ceiling. The music is German—accordions and happy singing.

Günther Gass started the restaurant out near Dixie Caverns in 1993 and moved here three years later. Jägerheim reflects his heritage.

Though the appetizers are pretty much American—cheese fries, breaded mushrooms, buffalo wings, onion rings—the lunch platters are all German. There's a bratwurst platter, a knockwurst platter and a summer sausage platter. German potato salad and a "Jägerheim Salad" are offered. Among the hot sandwiches are bratwurst, knockwurst, burgers and chicken Parmesan.

The schnitzels are popular at dinner, Wiener schnitzel and Jäger schnitzel topping the list. German pepper steak, sausages on cabbage and German goulash are offered, as are a vegetable lasagna, fillet of pork with homemade mushroom gravy, "Kasseler Rippensper" and other entrees. All dinners include salad. Sauerbraten is on the menu Friday and Saturday evenings on the last full weekend of the month.

The desserts include Black Forest cake, Black Forest cheesecake and, of course, German chocolate cake.

Mac and Bob's

Mac and Bob's

316 EAST MAIN STREET / SALEM, VA 24153
(540) 389-5999

Style	Family-style
Meals	Lunch and dinner, seven days a week
Price Range	Inexpensive/Moderate
Superlatives	The "Augustino," calzones, "Katie Salad"
Extras	Full bar

*M*ac and Bob's is slightly deceptive-looking. From the street, you might guess it to be a fern bar, thanks to the solarium room bordering the sidewalk. But once inside, you'll find several rooms with brick walls and smoky-glass partitions.

What started as a 10-stool bar up the street is now a 258-seat restaurant with a menu that has something for everyone. Since locating in this former restaurant, cake shop and taxi office, Mac and Bob's has slowly expanded back and sideways. The marble bar has close to 30 seats, and there are a few dartboards for customers. But a family atmosphere permeates the brick, pine and dark green interior.

Pizza, pasta, potato skins, a house quiche of cheese and broccoli, a quiche of the day and homemade French onion soup are available. The lunch and dinner menus are quite similar—you can go with subs and sandwiches anytime. A Reuben, a Philly, a French dip, a veggie and a club are listed among the sandwiches, but the most popular is the "Augustino," a house sub of ham, hard salami, bologna, provolone cheese, lettuce, tomato, mild peppers and onions.

The dinner menu features a variety of chicken entrees—Alfredo, linguine, piccata, Parmesan, Marsala. Baby back ribs, rib-eye steak, New York strip, stir-fry, catch of the day, burgers and salads are also listed. The "Katie Salad" is marinated grilled chicken, walnuts, cheddar, Monterey Jack and seasonal fruit on a bed of spinach.

Any meal can be finished with mud pie, a fudge brownie, "Chocolate Loving Spoon Cake" or a couple of kinds of cheesecake.

Mac and Bob's has retained its original name even though Mac is no longer part of the operation. Bob is Bob Rotanz. The "Katie Salad" is named for his daughter.

The Homeplace

The Homeplace

U.S. 311 / CATAWBA, VA 24070
(540) 384-7252

Style	Family-style
Meals	Dinner, Thursday through Sunday
Price Range	Inexpensive
Superlatives	Fried chicken, homemade fruit cobbler

*T*he name Catawba comes from the Choctaw Indian word for "separated." Perhaps the town's name thus honors the nearby mountain of the same name, which separates it from the larger towns and the main roads on the other side. The Appalachian Trail goes along the ridge of Catawba Mountain. A popular summer resort called Roanoke Red Sulphur Springs was located near here in the 1850s. A sanatorium for the treatment of tuberculosis was established in 1909. Neither is still in operation.

Guests at The Homeplace can't make a reservation, but they'll find the wait—and there almost always is one—very pleasant nonetheless. You can wait outside under the shade of majestic maple and oak trees, on the old country porch or in the gazebo. If you wait inside, you can sit in the Morgan Room, named for the previous owners.

The Homeplace is in a lovely white clapboard house with black shutters. Built in 1907, the home sits back from the road on 60 acres with a quintessential red barn and a pond. The restaurant opened in 1982, four years after the original dairy farm was divided into tracts and sold.

Harold Wingate bought two tracts—the one with the house and the one with the barn. He and his family renovated the interior by stripping varnish off the original oak trim and chestnut wainscoting, wiring new lights and refurbishing the walls. The floors are all wood. Most of the furniture is oak. Tables and chairs are always being moved to accommodate family gatherings of various sizes.

But even a restaurant in the nicest of settings must have the best of food to maintain its reputation and attract repeat business. Harold's son Kevin attributes The Homeplace's phenomenal success to "good food mainly, good value for the money, as well as good atmosphere and good service."

Once seated, you may choose among roast beef, fried chicken and country ham. Then other dishes come—mashed potatoes, gravy, green beans, biscuits with great apple butter, pinto beans, slaw. All of this is hot and tasty—and it's all replenished until you ask the waitress to stop delivering.

Of course, then she comes along with cherry or peach cobbler to finish what you'll likely admit was a wonderful dinner.

Afterwards, ask yourself this question: For a reasonably priced, family-style restaurant, what could The Homeplace do better? You'll probably draw a blank.

Greenwood Family Restaurant

U.S. 11 / TROUTVILLE, VA 24175
(540) 992-3550

Style	Family-style
Meals	Breakfast, lunch and dinner, seven days a week
Price Range	Inexpensive
Superlatives	"Dreamsicle Shake," pan-fried chicken, meatloaf

I wasn't starving when I happened to drive by the Greenwood, but I knew I'd be hungry in another half-hour, and the number of cars in the parking lot convinced me to stop. Good thing, too, because there's some fine home-cooked food here.

The decor consists primarily of wood painted green, white trim and wood paneling. There are large windows in both the front and back dining rooms. A model train runs around the back dining room near the ceiling. Overall, the place is attractive and very clean.

The Greenwood opened in 1952. It was purchased by Randy Marianetti in 1996. Randy wanted to be an electrician, but his father wanted him to go to college. He helped pay for his education at Virginia Tech by working in restaurants. He graduated in 1980 with a degree in communications.

Randy says there weren't many jobs in his field, so he went to work at something he knew, becoming district manager for a restaurant chain and getting involved in a number of restaurants in the Roanoke area. One lesson he learned is that you can take care of only one thing at a time if you want to do it right. So he now focuses all his attention on the Greenwood.

The place is very popular with truckers, whose main requirements are a large parking lot and good food. But don't let those 18-wheelers intimidate you. The Greenwood is just as popular with seniors, families and young folks, too.

If you're over 40, treat yourself to a "Dreamsicle Shake" for old times' sake. If you're under 40, well, you're in for a treat without the memories.

The comprehensive breakfast includes eggs, country ham, pork brains, traditional salt fish, pancakes, omelets and waffles with fruit and whipped topping. The bestseller is sausage gravy.

Sandwiches, sandwich platters, burgers, barbecue on a bun, chili, country-style steak, pot roast, soups and salads are offered at lunch.

Dinners include a variety of seafood, rib-eye steak, baked ham, pork tenderloin and the Greenwood's famous chicken, all served with two vegetables and bread. Meatloaf is also a local favorite.

The desserts are just what you'd expect—homemade and delicious. Among the choices are cobblers in season, "Grandma's Carrot Cake," rice pudding and an assortment of cakes and pies.

The waitresses are friendly and efficient, the food good and reasonably priced. And my car just might be in the parking lot when you stop.

To reach Greenwood Family Restaurant, take Exit 156 off I-81 and drive 1.2 miles south on U.S. 11.

Kaleidoscope Cafe

Kaleidoscope Cafe

895 MAIN STREET / BUCHANAN, VA 24066
(540) 254-3019

Style	Cafe
Meals	Baked goods and lunch, Monday through Saturday
Price Range	Inexpensive
Superlatives	White chocolate macadamia nut cookies

*B*uchanan was named for Colonel John Buchanan, the successful owner of Anchor and Hope Plantation in the mid-1700s. The Kaleidoscope Cafe may well be the oldest business building in town. Constructed in the 1820s, the building was vacant for nearly a decade before two enterprising local sisters, Donna Cox and Christy Rhodes, opened their cafe in the fall of 1996.

Actually, it was Donna and their dad, Kenneth Rhodes, who tossed around the idea for a restaurant while Christy was off studying biology at Radford University. In the fall of 1995, the three of them— along with their mother, Rita, and Donna's husband, Mike—were at a small cafe in Greensboro, North Carolina, when the idea took shape. Buchanan, they decided, needed a cafe like the one they were sitting in.

They bought the building the next spring. Donna, an avid auction-goer, scoured ads for an old oak counter and display cases. They found exactly what they wanted at an auction in Covington.

The sun was streaming through the windows in the late afternoon one day as the family tried to settle on a name for the place. With colorful rays playing on the walls, *Kaleidoscope* was the unanimous choice.

The ceilings are high, and the walls are navy blue on the bottom and white on the top. Each of the six round tables has a colorful tablecloth under glass and a creative centerpiece of cotton stuffed into a tall sundae glass with a straw. A little of the cotton at the top is dyed red, making a cute cotton parfait. Framed photographs, posters and prints hang on the walls.

Special coffees, cappuccino and espresso are brewed fresh daily. For cold drinks, the Kaleidoscope serves 25 flavors of Italian soda.

Two sandwiches and homemade soup are offered at lunch. Reuben, turkey and Swiss and tuna melt on a bagel are among the sandwiches. Vegetable beef, cream of potato or broccoli and New England clam chowder are some of the popular soups.

The baking starts around six o'clock each morning. You can just drive slowly through town with your windows down and find the place with your nose.

When you leave, remember to continue on U.S. 11 to the next access ramp to I-81; you cannot get back on at Exit 167. But this isn't out of your way, because you'll be going parallel to the interstate—and you'll be all refreshed thanks to the Kaleidoscope's home-baked goods and great coffee or tea.

BLUE RIDGE PARKWAY

Buck Mountain Grille

5002 FRANKLIN ROAD
(MILEPOST 120–121, BLUE RIDGE PARKWAY)
ROANOKE, VA 24014
(540) 776-1830

Style	Casual nice
Meals	Lunch, Tuesday through Friday; dinner, Tuesday through Sunday; Sunday brunch
Price Range	Moderate
Superlatives	Crab cakes, homemade tiramisu, vegetarian dishes
Extras	Full bar

*T*he Blue Ridge Parkway travels along 470 miles of the highest mountain ridges between Shenandoah National Park in northwestern Virginia and Great Smoky Mountains National Park on the North Carolina–Tennessee border.

When you take the U.S. 220 exit off the parkway, you'll find this superclean eatery at the bottom of the ramp. The outdoor awning and the carpeting are burgundy. The walls are white on the top and cream colored on the bottom. The plants are real and have little white lights in them. The fancy chandeliers are made of smoky glass and brass. Large windows provide a flood of daylight. Soft music plays in the background. It's all very refreshing.

Mushroom stroganoff, red beans and rice and angel hair pasta with marinara and feta cheese are some of the lighter lunch choices. Four vegetarian sandwiches and six salads—among them "Parkway Rice Salad" and crab salad—are also offered. The "Quarry Club," designed for big appetites, includes ham, turkey, bacon, Swiss cheese, tomato and lettuce. "Wonju Chicken" is named for Roanoke's Korean sister city. It's chicken marinated overnight in a homemade sauce that combines sesame, orange and ginger.

Five vegetarian entrees on the dinner menu cater to the meatless bunch. Angel hair pasta with pesto and polenta with marinara sauce are two of them. You can order a steak or a chicken dish, but seafood entrees outnumber all others. "Grecian Feta Shrimp," "Scallops Nantucket" and a fisherman's platter are a few of them. Some sandwiches are available for those not wishing to have a full dinner.

The brunch choices include sandwiches, vegetarian entrees, salads and breakfast items like omelets, pancakes and scrambled eggs. The French toast is made "the Roanoke way." Bananas, cinnamon and plain yogurt are added to the batter. The thick slices of

French bread are then served with real maple syrup and a fresh fruit salad with honey-yogurt dressing.

Peaks of Otter Lodge

MILEPOST 86, BLUE RIDGE PARKWAY
BEDFORD, VA 24523
(540) 586-1081

Style	Family-style
Meals	Breakfast, lunch and dinner, seven days a week
Price Range	Inexpensive/Moderate
Superlatives	Mountain scenery, country buffet
Extras	Full bar

*T*he name Peaks of Otter refers to three mountains located in a small geographical area. While there are several stories about the unusual name, no one seems sure how it came about.

Peaks of Otter Lodge was built in 1964 and is privately owned. However, because the Blue Ridge Parkway is operated by the National Park Service, the restaurants are authorized concessions operated under contract with the park service.

The rustic building has lots of wood and stone and a gorgeous view over a small lake. There are 63 overnight rooms, each with two double beds, a private bath and a private balcony or terrace.

The large dining room, open May through October, features spectacular buffets and regular menu entrees. The cozy coffee shop located off the main lobby is open year-round.

Breakfast is a hearty event featuring a variety of à la carte items and complete meals. French toast, ham biscuits and country ham steaks are among the offerings. There's a morning buffet during busy times.

Soup, salads, sandwiches, burgers, fried chicken, quiche, trout and roast turkey are some of the lunch options.

Dinner may feature a country buffet or seafood buffet, both smorgasbords of meats or fish, vegetables, salads and hush puppies. The entrees in the dining room may include prime rib, fried chicken, rainbow trout, roast turkey and dressing and a selection of sandwiches. The coffee shop has a hot roast beef sandwich, fillet of flounder, fried chicken and hamburger steak.

Southern favorites like bread pudding, cobbler, apple pie and pecan pie are among the desserts.

If you're tooling along the parkway, you can plan your day around a meal here. Or you might take one of Peaks of Otter's hearty picnic lunches with you on a midday hike or drive.

Fancy Hill

ROUTE 2, BOX 591 (EXIT 180 OFF I-81)
NATURAL BRIDGE, VA 24578
(540) 291-2860

Style	Family-style
Meals	Breakfast, lunch and dinner, seven days a week
Price Range	Inexpensive/Moderate
Superlatives	Steak Diane, twilight dinners
Extras	Beer and wine

Fancy Hill

According to legend, Natural Bridge was called "the Bridge of God" by the Monocan Indians, who worshiped it. Thomas Jefferson, the original American owner of the property, purchased Natural Bridge and 157 surrounding acres on July 5, 1774, "for 20 shillings of good and lawful money." "So beautiful an arch, so elevated, so light, and springing up as it were to heaven"—so goes Jefferson's description of the bridge.

Fancy Hill is an open, bright, clean family restaurant with a fantastic license-plate collection in the pine-paneled dining room. Plates are posted from all 50 states. I also found Nova Scotia, Newfoundland, British Columbia, New Brunswick, Quebec and the Yukon Territory. The oldest plate I could read was from 1922.

The photographs of sites in the Western United States filling one wall in the big dining room were taken by the owners during their travels. The interior is predominantly cream and mauve. Accordion blinds and lace cafe curtains soften the large front windows.

Fancy Hill's three "He-Man" breakfasts are steak and eggs, the "Big Boy" and country ham and eggs, each one as comprehensive a morning meal as you'll get anywhere. The extra large biscuits are just that.

Lunch features salads, flame-broiled burgers, sandwiches, pizza and hot or cold subs. If the soup of the day is homemade potato, I recommend it.

Entrees come with a house salad, bread and any two of several items—hush puppies, mashed potatoes and gravy, fried okra, french fries, pinto beans and others. The flame-broiled steaks are hand-cut by the chef. The house specialty is steak Diane—slices of tenderloin sauteed with mushrooms and onions and served with brown sauce. Chicken, pork, fish and a half-dozen Italian meals like manicotti and chicken breast parmigiana round out the menu.

The twilight dinner, available between 5 and 7 P.M. every day, is a specially priced meal offering five or so entree items accompanied by soup, salad, two vegetables, bread, a beverage and a dessert.

The parking lot here is large, so it doesn't matter what you're driving or hauling. And if you happen to stop at the end of a weary day, you'll be glad to know that the Fancy Hill Motel is right next door. The place may have been built in the 1950s or 1960s, but it sure looks like it belongs in the 1990s—it's clean, inviting and well maintained.

Eagle Nest

CROWS

Eagle Nest

U.S. 311 / CROWS, VA 24426
(540) 559-9738

Style	Family-style
Meals	Dinner, seven days a week
Price Range	Moderate/Expensive
Superlatives	Forest setting, seafood pasta, trout
Extras	Full bar

*L*ike so many towns, this one's name came from a man well known in the area. Actually, it's a variation, since his name was *Crow*—John Crow, the first colonel of the Alleghany Militia. He had 11 children, so everyone knew where *Crow's* place was. The community thus kept the *s* but dropped the apostrophe.

Since I arrived at the Eagle Nest on back roads, it seemed like I was in the middle of nowhere, but it's really less than five miles south of Exit 183 off I-64.

From the time you start your walk from the parking area, you'll be enchanted with the place. A fast-running stream spills over rocks into a deep pool right next to the wooden walkway. A tiny, one-room honeymoon cottage perches on a rocky outcrop on the other side of the water. Little cabins dot the hillside behind the main building.

This is an old hunting camp and looks every bit the part. The pitch of the floors gives testimony to its 60-odd years of history, and scores of initials carved in the log walls attest to the hundreds of folks who have passed through.

The hunting camp was built in 1929. The restaurant was originally next to the road. In 1950, it was moved up the hill and joined to a couple of other buildings to create the rambling log structure you see hugging the slope today.

Calling the Eagle Nest *rustic* would be an understatement. But the dining is, to quote the menu, "country gourmet." You'll note the navy-blue tablecloths and napkins, the little white lights around the windows on the porch and the cute little pierced-tin wall lamps in one of the dining rooms. The tables are set with blue-speckled tin plates, a basket of crackers and a lazy Susan with three pots of cheese, butter and apple butter.

Each dinner includes soup or salad, two vegetables, homemade bread and iced tea or coffee. The menu is comprehensive, from country-style entrees like fried chicken, cured country ham, veal liver and chicken livers to choice steaks and seafood. The steaks include New York strip, rib-eye, filet mignon and porterhouse. Among the seafood options are rainbow trout, catfish, sea scallops and frog legs. Daily specials like fried oysters, beef burgundy and trout stuffed with crabmeat are also offered.

The desserts include homemade brownies, bread pudding and even eclairs.

There's nothing rustic about the service, the food or the presentation here. Too bad the cabins aren't suited for overnight guests anymore. This would be a neat place to stay.

Cucci's

566 EAST MADISON STREET
COVINGTON, VA 24426
(540) 962-3964

Style	Italian
Meals	Lunch and dinner, Monday through Saturday
Price Range	Inexpensive
Superlatives	Bread, sauces, turnover pizza
Extras	Full bar

*O*riginally called Merry's Store or Merry's Stand, Covington was named for Peter Covington, the community's oldest resident at the time of the naming. The town was incorporated in 1833, but the incorporation was repealed six years later. Covington was incorporated again in 1849 and then again—perhaps for safe measure—in 1855. The Humpback Bridge, located just west of town, is the oldest covered bridge in Virginia. It spans 100 feet and is eight feet higher in the center than at the ends. The restored bridge is now part of a state wayside park.

Cucci's has been a Covington institution for over two decades now. Its story began at a pizza shop in New Jersey, where an impressionable teen named Janet met a young Italian named Victor Cucci. They got married and decided to open a restaurant. A brother of Victor's suggested they look around Covington.

They loved the town. The first Cucci's opened in 1977. Ten years later, Janet and Victor demolished their small building and constructed a new one on the same property. More than 10 years after that, Cucci's continues to enjoy a reputation for good food at a good price.

Everything still looks new inside. A huge central skylight allows abundant light into the dining rooms, which can seat around 100. Posters with Italian themes hang on the walls. You can learn a little about Italy from the place mats, which contain sketches of historic landmarks like the Leaning Tower of Pisa and the Colosseum, a map noting Italy's major cities and tidbits of information.

Of course, pizza is important here. There are a lot

Cucci's

of sizes, toppings and styles from which to choose. The "Cucci Special" has mushrooms, sausage, pepperoni, green peppers, onions, anchovies and garlic. Turnover pizzas are popular. The dough is folded over the toppings—which I guess are no longer toppings, since they're in the middle. Pizza can also be purchased by the slice. Cucci's 18 sandwiches come on homemade rolls. You can buy a single trip to the salad bar or all-you-can-eat trips. The "Vittorio Salad" includes cottage cheese, tuna, peaches, pineapple, tomato and lettuce.

Popular dinner entrees like spaghetti, lasagna, manicotti and ravioli come with bread and butter and one salad-bar trip. The bread is wonderful—it's yeasty, moist and tasty and has a nice crust. Many customers like to dip it into one of Cucci's sauces.

The desserts number exactly two—cheesecake and chocolate cake.

James Burke House Eatery

COVINGTON

James Burke House Eatery

232 WEST RIVERSIDE STREET
COVINGTON, VA 24426
(540) 965-0040

Style	Cafe
Meals	Continental breakfast, Monday through Friday; lunch, Monday through Saturday
Price Range	Inexpensive
Superlatives	Historic building, chicken salad, crème de menthe brownies

The property on which this restaurant stands was purchased at the original sale of town lots in 1818. Six years later, James Burke built a small, two-story brick home here—the second-oldest in town. A one-room brick addition was constructed on one side of the house soon afterwards. A similar addition was built on the other side in the early 1900s, perhaps to balance the appearance. In the 1950s, the house was expanded in the back. And finally, the 1990s brought an interior renovation.

Today, local girl Diane Maynard, Covington High School class of 1980, runs the business with her father and sister. Three tables are situated across from an old fireplace in the angled hall that connects the two dining rooms. The big windows in one of the dining rooms offer a view into a backyard of grass, maple trees, a sycamore and well-kept brick buildings. The windows have custom-made, multicolored valances. A few little quilts adorn the walls.

Salad platters, homemade soup (usually available from September through April) and stuffed potatoes are among the popular choices at lunch. The potatoes come loaded with such hearty combinations as roast turkey, bacon and muenster, or mixed vegetables, mushrooms, tomato and cheese. There's quite a sandwich selection. The "Mad Ann" is corned beef layered with sauerkraut and melted Swiss on rye. The "Highlander" is pita bread filled with garden vegetables, lettuce, tomato and fresh mushrooms, all of it topped with cheese. The really simple sandwiches are referred to as "Burke House Basics" on the menu. They include peanut butter and jelly, cheese, ham, tuna salad and turkey.

Though you'll see some of the homemade desserts on display, be sure to ask what's in the refrigerator, because some of the Burke House's most delightful sweets need to stay cool. The crème de menthe brownie is always an excellent choice.

You can also get picnic baskets and box lunches here. Rest assured that if you're on the road and whatever takeout items you order need refrigeration, there's an easy solution—you'll probably eat them before you leave the parking lot.

LOW MOOR

The Cat and Owl

KARNES ROAD (EXIT 21 OFF I-64)
LOW MOOR, VA 24457
(540) 862-5808

Style	Casual nice
Meals	Dinner, Monday through Saturday; closed on holidays
Price Range	Moderate/Expensive
Superlatives	Shrimp, char-broiled seafood, banana fritters
Extras	Full bar

Who's to say it wasn't fate that brought Bruce Proffitt to this place to run a restaurant and full bar just a quarter-mile from where his great-great-grandfather Patrick Fox once ran a saloon? Proffitt was born in nearby Clifton Forge but grew up in Pearisburg and went to college in Blacksburg,

The Cat and Owl

graduating from Virginia Tech in 1969. So how did he get back here?

His father and uncle heeded a prediction that the Clifton Forge–Covington area would grow in the next couple of decades. They surmised that if that was the case, establishing a good restaurant would be a smart move.

Their vision included a railroad theme. In fact, the walkway to the front door was created to look like a railroad platform. They wanted to call the restaurant The C & O, after the railroad company of the same name, but when they found they couldn't use the name, they chose The Cat and Owl, figuring it would get shortened to The C & O. Well, a few glitches along the way twisted the theme to barnboard and Victorian, and the name—it was just unusual enough to stick.

Bruce helped his father and uncle tear down barns and move the weathered boards inside the renovated brick house. Whatever isn't barnboard in here is red. Bright red. The carpet, the lamps, the chairs. The wallpaper is not only red, but fuzzy as well. *Eclectic* accurately describes the collection of antiques, old sports equipment, framed photos of women and American presidents and assorted odd pieces.

After an informal, two-week crash course at a friend's restaurant, Bruce began developing The Cat and Owl into a fine dining establishment with a great regional reputation. He eventually bought the place from his father. His cousin Scott is the chef.

The house appetizer is char-broiled shrimp. Shrimp is also available deep-fried. Catfish fillets, clam strips,

oysters and scallops are some of the other seafood choices. The steaks are hand-cut in the kitchen each day. You can order one of four sizes of rib-eye or one of three sizes of filet mignon. The "Best of Both Worlds" selections team rib-eye steak with shrimp, lobster tail, crab legs or scallops. Chicken, pork loin and beef kabobs are also available.

"Heath Bar Crunch Pie," deep-dish apple pie and lime sherbet are among the sweets, but banana fritters have become The Cat and Owl's signature dessert.

CLIFTON FORGE

Club Car Shop & Deli

429 EAST RIDGEWAY STREET
CLIFTON FORGE, VA 24422
(540) 862-0777

Style	Deli
Meals	Lunch, Monday through Saturday
Price Range	Inexpensive
Superlatives	"Club Car" sandwich, homemade cookies
Extras	Wine and beer

*T*here aren't too many towns that can say there's no other place by the same name. But Clifton Forge can—it's the only one in the United States. It was named by W. L. Alexander, who had a forge here and an ancestral home called Clifton up in Rockbridge County.

One of the newest attractions in town is the Club Car Shop & Deli. It was never in question that Maeve

Club Car Shop & Deli

ing on people, but they're all dressed."

The gourmet shop is at the front of a narrow space with an old tin ceiling painted black, contemporary track lighting and white walls. Maeve stocks fine chocolates, candies, gourmet sauces, Virginia wines, cookies, teapots, baskets, coffee, tea and fine gifts.

There are 10 tables in the back. You place your order at the counter on the right, get your drink from the cooler in the back and wait until lunch is delivered to your table.

Maeve offers soup, salads and freshly baked muffins. In keeping with the spirit of this railroad town, the sandwiches are named for trains—all of them, that is, except "Chessie's Favorite," Chessie being the feline logo for the C & O Railroad. "Chessie's" is tuna salad on your choice of bread. The "Allegheny" is a roast beef and provolone sandwich with roasted sweet red peppers, lettuce and herbal vinaigrette on a French roll. The "Fast Flying Virginian" has turkey, cheese, lettuce and tomato on marble rye.

Personally, I like the "Create Your Own" category and its three numbered instructions: (1) Choose a meat and a cheese; (2) Choose a bread; (3) Add the extras. This allows lots of combinations, as five meats, four cheeses, five breads and nearly a dozen extras are available.

The cookies are great—I tried one of each just to make sure. Cheesecake and German chocolate brownies are also available.

Archibald would have a little deli someday. She just didn't know exactly what it would be or when it would happen.

Once, on a trip to Farmville with her husband, Maeve expounded on her vision of a gourmet and wine shop with a deli. When they reached town, the couple strode into a little place called Cheese & Company (also included in this book). "It was exactly what I was describing," said Maeve.

Soon after that, a space in Clifton Forge occupied by a ladies' clothing boutique became vacant. On October 25, 1995, Maeve the registered nurse became Maeve the gourmet-shop owner. The deli opened the following June.

When asked if she missed being a nurse, Maeve quipped, "Oh, it's not much different. You're still wait-

Michel Cafe

Michel Cafe

424 EAST RIDGEWAY STREET
CLIFTON FORGE, VA 24422
(540) 862-4119

Style	Fine dining
Meals	Dinner, Monday through Saturday
Price Range	Moderate/Expensive
Superlatives	*Steak au poivre*, mountain trout, seafood
Extras	Full bar

*M*ichel Galand grew up in France and trained under well-known chef Paul Bocuse before coming to the United States to work at The Homestead Resort in Hot Springs. He later opened a restaurant in Covington, then Michel Cafe in Clifton Forge in the early 1980s.

Two restaurants proved one too many, so when Clifton Forge passed a law allowing liquor by the glass, Michel closed his Covington restaurant and concentrated his energies on Michel Cafe. In fact, it was through the restaurant that he met his wife, Carmen, who was challenged by her boss at a local newspaper to sell Michel an ad. She did, and six months after the sale, they were married.

Michel Cafe is as pretty from the outside as it is on the inside. Lace curtains, window boxes and attractive awnings make a favorable first impression. Inside, white linens adorn oak tables, and black-and-white photos of France from Michel's personal collection are displayed on the walls. The second floor has more dining space and room for private parties. The third floor has a bar and is used for private functions.

The menu is changed frequently. You may find escargots or shrimp and basil in a puff pastry among the appetizers. The soup du jour could be shrimp bisque.

Steak au poivre is a house specialty, as is mountain trout, which may be prepared with almonds or stuffed with crabmeat and topped with champagne sauce. Filet mignon with Bearnaise sauce, quail, veal chops with mushroom cream sauce, duck breast and lamb may be among the entrees, depending on the season.

Michel carries imported beers. The wine selection is subject to change, so the most convenient way to choose what you want is to make your way to the antique, solid oak, 12-foot-high walk-in cooler, which has been converted into a wine cellar and beer-storage unit.

Crème caramel or fresh fruit in a puff pastry with crème anglaise may be a sweet ending to your fine meal.

Recommended well beyond the limits of Clifton Forge, Michel Cafe lives up to its grand reputation.

Harb's

19 WEST WASHINGTON STREET
LEXINGTON, VA 24450
(540) 464-1900

Style	Cafe
Meals	Breakfast and lunch, seven days a week; dinner, Tuesday through Saturday
Price Range	Inexpensive/Moderate
Superlatives	Nachos with homemade sauce and sour cream, soups
Extras	Full bar

*L*exington is one of the prettiest, most compact, most delightful walk-around towns in Virginia—a place with great shops, beautiful bed and breakfast inns, live theater, equestrian events and free concerts. Actually, you don't even have to walk. From April through October, the Lexington Carriage Company will take you on a narrated tour.

Harb's didn't make the cut for this book the first time around because I didn't like the looks of the floor, which consists of the original black and white mosaic tiles discovered when another floor was torn up. Owners Dale Ferrebee and Marlene Smith have been told it's in very good shape for its age. One could say it adds character to the place.

The rest of the place also has character. The chairs are mismatched pieces acquired from the local universities and other places. The tables have red-and-white- or blue-and-white-checked tablecloths, a few colorful silk flowers in a clay pot and a candle. Artwork for sale is displayed on unevenly painted white walls. An old piano with a second-grade lesson book on it sees occasional use.

Despite my initial misgivings, Harb's reputation prompted me back. It's the only in-town place that serves breakfast. You can get muffins, freshly baked baguettes, fruit-filled croissants, jumbo bagels, Belgian waffles, eggs and omelets. Although the "Montepiano"—ground beef, spinach, mushrooms and onions scrambled with two eggs—is listed on the breakfast menu, it's available anytime.

Those who arrive on Wednesdays between 8 and 9 A.M. are in for a real treat—live bluegrass music. A local group—or some of its nine members—show up on Wednesdays to play for a muffin and coffee. It's a morning variation on singing for one's supper.

The soups here are homemade. New England clam chowder is a specialty. The salads are hearty. Harb's signature nachos with black beans come in small and large sizes. There are lots of sandwiches and some grilled items. The entrees include red beans and rice, rigatoni, a Mexican plate, a seafood platter, rib-eye steak and crab cakes.

Harb's has what it calls "Colossal Cookies," and they're colossally good. If I'd seen them before I saw the floor . . . Well, I no longer worry about the floor, now that I've eaten here.

Maple Hall

3111 NORTH LEE HIGHWAY (EXIT 195 OFF I-81)
LEXINGTON, VA 24450
(540) 463-2044 OR (540) 463-6693

Style	Fine dining
Meals	Dinner, seven days a week
Price Range	Moderate
Superlatives	Historical warmth, lobster bisque
Extras	Full bar

Set on 56 acres and flanked by majestic maple trees, Maple Hall was built as a plantation house in 1850.

Dining is at garden level in three intimate rooms, where double linens, fresh flowers, candles and fireplaces exude an elegant warmth.

The signature appetizer here is sausage pâté baked in pastry and served with sherry mushroom sauce. Other before-dinner treats may include smoked Virginia trout, a soup du jour, a special salad, or a chef's feature—crabmeat omelet the night I dined here. The lobster bisque stays on the appetizer menu all the time.

The menu is changed seasonally to take advantage of fresh produce and game, though the filet mignon is a stable item. The half-dozen or so entrees care-fully selected by chef Robert Dytrych will please a variety of different palates. A vegetarian dish is usually listed—like lasagna layered with a medley of carrots, spinach and broccoli in a cream sauce. The London broil comes from Virginia-raised Cervena deer and is marinated in bourbon and Worcestershire sauce and served with mushroom sauce. Sesame chicken marinated in teriyaki sauce comes with a sweet honey-and-pineapple glaze. A catch of the day is usually available. The pasta dish might be "Pasta alla Carbonara," which is diced prosciutto sauteed with garlic, shallots, peas and mushrooms. It comes in a cream sauce under crispy bacon and shredded imported cheese.

You'll have to have a ton of will power to resist Maple Hall's dessert tray. Like the appetizers and entrees, the desserts vary according to the chef's whim and the season, but be prepared for scrumptious carrot cake, pecan pie, Kentucky Derby pie and cheesecake.

The service is the superior sort you expect in fine restaurants. Attentive but not intrusive. Friendly but not cozy. Professional but not stiff. Very nice.

There's no need to get on the road after dining here. Maple Hall has lovely, antique-furnished guest rooms in the main building and a few outbuildings. A pool, a tennis court, walking trails and a stocked fishing pond are available, too.

The Palms

The Palms

101 WEST NELSON
LEXINGTON, VA 24450
(540) 463-7911

Style	Pub
Meals	Lunch and dinner, seven days a week; Sunday brunch
Price Range	Inexpensive/Moderate
Superlatives	"Hot Brown Sandwich"
Extras	Full bar

*P*eer recommendation carries a lot of weight in any industry, and I visited The Palms partly on the suggestion of an out-of-town restaurateur. It's a college-town type of place—lots of barstools, lots of noise and popcorn on the floor.

You'll understand the name once you get inside. There's a Deep South feel—high ceilings, slowly turn-ing fans, tan and green tones, palms on the wallpaper, tan stucco walls. The *Sommersby* poster calls forth the days when that movie was filmed nearby.

The building is 100 years old—and its tin ceilings probably are, too. The structure has seen service as a feed store, an antique shop and an ice cream place called the Palm Parlor. The bartender told us that lots of VMI and Washington and Lee alumni come in for ice cream. Something about reliving fond memories.

They should consider staying for lunch. The sandwich board offers the usual deli options—you choose the meat, cheese and bread. Burgers, Reubens, Italian subs, gyros, Mexican burgers on toasted pita bread, surf and turf burgers, steak sandwiches and char-broiled tuna fillet sandwiches are also offered.

Fettuccine Alfredo with ham, shrimp and steamed vegetables, homemade quiche of the day, a chicken plate, chicken or tuna fillet, spaghetti and crabmeat and shrimp au gratin are among the light dinner entrees. Full entrees include a pound of shrimp, broiled beef kabobs, mahi-mahi and baby back ribs. Dinners are accompanied by soup or salad, a vegetable and hot bread.

Just so you don't forget about the bar, 134 drinks are listed on the menu. That's not a typographical error—134. Some of the ones new to me were the "Blue Motorcycle," the "Forty-two Merc," the "Green Dinosaur" and "Lynchburg Lemonade."

Willson-Walker House

Willson-Walker House

30 NORTH MAIN STREET
LEXINGTON, VA 24450
(540) 463-3020

Style	Casual nice
Meals	Lunch and dinner, Tuesday through Saturday; lunch is not served on Saturday from January through March. Reservations are recommended.
Price Range	Moderate/Expensive
Superlatives	Historic house, local trout, veal
Extras	Full bar

William Willson's Classical Revival home was built in 1820. To lend some perspective, that was the same year Maine became the 23rd state, Daniel Boone died in Missouri and native Virginian James Monroe swept the presidential election. A postmaster and merchant,

Willson served as treasurer of Washington College, now Washington and Lee University.

The home was converted to a meat market and grocery store around 1911 by a fellow named Walker—thus the name Willson-Walker House. It is now owned by Josephine Griswald, who graduated from the New York Restaurant School and wrote her thesis on the creation of this restaurant. She opened it on June 25, 1985.

Stepping into the grand foyer, you can imagine the ladies and gentlemen of William Willson's generation descending the staircase in the fashions of the day. There's a formality to the Oriental rugs and the antique furniture upholstered in gold-striped fabric. The dining rooms have red walls, white trim, fireplaces and wall sconces. Champagne-colored table linens are complemented with burgundy napkins. Jazz plays softly during lunch and classical music during dinner.

Lunch is a comprehensive affair starting with a very expensive house salad. Well, maybe the $195 on my menu was a typographical error, the decimal point omitted between the one and the nine. The daily lunch special includes a cup of soup or a house salad, an entree, rolls, muffins and a drink. Even familiar items like burgers and open-faced chicken breast sandwiches are a little fancier than the norm here. For example, the burger comes on a multigrain roll with caramelized red onion, marmalade and Bearnaise mayonnaise.

Dinners vary with the seasons. Crab cakes and teriyaki shrimp kabobs are a couple of the appetizers. You can almost always find trout and veal specials, as well as a pasta dish like tortellini and a pork entree such as pork loin with sausage stuffing, topped with spicy baked apples.

Cobblers and tarts are among the popular desserts featuring fresh fruit in season, though chocoholics might prefer the "Chocolate Chocolate" dessert.

Sam Snead's Tavern

1 MAIN STREET
HOT SPRINGS, VA 24445
(800) 838-1766

Style	Casual nice
Meals	Dinner, Friday through Sunday from January to March and Wednesday through Monday from April to December. Reservations are required.
Price Range	Moderate/Expensive
Superlatives	Cozy setting, golf memorabilia, rainbow trout
Extras	Full bar

*I*n 1766, Thomas Bullitt built the first inn at Hot Springs because his house was being overrun by visitors to the 104-degree thermal springs. The inn changed hands in 1832 and soon began operating as The Homestead, which promoted the springs as a "cure for what ails you." Today, The Homestead is a world-class resort owned by Club Resorts, Inc.

Tucked in a former bank building, Sam Snead's Tavern was purchased by the legendary golfer in 1979 and was tastefully renovated by his son Jackie. The old vault is now a wine cellar. The Homestead owns and operates the restaurant.

If you love golf, as do many of the folks who frequent The Homestead, Sam Snead's doubles as a mini-museum. Golf clubs, assorted golf memorabilia and 35 of Snead's hole-in-one golf balls are on display.

The rich wood, the dark green and burgundy highlights, the gold picture frames containing golf-related prints and photographs—everything here evokes coziness. The stone fireplace crackles when the weather dictates, and the huge, triangular bar beckons.

In the fine tradition of The Homestead, the trout served at Sam Snead's is locally caught and the steaks cut from certified Angus beef. Sam's personal favorite is a full-pound porterhouse steak. The "Hole in One" is a jumbo beef rib chop. The other half-dozen or so entrees include steaks, chicken, shrimp and spare ribs. Wonderful pies and cakes are served for dessert.

Although Sam Snead's is the focus here, I'd be remiss not to mention the other eating options at The Homestead Resort. The Dining Room is a jacket-and-tie place serving continental cuisine in elegant surroundings. Slightly more casual is The Grille, which features tableside preparation of French and American entrees; jackets are required for evening dining. Cafe Albert, located among the neat shops on Cottage Row, offers lunch, baked goods and deli sandwiches. There's also a gourmet shop, a sports bar, a 19th-hole restaurant, a seasonal ski-lodge restaurant and clubhouses open to the public on three golf courses.

The Waterwheel

INN AT GRISTMILL SQUARE / VA 645
WARM SPRINGS, VA 24484
(540) 839-2231

Style	Casual nice
Meals	Dinner, Tuesday through Saturday from November to April and seven days a week from May to October; Sunday brunch
Price Range	Moderate/Expensive
Superlatives	Historic mill decor, trout
Extras	Full bar

*I*f you're keeping track of the springs in this part of the state, you might remember that Hot Springs maintains a temperature of around 104. There's a larger variety of minerals in the water at Warm Springs, where the temperature is a toasty 98.

The first mill at Warm Springs was constructed the same year Thomas Jefferson built his first house at Monticello, three years before the Declaration of Independence was signed. The present one was built in 1900. It operated for 70 years before being converted to this restaurant.

The big wooden wheel on the side of the building opposite the entrance once turned in Warm Springs Run. The creek still runs fast. If you look carefully, you may spot a turtle with a shell more than a foot in diameter. I've seen it.

The Waterwheel is part of the Inn at Gristmill Square, a unique assortment of 19th-century buildings renovated and opened in 1972 by the McWilliams family.

The pub at The Waterwheel is named for Simon Kenton, Indian fighter and friend to Daniel Boone, whose life he once saved. During his seven weeks in Warm Springs in 1771, Kenton worked diligently at the mill. A fugitive from justice for having killed a man, he anxiously continued his journey west. He returned to Virginia one time, so the story goes, and ran into the man he was supposed to have killed.

The beams in the mill have stretched with age but retain their strength and character. Whitewashed wood, original mill hardware, white and light mauve linens, candlelight and fresh flowers create an atmosphere of rustic elegance. In the wine cellar, the bottles are displayed among the gears of the old waterwheel.

Appetizers include bourbon shrimp and salmon mousse. Onion soup au gratin and a soup du jour are offered.

Trout is the specialty at The Waterwheel. You can order it pan-fried with black walnuts or baked and stuffed with shrimp, celery and onions. The cordon bleu is not prefaced with the word *chicken* because it's made with cutlets of veal, topped with béchamel sauce, sugar-cured ham and Swiss cheese. "Tournedos au Poivre," "Tenderloin en Croûte" and grilled rib-eye sound delicious, as do roast duckling with apricots and swordfish broiled with herb butter.

French toast with fruit filling, smoked chicken salad, eggs Benedict and grilled trout are some of the Sunday brunch offerings.

The Inn at Gristmill Square has 17 cozy guest rooms. Continental breakfast is delivered to your room in a basket lined with a red-and-white-checked linen.

Three tennis courts, a swimming pool, a sauna and the historic springs all contribute to the quiet, relaxing mood that reigns in Warm Springs.

Fort Lewis Lodge

HCR 3, BOX 21-A / MILLBORO, VA 24460
(540) 925-2314

Style	Family-style
Meals	Dinner, seven days a week from April through mid-October. Reservations are required; ask for directions when making reservations.
Price Range	Moderate
Superlatives	Setting, lodge atmosphere, great cooking
Extras	Full bar

*F*ort Lewis Lodge was recommended to me by the owner of another restaurant. I recommend it to you as the very definition of a getaway. Here is a place to truly *get away*.

Yes, you can hike, hunt, bicycle and play basketball, but some of us could spend many happy days simply moving among the Cowpasture River (with or without a rod and reel), the massage room, the hot tub, the pond, the sitting room in the lodge and—of course—the dining hall.

Set on 3,200 acres of western Virginia valleys and ridges, Fort Lewis Lodge was originally Fort Lewis Plantation, settled by Colonel Charles Lewis in 1754. More than two centuries later, in 1986, John and Caryl Cowden realized their dream of owning an inn

that showcased the natural beauty of the land and provided comfort and low-key elegance for guests.

The dining hall, a rustic two-story building constructed in the late 1980s, has beams, old wood and a rebuilt stone foundation from the original mill on the site. Dinner is available to the public by reservation. The menu is always "Innkeeper's Choice," meaning that an entire meal is planned, prepared and served buffet-style. There are no menu choices, although you may call ahead a day or two to see what's going to be cooking the night of your visit.

The bar opens around 6:30 for drinks and snacks. Iced tea and lemonade are served with dinner. Heavily dependent on local game and produce, the food here varies as often as the sky and the weather. The night I visited was steak night. Perfectly grilled, thick, tender steaks were accompanied by German hot potatoes, corn on the cob, fresh salad, pumpkin muffins and a scrumptious pecan bar with ice cream. Pork, chicken, fish, seafood, barbecue and appropriate side dishes are served on other nights. You can trek to the buffet as many times as you wish. It's right off the open kitchen, so you can see everything that's going on.

The guest rooms are immaculate. You're a long way from anywhere, so if you're staying overnight, be sure to bring your shampoo and other necessities. And some reading material, needlework or whatever you enjoy for relaxation, as there are no televisions or telephones here.

I'm going back—for the food and the ultimate chance to *get away*.

Suzy's Country Cafe

Suzy's Country Cafe

U.S. 11 / FAIRFIELD, VA 24435
(540) 377-6284

Style	Cafe
Meals	Breakfast and lunch, Monday through Saturday; dinner, Monday through Saturday in summer and Thursday through Saturday in winter
Price Range	Inexpensive
Superlatives	Hand-pattied burgers, fresh tuna and chicken salads

Suzy's, located off I-81 at Exit 200, is named for owner Caroline Ramsey, whose name was shortened to Suzy. No, it doesn't make any sense, but that's exactly the way I heard it from my waitress, Shelly Ramsey, who is also Suzy's daughter-in-law.

Although Suzy has only recently secured a sign on I-81, the cafe has been here for years. It was originally owned by the same folks who had the Foodliner next door. Suzy purchased it when it became too much for the owners to run both the grocery store and the cafe.

It's a simple place with nice country touches like handmade crafts and sunflower print valances. The floor is gold linoleum, and the booths have orange seats. Natural light fills most of the place, and fluorescent lights take care of the rest. There's a large television that was tuned to *CNN Headline News* the day I stopped for lunch.

The homemade biscuits come loaded with country ham, tenderloin, sausage, egg and cheese or just plain egg. The "3 x 3" breakfast includes three eggs, three pancakes and three bacon strips or sausages. You can figure from that what's in the "2 x 2" breakfast. The best part about breakfast? It's served all day long.

The burgers are good. They're billed on the menu as the biggest in town, but let me put that into context. Shelly pointed out the window. "There's the bank down there, lumberyard over there, four gas stations and the school at the top of the hill," she said.

"You're in and out of it before you know you've been here," quipped Rosa Blackwell, the cook.

So these may indeed be the biggest burgers in town. They may also be the only ones!

The dinner menu is brief—chicken, chopped steak and pork chops, served with two vegetables and a roll.

The desserts—coconut cream pie, apple crisp, chocolate cream pie, carrot cake and ice cream—are homemade.

The Purple Foot

The Purple Foot

1035 WEST BROAD STREET
WAYNESBORO, VA 22980
(540) 942-WINE

Style	Cafe
Meals	Lunch and afternoon refreshments
Price Range	Inexpensive
Superlatives	Classy gourmet shop, "Lavender Lemonade"
Extras	Wine and beer

*F*ounded in 1797, Waynesboro was originally known as Teesville, after the Tee brothers, local tavern keepers. It was eventually renamed for Revolutionary War general Anthony Wayne, better known as "Mad Anthony."

It's hard to imagine that the cute chalet that houses The Purple Foot was home to a dry cleaner before Erwin Bohmfalk opened the cafe in 1978.

The first decision you'll have to make when you get here is whether you'll browse the gift shop on your way to lunch or on your way out. This is the place to buy a cuckoo clock, imported cheese, Virginia wine, salt and pepper shakers or a Virginia T-shirt.

Assuming you'll wait until after lunch to browse, just walk straight through to the back room. There are seats for around 50 here and another 50 on the garden terrace. The interior features regional artwork that is rotated monthly. The charming terrace has rock gardens, hanging flower baskets and a water fountain with a statue that looks like it's had a little too much grape juice, if you catch my drift.

Even after you've decided what you want to eat, read the entire menu. When you least expect it, it'll make you chuckle. The first item under "Very Special Sandwiches," for example, is a sub whose description is quite normal until the last sentence: "Hot, chopped peppers may be added for those of you with dead tongues." "Bush's Nightmare," one of the "Dream Potatoes," is a baked potato topped with—you guessed it—broccoli and melted cheddar. Other "Dream Potatoes" have Irish, French, German or Mexican toppings.

Instead of using the word *homemade*, The Purple Foot describes its French bread as "baked-ourselves," in case there's any doubt about where it's made. The cafe also offers "Pita Principals" and "Pita Puns." The crepes come in pairs, filled with turkey and broccoli, snow crabmeat and whitefish or knockwurst and sauerkraut.

Desserts are made on the premises. The regulars are cheesecake, baklava, frozen yogurt and my personal favorite lunch dessert—cookies. Ask about the "Special Disgustingly Sinful Dessert" of the day.

Enjoy your lunch. Then go to the gift shop.

Weasie's Kitchen

WAYNESBORO

Weasie's Kitchen

130 EAST BROAD STREET
WAYNESBORO, VA 22980
(540) 943-0500

Style	Family-style
Meals	Breakfast, lunch and dinner, seven days a week
Price Range	Inexpensive
Superlatives	Breakfast served anytime, pancakes

*F*ull parking lots at restaurants always get my attention. It was 5:30 or so on a Monday afternoon when I noticed all the cars here. There was no meet-ing going on inside, just lots of contented-looking local folks chatting and eating. Most of the 16 booths were occupied, so I sat at the counter.

The building was first a car dealership and then a Dairy Queen before Eloise "Weasie" Roberts opened her restaurant. Joyce Campbell started working at Weasie's in 1985 and bought the business a decade later.

Breakfast is served anytime. The pancakes are famous among Appalachian Trail hikers, who pass within five miles of Weasie's on the 2,144-mile trail. They are encouraged to sign a hikers' guest book, and records are kept of the most pancakes consumed in one sitting. Currently, a 1990 hiker called "The Pope, John Paul" holds the title with 21 pancakes.

If you want something other than pancakes, try the "Apple Roll-Ups," which are thin crepes with spiced apples, or a "Breakfast Club," which is a toasted ham, cheese and egg sandwich.

This is a casual place where appetizers are called "snacks" and the biscuits are made in the back. Dinners range from pepper steaks and spaghetti to fish platters, shrimp dinners, veal patties, pork chops and grilled liver and onions. You get a roll and two vegetables, but the word *vegetables* carries a loose translation, since peaches, apples and cottage cheese are on the list.

The sign outside looked a little worn, but you couldn't miss the message on it: "Where friends meet to eat." It sure seemed that way that Monday around 5:30 P.M.

66   Region 2 / Shenandoah Valley

Edelweiss

Handwritten notes: ✓ Hungarian goulash / Sampler salad / garden salad / German potato salad (◉ Try vegetarian entree didn't have) ✗ no roast pork

Edelweiss

U.S. 340 AT U.S. 11 /GREENVILLE, VA 24401
(540) 337-1203

Style	German
Meals	Lunch and dinner, seven days a week
Price Range	Inexpensive/Moderate
Superlatives	"German Sampler," Black Forest cake
Extras	Wine and beer

*E*delweiss the flower is the national flower of Austria, and one of the prettiest songs in *The Sound of Music* bears its name. Edelweiss the restaurant is an inviting log cabin perched on a hilltop. It's less than a mile from Exit 213A off I-81—just far enough off the highway to let you be enveloped in the aura of Europe.

Ingrid Moore and her former husband spent 16 years in New York City in the delicatessen business.

They spent vacations camping in Virginia, which reminded Ingrid of Germany, her homeland.

In 1981, they opened Edelweiss in a building constructed the year before. Wood enhances the inside and is complemented by beige and mauve linens. Four wagon-wheel lamps softly illuminate a dining area that seats 60.

If it's a popular German dish, it's on the menu—sauerbraten, Hungarian goulash, several entrees with the suffix *braten* or *schnitzel* or *wurst*. There's a vegetable plate for those who don't eat meat and a variety of pork, veal and beef for those who do. Fillet of flounder and chicken are also available.

For a comprehensive German dining experience, order the "German Sampler," which includes five favorite German dishes. "The 'German Sampler' was introduced because so many repeat guests ordered the same thing over and over. I wanted them to try something different, but they resisted an entire meal of something they weren't sure of," explained Ingrid.

Fresh vegetables like apple-flavored red cabbage, German fried noodles, green beans, Bavarian-style cabbage, sauerkraut and mashed potatoes are served family-style with all meals. Children under 12 eat for half-price.

Most German meals are consumed with beer, so Edelweiss offers an interesting selection of light and dark beers, as well as wines.

Black Forest cake is a specialty, as are German-style tortes and rice pudding with meringue topping. The German-style cheesecake, made with cottage cheese, is not as heavy as New York–style cheesecake.

Ingrid's son Stephan Roscher helps out at the restaurant. He can verify that, in the best German tradition, recipes have been handed down through the generations, and that anything that can be made from scratch is.

Pink Cadillac

Pink Cadillac

U.S. 11 (EXIT 213A OFF I-81)
GREENVILLE, VA 24440
(540) 337-4315

Style	Diner
Meals	Breakfast, lunch and dinner, seven days a week
Price Range	Inexpensive
Superlatives	Decor, rotisserie chicken
Extras	Wine and beer

*T*here must be something really special about pink Cadillacs or Mary Kay wouldn't have chosen them as the symbol of her makeup empire. Besides the 1953 model in the front yard here, there are several toy ones in the glass case by the front door.

Originally a Howard Johnson's, the place was purchased in 1990 by Ray Ferguson, who started Fergie's Steakhouse. When that didn't go over too well, he tried a bar, with the same lousy results. Then he hit upon the pink Cadillac idea. He and partner Madeline Pitkin, whom Ferguson refers to as "the boss lady," soon began to see results.

The Pink Cadillac is definitely 1950s. The exterior is bright pink and the interior turquoise with black and white tiles. It has booths for 50 or so and more than a dozen counter stools. A party room in the back has an ice cream parlor in one corner. You'll also find an old Coke cooler, a 1938 Harley motorcycle, pink mugs, an old Texaco gas pump and an Elvis lamp. "You can't have too many Elvis lamps," quipped Ferguson, a gourmet chef who now enjoys cranking out hamburgers and french fries.

If you can't find something you want on this menu—well, that's not likely. There are omelets, cold sandwiches, hot sandwiches, seafood baskets, hearty bowls of spaghetti, soups, salads, pasta dishes.

The dish known as "The Cadillac of Rotisserie Chicken" is basted with the diner's own blend of herbs and fruity spices. Meatloaf, liver and onions, country-fried steak, ham steak with pineapple and hot turkey are among the "Cadillac Plates."

The diet platters include a salad and a side of fruit with either a four-ounce tuna steak or the same measure of grilled chicken. The trio of vegetarian specials includes a meatless spaghetti with marinara sauce.

Prime rib isn't one of the diet dinners. You'll note that the management hasn't instituted a portion-control policy. You can order five ounces for $5.95, six for $6.95, seven for $7.95 and so on—up to 100 ounces for $100.95. That would be some serving of prime rib!

L'Italia

23 EAST BEVERLEY STREET
STAUNTON, VA 24401
(540) 885-0102

Style	Italian
Meals	Lunch and dinner, Tuesday through Sunday
Price Range	Moderate
Superlatives	Tiramisu, chicken rollatini, "Saltimbocca alla Romana"
Extras	Full bar

Women still make news when they become firefighters, but when Staunton's first volunteer fire department was organized in 1790, it had a female member. Talk about being ahead of the times! Named for Lady Rebecca Staunton, the wife of Governor William Gooch, the town was incorporated in 1801. It appointed its first two police officers the next year. The annual salary? Ten dollars. Woodrow Wilson, the 28th president of the United States, was born in Staunton in 1856. His birthplace is open to the public.

Emilio Amato, the owner of L'Italia, hails from Sicily. Most of the restaurant is a former men's store, as is evident in the display shelves and the drawers on both sides of the first-floor dining room. Between the restaurant's two floors, Emilio can host more than 100 guests.

L'Italia offers a tantalizing selection of tomato sauces, a staple in Emilio's native southern Italy, and cream sauces, which are more characteristic of northern Italian dishes.

The lunch specials include lots of pasta favorites—baked ziti, manicotti, linguine with red or white clam sauce and others—as well as things like eggplant parmigiana and veal parmigiana. Appetizers, soups, salads and subs are also available. One of the house specials—chicken rollatini—is available for lunch or dinner. It features slices of chicken breast filled with herbs, three cheeses and ham, then sauteed in a cream sauce and served with spaghetti.

L'Italia

More than two dozen dinner entrees are offered, including "Saltimbocca alla Romana"—layers of veal with prosciutto and wine sauce, served on a bed of fresh spinach and mushrooms. Poultry, pasta and seafood items are also available.

Not surprisingly, many of the wines are from Italy, but Virginia and California are also represented.

[handwritten: pork chops—only ok; turkey—kind of good (hold gravy)]

STAUNTON

Mrs. Rowe's Family Restaurant and Bakery

[handwritten: ✓]

[handwritten: spoon bread; baked apples; cole slaw; baked tomatoes; au gratin potatoes]

ROUTE 4, BOX 88 (EXIT 222 OFF I-81)
STAUNTON, VA 24401
(540) 886-1833

[handwritten: ✗ candied yams]

Style	Family-style
Meals	Breakfast, lunch and dinner, seven days a week
Price Range	Inexpensive/Moderate
Superlatives	Baked goods
Extras	Wine and beer *[handwritten: chardonnay & white zinfandel—ok]*

When Mrs. Rowe was traveling in Canada some years back, she met some Canadians who raved about a red restaurant they stopped at every year going back and forth to Florida. "When I found out it was my place, I started flying the Canadian flag," she recalled. That's why you'll see the distinctive maple leaf waving next to the Stars and Stripes at this one-of-a-kind restaurant.

Mrs. Rowe and her late husband opened the place in 1947. Since then, it has been featured in *Boston Globe Magazine*, *Restaurants & Institutions*, *Good Food* and other publications.

Among all the rooms, 230 guests can be seated. Children's art and P. Buckley Moss prints are on the walls. The service is friendly and efficient.

Home cooking is the specialty. Bread, biscuits and pies are prepared from Mrs. Rowe's own recipes, many of which are included in a cookbook on sale here, *Mrs. Rowe's Favorite Recipes*.

Breakfast is standard Southern, with a few variations. Pumpkin, blueberry and plain pancakes are available. The creamed chipped beef is homemade, as is the bread for toast. The cinnamon rolls and sticky buns are divine.

At lunch, regular sandwiches are served with potato chips. Deluxe sandwiches—like "Hot Minute Steak" and a hot turkey sandwich—are served with mashed potatoes and gravy.

Dinner specials come with two vegetables or one vegetable and a garden salad. The vegetable choices include cucumbers and onions (that's one dish), baked tomatoes, turnip greens, pickled beets, lima beans, green beans, mashed potatoes and applesauce. T-bone steak, baked pork tenderloin, deviled crab cutlets, country ham steak and Southern fried chicken are generally among the entrees.

The recommended dessert is warm apple pie with cinnamon ice cream. You can also have gelatin with whipped cream, pecan pie or other baked goods. Catherine Eckel of Blacksburg, a Virginia Tech employee who occasionally travels to Washington, D.C., said that Mrs. Rowe's has "the best mincemeat pie with rum raisin sauce—the kind made with real meat." Eckel probably doesn't stop for just one piece on her trips up and down I-81. If she's like many longtime fans of Mrs. Rowe's, she buys a whole pie.

The Pullman

36 MIDDLEBROOK AVENUE
STAUNTON, VA 24402
(540) 885-6612

Style	Casual nice
Meals	Lunch and dinner, seven days a week
Price Range	Inexpensive/Moderate
Superlatives	Antiques, "Katy Chicken Pie"
Extras	Full bar

At The Pullman, you may find yourself dining at a window 15 or so feet from the track when a train rolls into town. Freight trains pass through daily. Amtrak comes in three times a week and stops for passengers right outside.

The building was constructed in 1857 and modernized in 1902 but had fallen into a state of disrepair prior to being renovated for the restaurant, which opened in 1993.

You actually enter an old-fashioned ice cream parlor first. The counters are marble. The player piano in the far corner rolls out old-time tunes on weekends. The exquisite trim and the huge antiques are classic examples of fine wood craftsmanship. One piece from a West Virginia pharmacy stands around eight feet high and almost as many feet wide. The dining areas offer some marble tables, stained-glass lamps and brass rails. Attractive partitions and table arrangements contribute to the intimate dining here.

An array of salads, fresh greens, breads and soups are available at the soup and salad bar. "Katy Chicken Pie" is a hearty serving of chicken chunks and vegetables in a flaky crust. The spinach and mushroom lasagna served at lunch is made from scratch and topped with homemade tomato sauce.

Dinners run the gamut—chicken entrees, pasta, catch of the day, choice beef. The Pullman's specialties include marinated lamb chunks grilled on a skewer, pork loin seared with Thai spices and blackened medallions of spiced beef.

Of course, the ice cream parlor can make just about any ice cream dessert you wish. Apple dumplings or a hot fudge brownie may also tempt you.

The restaurant's "Assorted Policies" are printed toward the end of the menu. Under "Dress code," it says simply, "Come as you are." But the following policy is my favorite: "Diets, desires and dilemmas: We will do our best to accommodate any special requests that are made."

It's a nice touch at a nice restaurant.

Wright's Dairy-Rite

346 GREENVILLE AVENUE / STAUNTON, VA 24401
(540) 886-0435

Style	Drive-in
Meals	Lunch and dinner, seven days a week
Price Range	Inexpensive
Superlatives	Nostalgic atmosphere, onion rings, foot-long hot dogs with homemade chili

*I*n the year 1952—and not necessarily in their order of importance—Queen Elizabeth II was crowned, Dwight Eisenhower won the presidential election and the Wright family opened its drive-in. The current owner, James E. Cash, was married to a Wright. His son, James R. Cash, is the manager. Cash the elder is looking into the possibility that this may be the country's oldest drive-in restaurant under the continuous ownership of a single family.

Twice during the year, Wright's hosts a "Cruise-in," when people roll in with their beloved vehicles—old, new, truck, sedan, roadster. Votes are cast for the best vehicles, with dash plaques awarded to the ten favorites. Not to be left out, motorcyclists have started a midsummer "Cruise-through" at the drive-in.

Curbside service is always available, although trays are no longer perched on car windows. Now, orders come on a tray that is set on the speaker, which is then pulled over to the car window.

If you go inside to eat, you'll most likely sit in the addition built in 1991. The Statler Brothers, native sons who keep a low profile in the area, came for the ribbon-cutting ceremony when this, the Annie Small Room, opened. Annie Small was a longtime employee who died of cancer in 1991. No doubt, she served each of the brothers at one time or another. It's equally likely she served their kids, who also frequent the drive-in.

There are phones at the booths and tables for placing your order. Curb-service menus from 1958 and 1961 and a working Wurlitzer jukebox loaded with 1950s music provide nostalgic touches.

Wright's Dairy-Rite

The menu is what you'd expect—hamburgers, hot dogs, chicken or fish on a bun and so on. A low-fat section includes half a dozen items, among them a garden burger, a vegetarian sub and a chicken pita. The "Super Burger" is very popular.

My husband, John, was happy because Wright's has pineapple malted milk shakes. All the shakes, cones, floats and splits contribute to the atmosphere of a 1950s drive-in.

The neon sign is the third one on the premises, the first two having rusted out. It's identical to the original sign. Just spotting it is a reminder of simpler times.

MJ's Cafe

U.S. 250 / CHURCHVILLE, VA 24421
(540) 337-6427

Style	Cafe
Meals	Breakfast, lunch and dinner, Monday through Saturday
Price Range	Inexpensive
Superlatives	Homemade soups, coconut cream pie, chocolate turtle pie

*G*etting out of city life on the edge of Washington, D.C.—that was all the motivation Charles and Mary Jo Forbes needed for moving with their three sons to this small enclave close to 10 years ago. Mary Jo bought the restaurant, and with help from Chuck and the kids, she's created a comfortable 54-seat cafe.

The building was a pool hall, a barbershop and a doctor's office before its first days as a restaurant, when it was known as the T-Bone Tooter. According to a copy of the Tooter's menu, barbecue was 25 cents, a hamburger 15 cents, and a piece of pie 10 cents.

A hunting theme is prominent inside MJ's today—the restrooms are marked "Does" and "Bucks." A biplane with a wingspan of about four feet hangs from the ceiling. Chuck bought it at a flea market, built the propeller and gave the craft a new coat of paint. A few lobster traps have found their way into this rather eclectic mix of things.

The menu doesn't leave much room for guessing. It tells you exactly how many you get or how much something weighs. If you want a side order of bacon, for example, you get three strips. A side of sausage is composed of two patties. French toast and buttermilk pancakes come three to an order, and fresh-baked Parmesan breadsticks come in a group of four. Hamburgers are a half-pound or a quarter-pound, and dinner steaks range from a four-ounce rib-eye with fried shrimp to a 12-ounce T-bone or hamburger steak. You can get a five-ounce mesquite-grilled chicken breast or fried chicken measured in three pieces—breast, thigh and leg.

Check the dessert board for the current pie flavors. There are usually a couple of cream pies, a couple of fruit pies, a couple of cakes and apple turnovers, served with or without ice cream. Sundaes, milk shakes and ice cream sodas are also available.

The Forbes boys are in their early 20s now. Jeremy, the middle son, had this to say about the family's move to Churchville from the hustle and bustle and traffic of city life: "The people are real friendly here, and I've always found plenty to do."

Highland Inn

MAIN STREET / MONTEREY, VA 24465
(540) 468-2143

Style	Casual nice
Meals	Lunch, Friday and Saturday; dinner, Monday through Saturday; Sunday brunch
Price Range	Inexpensive/Moderate
Superlatives	Old-fashioned atmosphere, trout
Extras	Full bar

Located 3,000 feet above sea level, Monterey is the county seat of, and the largest town in, Highland County. The county is often referred to as "Virginia's Switzerland" for its gorgeous rolling hills, pastoral views and mountains as high as 4,500 feet. Monterey boasts more than a dozen historic buildings. The oldest of them is a cabin built around 1790 and first used as a tavern. Several Victorian structures with classic gingerbread trim date from the 1800s.

The Highland Inn is one of them. It was built in 1896, the same year that the first modern Olympic games were held in Athens. Now, more than a century later, the inn is listed on the National Register of Historic Places and is a Virginia Historic Landmark. In that time, the United States has hosted the Olympics seven times.

The inn still has its original porches and gingerbread trim. Its old-time charm has been retained while new-time amenities have been added. Each of the 17 guest rooms now has a private bath, for example.

The inn is white with dark green trim and matching rockers along the porch, which spans the entire front of the building. Hanging baskets and flowers lend a country look.

The floors inside have the obligatory squeak of wood a century old. The Black Sheep Tavern features antiques, old quilts, old typewriters and lace on the windows. A small piano room has books, games and puzzles. In the Monterey Room—the main dining room—the linens are pink and white in the warm months and green and white during winter. Red is added at holiday time. Single candles adorn each table in the room, which seats 50. A large potbelly stove adds warmth on winter evenings.

The dinner menu is changed daily to maximize quality and freshness of ingredients. Prime rib, trout, quail and chicken are popular entrees. A country buffet is offered on Wednesday nights.

Sunday brunch may include chicken and dumplings, flank steak and a bountiful soup and salad bar.

The complimentary continental breakfast is available only to overnight guests. So when you call here, you'll be wise to make two reservations—one for dinner, one for the night.

Karl's

101 NORTH MAIN STREET
BRIDGEWATER, VA 22821
(540) 828-3002

Style	Home-style
Meals	Breakfast, lunch and dinner, Tuesday through Sunday
Price Range	Inexpensive
Superlatives	Meatloaf, turkey dinners, "Mother's Cheesecake"

Bridgewater is the home of Bridgewater College, a beautiful small campus of classic brick buildings with bright white trim.

Karl Kwolek, Sr., began his restaurant in the summer of 1997. "Opening a restaurant is the hardest thing I've ever done, but the most satisfying," he noted.

Although it's hard work, Karl is certainly well qualified for it. For more than 30 years, he was employed in college and university food-service operations, where he learned the millions of tasks that go into delivering quality food to hundreds of people.

The windows in the front of his restaurant have lace cafe curtains. The back room, which is mostly brown brick with coach lights, has five booths and captain's chairs at the tables. The television behind the counter wasn't on when I visited in midafternoon but apparently is tuned to a country-music channel in the evenings.

Breakfast is served all day at Karl's. You can get any combinations of eggs, meat, biscuits and hot cakes you can imagine. Of course, there's also sausage gravy, French toast, omelets, fresh fruit in season, banana nut bread and just plain cereal.

At lunch, you can order sandwiches, burgers, subs or spaghetti. Karl's offers "In a Hurry" sandwiches for those on the go.

The dinner salads include a Caesar and a house salad. Rainbow trout, chicken and ground chuck steak are available from the broiler. Another favorite is the oven-roasted turkey dinner.

"Mother's Cheesecake" is a specialty dessert, and apple pie, strawberry pie and an assortment of cakes are also served.

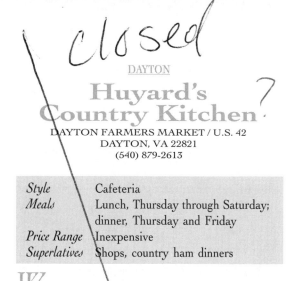

closed

DAYTON

Huyard's Country Kitchen?

DAYTON FARMERS MARKET / U.S. 42
DAYTON, VA 22821
(540) 879-2613

Style	Cafeteria
Meals	Lunch, Thursday through Saturday; dinner, Thursday and Friday
Price Range	Inexpensive
Superlatives	Shops, country ham dinners

With Huyard's and the assortment of shops clustered at the Dayton Farmers Market, it's hard to say whether this is the kind of place you'd come to eat or to shop. Most likely both.

More than 20 shops carry all sorts of home accessories, craft items, kitchenware, toys, jewelry and quilts. Several are operated by members of the Amish community. Swiss Valley Lace carries an incredible selection of lace and china. Ten Thousand Villages stocks handicrafts from around the world. You can find Amish collectibles, books, unusual cards, pottery, rugs and even mailboxes.

Though a number of shops sell gourmet food items, pretzels, fudge, candy, freshly baked cookies, jams, jellies, cheese, donuts, ice cream or gourmet coffee and tea, Huyard's Country Kitchen is the place to go for your main meal.

Everything looks very good at this cafeteria-style restaurant. Sandwich meats are sliced right when you order them. Barbecue, chicken, ham, turkey, mashed potatoes, macaroni and cheese, spiced apples, rice and a variety of vegetables are among the offerings. You can buy a sandwich, a meat plate, a vegetable plate or a dinner plate, each for a set price. Or you can choose individual items. There are plenty of tables, each with a flowered tablecloth and a vinyl clear one on top.

It's an easy detour off I-81. Take Exit 245 and go west, then turn south on U.S. 42. Or you can take Exit 240 and go west, then turn north on U.S. 42. Either way, you'll arrive in about 10 minutes. Look for the yellow metal building on the western side of U.S. 42 about three miles south of Harrisonburg.

The Brookside

2978 U.S. 211 EAST / LURAY, VA 22835
(540) 743-5698

Style	Family-style
Meals	Breakfast, lunch and dinner, seven days a week
Price Range	Inexpensive/Moderate
Superlatives	Spaghetti, catfish, buffets
Extras	Wine and beer

*F*orty-seven carillon bells at the Luray Singing Tower bring musical beauty to the mountain air. Rolling hills, pastures and valleys framed by the Blue Ridge and Massanutten Mountains lend the area visual serenity. The Luray Caverns are a major tourist attraction here, but there are also other things to see in this gentle mountain region, like the Historic Car and Carriage Caravan, which has more than 140 antique cars on display.

Bob and Cece Castle are the fourth owners of The Brookside and The Cabins at Brookside, located on U.S. 211 four miles east of Skyline Drive. To the best of their knowledge, some little cabins were built here in 1924, and the restaurant opened 13 years later. The original logo was a peacock, and there's a peacock on the property even today. It's "sort of a kid's attraction," Bob says.

With 17 years in the restaurant business and more than a decade in construction, Bob was well prepared to buy The Brookside in the winter of 1989. The cabins have since been renovated and expanded or completely rebuilt.

The spotless restaurant has cream and green calico curtains, wooden tables and chairs with green seats. Shelves with samples of gift-shop items separate the two main dining areas. The walls are decorated with dried flower arrangements, prints, paintings and photos.

Breakfast is traditional country fare. The buffet is especially popular.

At lunch, you'll find all the sandwiches you'd expect—hot roast beef, hot turkey, burgers, grilled ham and cheese, BLTs, club sandwiches and pork barbecue. It's noted on the menu that the grilled Virginia ham sandwich is "salty"; it comes on a toasted bun. The pita sandwich is filled with shredded beef or chicken and stir-fried vegetables.

In the evening, there's beef liver, chopped sirloin, rib-eye steak, pork chops, chicken served several ways, lots of seafood selections and spaghetti. Among the healthy choices is a platter in which skinless chicken is basted with a nonfat vinaigrette and served with fresh fruit and vegetables. The baked potatoes come with broccoli and cheese, chili and onions or chili, onions and cheese. For vegetarians, there's a garden burger. Among the salads are a Greek salad and a grilled chicken salad.

The desserts include homemade pies, cakes and cobblers.

Great! Pork chops great! Good Prime Rib?

Dan's Steak House

U.S. 211 / LURAY, VA 22835
(540) 743-6285

Style	Family-style
Meals	Dinner, seven days a week from April through October and Wednesday through Sunday from November through March
Price Range	Moderate/Expensive
Superlatives	Sirloin for two, steaks
Extras	Full bar

*T*here are a few restaurants around the state named for one of the owner's children. But in this case, owner Earl Vaught named his son Dan for the restaurant he already owned.

He bought the place in 1980, when it was a beer joint named Dan's. It seated fewer than 100 people and served steaks on Saturday nights only. Earl expanded the restaurant, which was built in 1937, and it now accommodates more than 200. He cuts the beef daily and serves steaks all the time.

The original road ran right in front of the building. Now, the new road is a few feet away and the original one is the parking lot. Dan's is white outside and has a red sign. The inside is knotty pine cut from trees right here in Page County. You'll note the wagon-wheel hanging lamps and the oldies playing in the background. From the front dining room, there's a nice view down the mountain and across Page Valley and the town of Luray.

The sirloin for two is billed as a "Valley Tradition." It includes more than two pounds of aged beef broiled the way you want and served with a salad, potato and fresh bread. Other choices include T-bone, porterhouse, New York strip, filet mignon and prime rib. You can get most anything cut extra thick.

A couple of sandwiches, chicken breast and pork chops are offered. Seafood dinners include catch of the day, fried oysters, fresh scallops and steamed

Dan's Steak House

spiced shrimp. The menu tops out with the surf-and-turf combination of steamed spiced shrimp and filet mignon. The daily specials include Monday's surf and turf, Tuesday's prime rib, Wednesday's crab legs and Thursday's New York strip dinner for two.

Dan's is the kind of place—and Earl and his staff the kind of people—that will make you feel like you've stepped into a group of old friends.

The restaurant is on the northern side of U.S. 211 five miles east of Exit 264 off I-81 and 12 miles west of Luray Caverns.

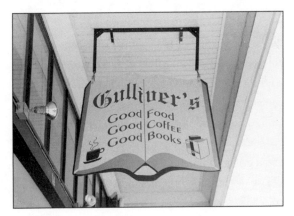

Gulliver's

Gulliver's

55 EAST MAIN STREET / LURAY, VA 22835
(540) 743-4460

Style	Cafe
Meals	Breakfast, Monday through Saturday; lunch, seven days a week
Price Range	Inexpensive
Superlatives	"Awesome Apple Cake," salads
Extras	Wine and beer

*I*n this old hardware store with original floors, a tin ceiling and floor-to-ceiling shelves accessed by a sliding ladder, Joanne Lee has created an interesting combination of an art gallery, a shop and a cafe.

The huge, open second floor—reached by climbing stairs painted like yellow bricks and dubbed the "Yellow Brick Road"—is divided into wire cubicles. Each one is rented to an artist who displays work for sale, like dealer spaces in an antique mall. I found an attractive little painting of bluebirds and purchased it. The concept is great. Hopefully, an increasing number of artists will participate in the future.

The shop downstairs stocks a few books, a few crafts and a little of this and that, displayed on shelves against the walls. The cafe occupies the middle of the room and has about eight tables with green tablecloths under glass.

Breakfast goodies include cinnamon rolls, muffins, waffles, egg biscuits and bagels.

The lunch sandwiches include a Reuben, smoked turkey and cheese, tuna salad, chicken, barbecue, BLT, pimento cheese and a garden burger. Salads, baked potatoes, fruit cups, potato salad and soup by the cup or bowl are also offered.

For dessert, there's homemade bread pudding, chocolate chip or peanut butter cookies, "Awesome Apple Cake" and "Chocolate Lover's Spoon Cake." By the way, the plastic spoon taped to the pen at the counter has nothing to do with the spoon cake. The idea came from a doctor's office where Joanne once noticed a plastic spoon taped to a pen. "No one takes a pen with a spoon taped on it," was the receptionist's explanation. Apparently, it works.

A few kinds of coffee are available. If you're not sure which to order, the menu suggests that you "ask for a short course and a sample anytime."

And if you're looking for an evening out, you can find entertainment here each Saturday from 8 to 10 P.M. It might be music, or it might be a play. Desserts and drinks are served along with the entertainment.

changed — no good

Parkhurst

2547 U.S. 211 WEST / LURAY, VA 22835
(540) 743-6009

yes

Style	Fine dining
Meals	Dinner, seven days a week
Price Range	Expensive
Superlatives	Fettuccine with shellfish, <u>fillet of sole</u>
Extras	Full bar

*I*n the late 1970s, George and Nita Weddleton sold their restaurant in California and went to Bethesda, Maryland, to visit some friends. On a drive through the countryside, they stumbled onto a 1950s motel with weeds all around it just two miles west of Luray Caverns. Originally a two-story building, it had been constructed in 1938 but burned down three years later. It was then rebuilt as a single story.

Only creative people with a knack for seeing the potential in such a place could have transformed the old motel into a fine restaurant. The Weddletons have that knack.

The Parkhurst opened in 1979. The exterior is bright white brick. You walk into a foyer, then step on soft carpeting into the restaurant. To the left is a dining room with a lovely red, gold and pink stained-glass window, cream tablecloths, fresh flowers, little oil lamps and window dining. To the right of the entry is a dining room with a little glassed-in room off it. It's all attractive, immaculate and inviting.

Among the many appetizers are fried calamari, spinach-stuffed mushroom caps, cheddar jalapeños and lobster- and crab-filled ravioli. The Parkhurst's signature soup is a tasty tomato shrimp bisque. It also offers French onion and a soup of the day. Several dressings are available for the five salad options. Each of the large salads constitutes a meal in itself.

The Parkhurst offers more than two dozen entrees, which run the gamut from sole and the very popular fettuccine with shellfish to vegetable curry, broiled lamb chops, grilled quail, veal piccata, *steak au poivre* and Châteaubriand.

The Parkhurst maintains a nice wine list. It also offers champagne, cider and a variety of beers. The desserts are changed daily.

There's a minimum charge per person and an extra charge for sharing an entree, so plan on enjoying an entire dinner here. The setting is nice, the staff well trained and the food delicious.

K.S.K.'s Harmony Garden

K.S.K.'s
Harmony Garden

5939 KING STREET / MOUNT JACKSON, VA 22842
(800) 213-8464

Style	Cafe
Meals	Breakfast and lunch, Tuesday through Saturday; dinner, Tuesday through Saturday during winter and Tuesday through Sunday during summer; Sunday brunch during summer
Price Range	Moderate/Expensive
Superlatives	Chocolate macadamia nut–filled croissant, shellfish medley
Extras	Wine and beer

*T*his town's name was changed from Mount Pleasant to Mount Jackson after Andrew Jackson's victory at the Battle of New Orleans in the War of 1812.

A small town with around 1,500 residents, Mount Jackson boasts one of the last remaining covered bridges in the state, the Meems Bottom Bridge, which spans the north fork of the Shenandoah River.

K.S.K.'s Harmony Garden is a small cafe owned by a young couple who are very knowledgeable about coffee, tea and food. David and Danielle Fansler met as teens cruising around town. David was raised in New Mexico and moved here as a teenager. Danielle is a native Virginian.

The initials stand for Koffee Service Knowledge—and the Fanslers provide all three. According to David, coffee was discovered around 675 A.D. and was originally spelled with a *k*. The "Harmony Garden" portion of the name suggests a place of relaxation.

Inside, the bright yellows and reds are intended to energize the spirit. On the walls is an eclectic mix of prints, photos and odd items like a rod and reel, some hats and a few musical instruments. The curtains are green, and the floors are a gray faux marble vinyl.

The building—which houses both the cafe and the Fanslers' national mail-order coffee, tea and gift-basket business—was once the local train depot. Livestock was paraded through on the way to or from the trains.

It's a small place in terms of seating—there's room for about 28. But it's a big place when you're talking coffee or tea. The Fanslers stock more than 150 different coffees—coffees from around the world, organic coffees, flavored coffees—as well as dozens of bulk teas.

The focus here is on healthy food—fresh ingredients, no preservatives, no MSG. David cuts the potatoes for the french fries and is as fluent in herbs and spices as he is in coffees and teas. He creates all the dishes, many of which have Irish and Scottish roots.

In the mornings, you can have French toast, eggs, potatoes, pancakes, country ham, biscuits and gravy and a variety of other things. At midday, the cafe offers a selection of sandwiches, burgers and salads. All the appetizers I saw on the dinner menu were fish, as were all the entrees except a New York strip steak. The menu varies, and each entree is individually prepared.

David's first cooking experience came early, when he prepared filet mignon over the full flame of a gas stove, holding the meat on a fork. He was three. By age five, he was making surf and turf, which he considers his first real dinner.

And he still makes it—with some refinements, of course.

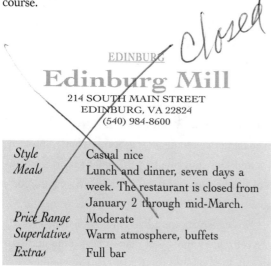

closed

EDINBURG
Edinburg Mill
214 SOUTH MAIN STREET
EDINBURG, VA 22824
(540) 984-8600

Style	Casual nice
Meals	Lunch and dinner, seven days a week. The restaurant is closed from January 2 through mid-March.
Price Range	Moderate
Superlatives	Warm atmosphere, buffets
Extras	Full bar

Edinburg Mill

This pretty little town was first called Stoney Creek, then Shryock. When Swiss settlers came, they named it Edenburg for the biblical garden paradise. Somewhere along the way, the spelling was changed to Edinburg. There's great fishing nearby in the North and South Forks of the Shenandoah River.

Hank Steed was retired and living on his sailboat off the coast of North Carolina when he learned that the Edinburg Mill was for sale. He tied up and came ashore in February 1996. He opened that spring, then again the following spring. He plans to continue for many springs to follow.

The mill is a magnificent four-story building along Stoney Creek. Old grain bins have been converted to private dining areas, and gears and beams can be seen throughout. Built in 1848 by George Grandstaff, a major in the War of 1812, the mill supplied grain to Confederate soldiers during the Civil War. It was set on fire twice but was ultimately spared after two of

Grandstaff's granddaughters pleaded with General Philip Sheridan not to burn it.

The mill remained in production until 1978, when it became a restaurant. "Still feeding the Shenandoah Valley" is its motto.

The downstairs tavern is warm and cozy. Dining areas are on the second and third floors. The fourth floor has been renovated into an apartment. On the tables, you'll find white vinyl tablecloths with place mats and burgundy napkins. The place has the warmth that only old wood can give.

It's not a formal restaurant. Lunch buffets are often offered, but if you're not in the mood, you can choose an entree like a catfish sandwich, a prime rib sandwich, a Greek or Caesar salad, homemade soup, chili or a burger from the attractive menu.

A country buffet is featured on Wednesday evenings. The buffet on Friday and Saturday nights includes chef-carved prime rib, shrimp, clams, fish, baked chicken, crab bites, clam chowder, vegetables, salad bar and dessert. The Sunday-evening buffet features three meats, fresh vegetables, soup, salad and desserts. Dinner entrees that may be ordered off the menu include prime rib, "Chicken Nantucket," medallions of beef tenderloin, rainbow trout and country ham.

Nana's Gift Shop, located near the restaurant's entrance, carries the Edinburg Mill sweatshirts worn by servers and a selection of art and crafts by local artisans.

WOODSTOCK

The Spring House

325 SOUTH MAIN STREET
WOODSTOCK, VA 22664
(540) 459-4755

Style	Casual nice
Meals	Breakfast, lunch and dinner, seven days a week
Price Range	Inexpensive/Moderate
Superlatives	Antiques, design, "Spring House Steak"
Extras	Full bar

*T*he county seat of Shenandoah County, Woodstock lays claim to having the oldest courthouse in continuous use east of the Blue Ridge. The steeple and porch of the structure were built of native limestone in 1795. The town and the surrounding valley can perhaps best be seen from Woodstock Tower, a 40-foot tower built by the Civilian Conservation Corps in the 1930s. From it, one can also see the seven bends of the Shenandoah River.

It was in the late 1970s that Dan and Sue Harshman sold their retail business in Pittsburgh and relocated to Virginia to start a not-yet-defined enterprise, perhaps a wholesale print business. Over a drink one evening in the lounge of The Spring House, the owners told Dan and Sue that they planned to open another restaurant and sell this one. "We were thinking about offering it to you," Dan and Sue were told.

Owning a restaurant had only crossed their minds as a retirement thing—perhaps a little mom-and-pop place a long way in the future. But remember that line about the best-laid plans of mice and men? Before the new year, the Harshmans found themselves the owners of a restaurant.

They've created an atmosphere that's most comfortable. Although the original structure is only a small portion of today's building, the entire restaurant—the old beams and floorboards, the phenomenal antique collection, the cozy rooms, the soft instrumental and vocal music of the 1930s, 1940s and 1950s—exudes historical flavor. Both Dan and Sue are interior designers, and it shows.

Omelets, pancakes, French toast, country ham and freshly baked pastries are offered for breakfast. A European breakfast buffet is served on Sundays.

The sandwiches include a Reuben, a BLT, roast beef and ham and the "Tomato in a Squeeze." In case you're wondering what's squeezing the tomato, it's between roast beef and cheddar cheese on one side and ham and Swiss on the other.

No matter what you're thinking of ordering, include a basket of walnut rolls. Or at the very least, buy some to take with you. These light rolls with crushed walnuts are served with honey butter. They're fabulous.

Close to three dozen dinner entrees are available. "Le Bleu Filet" is a tender fillet sauteed and served in a ramekin topped with bleu cheese and bacon. Salmon cakes, grilled trout and "Chicken Virginia"—a chicken breast over thinly sliced ham, grilled and served with apple cider and lemon sauce—are also offered.

The "Double Devil Dessert" is the restaurant's most popular. It's chocolate spice cake with ice cream, whipped cream, hot fudge and a cherry.

Being at the Spring House is like eating at a favorite aunt's house—and you don't have to help with the dishes.

The Apple House

LINDEN

The Apple House
VA 55 (EXIT 13 OFF I-66) / LINDEN, VA 22642
(540) 635-2118

Style	Home-style
Meals	Breakfast and lunch, seven days a week
Price Range	Inexpensive
Superlatives	Barbecue, donuts, Alpenglow

*I*f you like country gifts, barbecue, donuts and sparkling cider, you don't want to miss The Apple House. The place opened in 1963 as a processing plant for apples, but little by little, the retail side of the business grew.

In 1980, Ben and Jean Lacy created Alpenglow, a nonalcoholic sparkling apple cider. Daughter Betsy Quarles managed the bottling plant until relocating to Fredericksburg. Daughter Debbie Hunter stepped in as sales manager. Son George McIntyre runs the gift shop and restaurant with his mother. It's a real family affair.

Alpenglow is now distributed nationally. It's a fabulous drink, but don't take my word for it. There's a tasting station in the gift shop, and any one of the friendly staff members can assist you. Gifts ranging from cassette tapes and candles to quilts, T-shirts, chimes, throws, toys and country crafts are available here.

The little restaurant, located to the left, has room for around 28. It's cream with wood trim, lace valances and red-and-white-checked curtains.

There's a lot of barbecue to be had in Virginia, but there's none like George McIntyre's. Cooked over hickory, apple and oak and served on a croissant, it has a wonderfully spicy flavor.

There's a lot of donuts to be had, too, but George's are special. These cake donuts made with apple butter and rolled in cinnamon and sugar are fabulous.

You can get breakfast all day at The Apple House.

At lunch, you can choose from among hot dogs, hamburgers, a roast beef sandwich, a turkey sandwich, a BLT, a grilled cheese and other sandwiches.

This is a great place to stop for gift shopping and a sample—or a few bottles—of Alpenglow. But it's a must stop for barbecue and donuts.

The Apple House is a long, low, red building just off I-66 at Exit 13. If you're going east on I-66, bear right at the bottom of the ramp and right again at the stop sign onto Va. 55. The Apple House is just on the right.

Fox Diner

FRONT ROYAL

Fox Diner

2 SOUTH STREET / FRONT ROYAL, VA 22630
(540) 635-3325

Style	Diner
Meals	Breakfast, lunch and dinner, seven days a week
Price Range	Inexpensive
Superlatives	"Next-Best-Thing-to-Sex Cake"

Originally called Lehew Town for a Frenchman named Peter Lehew, this community was known as Front Royal as early as 1788. The name honors its royal oak tree. The entrance to Skyline Drive and Shenandoah National Park is here, as is Skyline Caverns, home of the world's only known anthodites—six-sided crystals with white spikes going out in all directions. Front Royal's restored downtown is delightful.

The Fox Diner is one of those little places built in

the 1950s that hasn't changed much. But it's been discovered. A photo and story appeared in the June 1996 issue of *Motorcyclist* magazine. NBC News dropped in to gather local opinions on how much the government is spending fighting cigarette use. A feature appeared in a Swedish newspaper. And the premiere issue of the adventure magazine *Unlimited* mentioned the Fox Diner's fried chicken.

The inside of the diner is tan and blue with light wood-grain paneling and lace valances. There are 11 stools at the counter, three booths and three small tables for two. Silk flowers add a few small splashes of color.

"Running a little restaurant was always something I wanted to do," Loretta Fox Wines told me. She bought this diner in 1987, after 34 years as a high-school secretary.

Her gentleman friend Lewin Williams was seated on the same stool where I'd left him after my first visit five months earlier. "I just sit here in case we get busy," he said.

Omelets, egg sandwiches, hot cakes and French toast are available for breakfast.

Pinto beans with onions and cornbread ranks high on the popularity scale at lunchtime. This may be the only menu on which I've seen a bologna sandwich. Other midday choices include a BLT, a steak sub, grilled ham and cheese, the "Fox Hound" (a quarter-pound beef hot dog with special relish) and the "Fox Burger" (a patty decorated with cheese, bacon, lettuce, tomato and onion).

The dinner menu lists rib-eye steak, haddock, crab cakes, fried chicken, pork chops and other meats, all of which come with two vegetables and rolls. You may also order a hot roast beef or turkey sandwich with mashed potatoes and gravy.

You can get pie, cake, cobbler in season or brownies for dessert, but rumor has it that the "Next-Best-Thing-to-Sex Cake" is the preferred sweet ending. Far be it from me to register an opinion on this. Besides, there wasn't any left on either of my visits.

FRONT ROYAL

Main Street Mill

500 EAST MAIN STREET
FRONT ROYAL, VA 22630
(540) 636-3123

Style	Family-style
Meals	Breakfast, lunch and dinner, seven days a week
Price Range	Inexpensive/Moderate
Superlatives	Crab cakes, Southern-style vinegar-based barbecue
Extras	Full bar

*F*ormer Front Royal mayor Stan Brooks and his partner, Alice Barnhart, opened the Main Street Mill in February 1996. Their goal was to bring their community the kind of food people were going out of town to find.

The old mill itself is interesting—big rooms, tall ceilings, massive beams. Actually, the beams are less massive than they used to be. A fire in the 1920s damaged the interior. The beams have been sanded down, but it's still obvious they were scorched by flames.

The bar, located to the right, is surrounded by green walls. The sizable dining area has a fence painted around the middle of the room and a mural of country life on the upper half of the walls. In a couple of places, there's a horse looking over the rail. A rooster stands on it, a cat is curled up on it, and a painted saddle hangs over it. At the top of a painted lamp base is a real sconce. It's an interesting piece done by local artist Pat Windrow, who has taken some artistic liberties with the sun and shadows. Framed black-and-white photos of local people and places are displayed on the walls. Brooks is as fond of this photo collection as he is of Front Royal, his hometown.

The breakfast menu lists a variety of pancakes—blueberry, apple-cinnamon, chocolate chip—omelets, biscuits and gravy, Belgian waffles and other things. The "Fruity Tooty" is touted as the freshest fruit plate in town.

At lunch, the deli sandwiches come with a pickle and your choice of a side item. The burgers are named for places in the immediate area—"The Mill," "The Blackened Mill," "The Downtowner," "The West Main," "The East Main" and "The Uptowner." Soups, salads, potatoes and grilled sandwiches are also available.

Dinner entrees range from bacon-wrapped filet mignon and homemade crab cakes to barbecue platters and pasta dishes. Hometown favorites include a Virginia country ham dinner, pork chops, roast beef and roast turkey.

Located next door to Front Royal's visitor center, the Main Street Mill can be seen for blocks because of its height. In fact, after I left, I used it to gauge where I was relative to where I'd been and where I wanted to go. But don't worry, you won't get lost in Front Royal. It's not that big.

FRONT ROYAL

The Mills House ?

122 NORTH ROYAL AVENUE
FRONT ROYAL, VA 22630
(540) 636-4256

Style	Casual nice
Meals	Lunch, Monday through Saturday; dinner, Friday and Saturday
Price Range	Inexpensive/Moderate
Superlatives	Candy store, gift shop, chef's specials
Extras	Wine and beer

There are two good reasons to stop here. One, of course, is to have lunch or dinner. The other is to browse the gift and Christmas shops and the candy store downstairs.

The restaurant is a little more than 10 years old and has been located in this turn-of-the-century brick house since 1993. The front room is decorated in soft green and pink with wall lamps and lace curtains. The back dining room has colorful wallpaper in shades of brown, cream, gold and dark green over a chair rail.

At lunch, the sandwiches come with a pickle spear and your choice of potato chips, carrot sticks, slaw or potato salad. Fat grams are listed next to each hot, vegetarian, deli and club sandwich. Little hearts des-

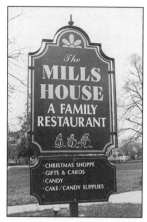

The Mills House

In the candy shop downstairs, you'll find a plethora of candy-making supplies and cake-decorating items, as well as fine candies and a complete line of kosher candies. In fact, the restaurant was called Sweet Time until 1997. Indeed, this candy shop remains the place to have one sweet time.

ignate which ones have been deemed heart-healthy. The cold plates, served with sourdough bread, include turkey, ham, roast beef, tuna salad, chicken salad and egg salad.

The dinner entrees include rib-eye steak slow-roasted with a sauce of port wine and mushrooms. The "Atlanta Salmon Fillet" is pan-seared with ginger butter and served with angel hair pasta. The grilled portobello mushroom comes with roasted tomatoes in a light garlic sauce. The turkey meatloaf with bourbon cranberry relish shares its plate with celery-studded mashed potatoes. The chef's specials include grilled pork loin with roasted red potatoes and sauteed tuna steak in a cognac-thyme cream sauce over pasta.

Desserts include apple pie, Black Forest cheesecake, Kentucky Derby pie and chocolate cake. And you and the others at your table won't have to agree on what type of tea you'd like, because you'll each receive your own teapot.

Sandy's Diner ?

1718 SHENANDOAH AVENUE
FRONT ROYAL, VA 22630
(540) 635-2911

Style	Diner
Meals	Breakfast, lunch and dinner, seven days a week
Price Range	Inexpensive
Superlatives	Diner atmosphere, omelets
Extras	Wine and beer

*A*mong all the diners I've been in, this one is a classic. It's also the largest and very likely the cleanest.

There's a lot of stainless steel inside and out. On a sunny morning, light streams in through miniblinds all across the front and brightens a spotless interior. Fluorescent lamps behind wooden valances provide soft indirect light. The strips of mirrors on the ceiling and the terrazzo floors are original. There are 16 stools, 10 booths and two tables for four. The stools and most of the booth seats are dark green with rows of silver rivets. For 25 cents, you can make two country-music selections at your table on the "Wall-O-Matic" machine.

Sandy's Diner

but there's also a note suggesting that customers "ask about other homemade pies and cakes." These might include coconut pie, chocolate cream pie, pound cake, chocolate cake and carrot cake. Ice cream is also served.

This place is popular among locals, most of whom are addressed as "honey" by the friendly waitresses.

STRASBURG
Hi Neighbor
192 WEST KING STREET / STRASBURG, VA 22657
(540) 465-9987

Style	Home-style
Meals	Breakfast and lunch, seven days a week; dinner, Monday through Friday
Price Range	Inexpensive/Moderate
Superlatives	Local color, scrapple
Extras	Wine and beer

Built in 1955, the diner was moved here from Cumberland, Maryland, in 1963. Front Royal native Sandy Williams relocated her downtown Sandy's Restaurant here in 1994 when a group of investors bought the diner at auction and approached her about operating it.

Breakfast comes hot and fast. Home fries can be ordered with or without onions. Hot cakes, scrapple, breakfast meats, omelets with various things inside and corned beef hash are offered. The breakfast special includes two pancakes, two eggs, a sausage, two bacon strips and potatoes.

Sandwiches, subs, burgers and complete meals are available at lunchtime. Grilled pork chops, ham steaks, a seafood platter, spaghetti, lasagna, haddock and fried chicken are among the entrees.

Two of the popular selections at dinner are roast beef and turkey, either served with mashed potatoes and gravy. Homemade pot pie is also available.

Apple pie and cherry pie are listed on the menu,

*T*he town of Strasburg is synonymous with antiques. It's noted not only for the Strasburg Emporium and its 100 or so dealers, but also for the small antique shops scattered around town. The Strasburg Museum, located in a train station built in 1891, and the Museum of American Presidents, opened in 1996, are popular among visitors as well.

Look for the one-word banner hanging outside Hi Neighbor above the sidewalk. Its message is simple and direct: *Food.*

At noon, you'll find just about every kind of person—blue-collar people, white-collar people, people in uniforms, people in blue jeans, children. Some dressed up, others dressed down. Lots of just plain chatty folks and the friendly waitresses who serve them.

The dining room dates to the Civil War. Union general Philip Sheridan stayed here for several weeks, paying the owners with sugar, coffee and other scarce items. At the turn of the century, the building became the Massanutten Hotel. Now, there's just the restaurant on the site.

If you don't want to order a full breakfast, you can choose from among 17 side orders, including egg substitute for the cholesterol-conscious. The cholesterol-unconscious will probably lean more toward the biscuits and gravy or the corned beef hash. Among the more than a dozen breakfasts is the "Sportsman's Breakfast," which features rainbow trout.

But the specialty here is scrapple. Originally a Pennsylvania Dutch dish, scrapple is finely chopped pork scraps with cornmeal and pork liver added. The concoction is cooked into a mush, pressed into a loaf pan and cooled. A serving is then sliced, fried in butter and served hot, most often on toast or pancakes. Puddin' meat, also available here, is similar to scrapple but without the cornmeal and liver. It's a coarse, crumbly food.

The sandwiches range from peanut butter and jelly to crab cake. Both pork and beef barbecue are available. Platters are served with french fries and slaw.

Everyone seems to know everyone else here, but they're friendly enough to make you feel part of it all, too.

Hotel Strasburg

213 SOUTH HOLLIDAY STREET
STRASBURG, VA 22657
(800) 348-8327 OR (540) 465-9191

Style	Fine dining
Meals	Breakfast, Saturday and Sunday; lunch, Monday through Saturday; dinner, seven days a week. The Depot Lounge serves lunch and dinner seven days a week.
Price Range	Moderate/Expensive
Superlatives	Victorian atmosphere, antiques, Mediterranean-style food
Extras	Full bar

The Hotel Strasburg combines Victorian style and friendly warmth. Constructed in the 1890s as a private hospital, the building was converted to a hotel in the early 1900s. The interior was completely restored to elegance in 1977.

On New Year's Day 1994, Gary and Carol Rutherford bought the hotel, after having leased it for three years. The small front door belies the grandeur inside. To the left is the large walnut front desk. You'll note the huge Belgian sideboard standing behind it. To the right is the Depot Lounge, a cozy little spot with a bar and tables for about 35 people. Soup, salads, focaccia, nachos, appetizers, burgers, sandwiches and desserts are available here all afternoon and evening. Dinners are available during dinner hours.

The halls and the dining rooms are cream with green trim. Artwork and mirrors with ornate gold frames grace the walls, as do antique plates.

Hotel Strasburg

Entrees" include trout, crab cakes, catch of the day and a vegetarian dish.

The guest rooms at the Hotel Strasburg are exquisite. They feature lots of dark walnut, marble and fabulous headboards, all complemented by modern amenities like private baths, telephones and televisions. With all the classic Victorian decor around here, you might expect an atmosphere of stiff formality, but it's just the opposite. Here as elsewhere, the owners set the tone for their business, and Gary Rutherford just happens to be a cheerful, friendly fellow. His easy manner is reflected in the entire staff.

Breakfast is available to the public on Saturday and Sunday mornings. Overnight guests receive a continental breakfast each morning.

Chef Frank Asaro has been here close to a decade. He specializes in Mediterranean-style cuisine, although his signature lunch entree is chicken pot pie, a made-from-scratch little casserole under a puff pastry. Other choices include an Italian steak-and-cheese sandwich, "Sea and Garden Focaccia" and "Focaccia Rustica"—grilled portobello mushroom with pesto, roasted sweet red pepper and melted provolone.

There are four sections to the dinner menu. The section called "From the Saute Station" includes pan-seared lamb chops, butter pecan chicken and "Veal Gremolata." The "From the Charcoal Grill" section includes grilled pork chops, surf and turf and veal cutlets. The items in the "Pasta Entrees" section come with a garden salad. The "Seafood and Vegetarian

MIDDLETOWN

The Wayside Inn

7783 MAIN STREET / MIDDLETOWN, VA 22645
(540) 869-1797

Style	Fine dining
Meals	Breakfast, Monday through Saturday; lunch and dinner, seven days a week; Sunday brunch
Price Range	Moderate/Expensive
Superlatives	Historical atmosphere, peanut soup, trout
Extras	Full bar

*M*iddletown is a pretty little town with historic houses and the second-oldest professional theater company in the state. Wayside Theatre presents more than half a dozen productions between June and December. One of the town's most interesting buildings is Grace United Methodist Church over on Main Street, which has a 75-foot tower with a carillon and unusual sliding stained-glass windows in the sanctuary.

The Wayside Inn bills itself as the "oldest motor inn" in the country, having opened in 1797. Of course, there weren't any automobiles then. It would be another 99 years before Henry Ford made his first car. But the place has indeed provided food and lodging to travelers for more than two centuries.

Though he was probably not the first guest to motor in, John D. Rockefeller was certainly among the most famous. The 1922 telegram in which he requested two rooms—one for himself and the other for his driver—is now framed and displayed on a wall.

In the early 1990s, a third floor and new wings were added and the name was changed from Larrick's Hotel to The Wayside Inn. The inn is owned by a corporation that also operates the Henley Park Hotel, the Morrison-Clark Inn and a few other fine Washington, D.C., properties.

When Keith Deering took over as executive chef at The Wayside Inn in 1996, he carefully evaluated the menus. He kept some of the traditional favorites, modified others and eliminated heavy stuff like biscuits smothered with chicken and dumplings, thick stews and casseroles. His approach is to use local ingredients and prepare them in a light, innovative fashion. He prefers fresh herbs and often uses Virginia apples, oysters, peaches and quail.

Eggs, meat, hot cakes and French toast are offered at breakfast.

The midday bill of fare includes salads, sandwiches and entrees. Among the soups are The Wayside's signature peanut soup and a cabbage and black-eyed pea soup with country ham.

The dinner appetizers include warm artichoke hearts stuffed with cheese and bell peppers. Homemade spoon bread, a traditional favorite, is still offered. The roast pork entree is marinated and served with a sauce of pureed apples and bourbon. The Shenandoah Valley rainbow trout comes with lump crabmeat, butter, chive sauce and a corn cake. Classics like roasted turkey and Virginia country ham steaks are also available.

Sunday brunch is a table event, not a buffet. Among the novel options available are "Amaretto French Toast" and "Eggs Belle Grove." Such items as corn-fried catfish, baked salmon and eggplant are also offered.

The Wayside Inn is a pretty place with a friendly staff, nice accommodations and fine food.

WHITE POST

L'Auberge Provençale

U.S. 340 / WHITE POST, VA 22663
(800) 638-1702 OR (540) 837-1375

Style	Fine dining
Meals	Dinner, Wednesday through Sunday. Reservations are strongly requested.
Price Range	Expensive
Superlatives	Pastoral setting, food quality and presentation
Extras	Full bar

*T*his town was named for a white post that marked the way to Greenway Court, the home of Thomas, Sixth Lord Fairfax. It is said that the post was whitewashed frequently to enhance its visibility and probably its appearance as well, as a chipped or peeling post would not have made a favorable first impression.

If you can't get over to the south of France, L'Auberge Provençale is a superb place to experience the food, drink, amenities and loveliness of that region.

The manor house was built in 1753 from fieldstones found in the area's pastures and valleys. The building rambles down a small slope; additions were constructed in 1890 and 1990. Eleven very nice guest rooms are available.

Alain and Celeste Borel bought the property in 1981. On the grounds, you'll find hanging baskets, colorful flowers in Celeste's collection of antique olive jars, the chef's vegetable and herb gardens and more than three dozen fruit trees. A fourth-generation gourmet chef from Avignon, Alain makes good use of his fresh produce.

Inside the front door are framed awards and articles. Magazines that portray the finest in food—*Bon Appétit, Gourmet, Food and Wine*—have not missed L'Auberge Provençale.

Celeste is responsible for the fabrics and decor. The intimate dining rooms have their own color schemes. A rich royal blue is prominent in the front room, which has a fireplace. The large solarium room, built in 1986, is done is soft peach, a perfect backdrop for the copper pots and pans that belonged to Alain's great-grandmother.

Dinner is a five-course event.

It all starts with an *"Amouse Bouche,"* translated as a little something "to amuse your mouth." Not considered a course in itself, this might be a small salmon crepe—just a little nibble to enjoy while you scan the menu.

The first course is the Entree. Here, however, the familiar term simply means the entry to the meal—an appetizer. One possibility is sauteed frog legs with raspberry cream in puff pastry.

The *"Deuxième Suite,"* or second course, is soup or salad.

The Intermezzo is the third course. It may be a sorbet, the most common palate cleanser.

The fourth course is the main course. It might be lamb with carrot ginger sauce or sea bass with fish mousse.

An optional cheese course is offered after the dinner.

Dessert completes the dining experience. Among the possibilities are crème brûlée or a "Chocolate Tower," filled with raspberries and white chocolate mousse.

You don't wait for a special occasion to come to L'Auberge Provençale. Coming to L'Auberge Provençale creates a special occasion.

The Battletown Inn

102 WEST MAIN STREET
BERRYVILLE, VA 22611
(800) 282-4106

Style	Casual nice
Meals	Lunch, Tuesday through Saturday; Dinner, Tuesday through Sunday; Sunday brunch
Price Range	Moderate
Superlatives	Lovely atmosphere, peanut soup, "Rum Buns"
Extras	Full bar

The Battletown Inn

*O*ne of the attractions around Berryville is Holy Cross Abbey, a Cistercian monastery that began in France in the year 1098. Another attraction—and an unusual one at that—is the Enders Mortuary Museum, which exhibits old caskets, embalming implements and a horse-drawn hearse from 1889. Berryville was originally called Battletown because of its many tavern brawls. That may explain the museum, but what about the monastery?

It was in 1809 that a house was built in Berryville for Sara Stribling, daughter of the town's founder and namesake, Benjamin Berry. That house is now The Battletown Inn. Susan Bailey, a Berryville native, bought the business and reopened the restaurant and the 12-room inn next door in April 1994.

The inn looks important in its crisp white paint and dark green trim. The columns are elegant. Flags wave in the breeze. The Stars and Stripes flies next to the navy-blue Virginia flag, adopted in 1861. A Clarke County flag and a hospitality banner are also displayed.

This place feels special the minute you walk in the door. It's light and bright, with fresh table linens and soft music. Windsor chairs are clustered around tables in intimate dining rooms on the first and second floors.

A smothered chicken dish is one of the popular items at lunch. Prime rib on garlic toast and the "Chicken Blanquette"—creamed chicken and vegetables in a puff pastry shell—can be ordered with or without buttermilk-fried onion rings and what the menu bills as The Battletown Inn's "World-Famous Rum Buns." Soup, sandwiches and burgers are also available.

Trout pâté and broiled mussels are among the appetizers. Dinners are served with a relish tray of apple butter, cottage cheese, watermelon pickles and Jamaican relish, along with "Rum Buns," dinner rolls and a sorbet intermezzo—often an apple cider sorbet made on the premises. The entrees include chicken, baked ham, roast pork, prime rib and broiled flounder. Those who enjoy sirloin or shrimp can order either or both *en brochette*.

Desserts like chocolate mousse, berry tarts and

bread pudding with white chocolate sauce provide the perfect ending.

The Gray Ghost Tavern, which opened upstairs in 1997, features fare such as pork barbecue, French dip and black bean and sirloin chili. Two popular items are the seven-layer shrimp salad and cheese fondue with crabmeat and artichoke hearts.

Bon Matin
Bakery & Cafe

BERRYVILLE

Bon Matin
Bakery & Cafe

1 EAST MAIN STREET
BERRYVILLE, VA 22611
(540) 955-1554

Style	Cafe
Meals	Breakfast and lunch, Tuesday through Saturday; Sunday brunch
Price Range	Inexpensive
Superlatives	Baked goods

*T*he name Bon Matin, French for "good morning," certainly fits this cafe. You're almost guaranteed to have a good morning if you start it here.

The most prominent color inside is pink. The entry is bordered by white lattice with real plants climbing up. Fluorescent lights on a wooden ceiling brighten an already well-lit space. The original pencil prints on the walls may be purchased. Local artists can bring their work in here to display for sale.

There's seating for a couple dozen people at the round tables. You place your order at the bakery counter below the posted menu. It's then made fresh and delivered to you at your table or in a bag to go.

If you come for a morning repast, you can select a muffin or an eclair with juice, coffee—fancy or plain—or tea.

If you're here for lunch, it's a little more comprehensive. The house soup is tomato bisque, and there's a soup du jour, like split pea or "Mulligatawny"—a curried chicken, rice and vegetable soup. The salad du jour might be navel orange on spinach with sliced red onions, strawberries and strawberry vinaigrette. Regular salads include the "Mandarin Spinach Salad" and the "Savory Sampler." Among the sandwiches are turkey, chicken salad, tuna, ham and Swiss on sourdough, beef and herb cheese on French bread and a seafood croissant.

And you can always get my favorite dessert—a cookie.

Sunday brunch consists of omelets, crepes, quiche, a cheese plate, pastries and assorted breads and muffins.

It's not a fancy place, but the food is prepared with care and fresh ingredients. And they have cookies!

Amherst Diner

334 AMHERST STREET
WINCHESTER, VA 22601
(540) 667-8222

Style	Diner
Meals	Breakfast, lunch and dinner, seven days a week
Price Range	Inexpensive
Superlatives	Superclean atmosphere, real potatoes, fresh sausage

*A*pples are big here—as the Apple Blossom Festival each spring and the Apple Harvest Festival each fall attest—but there's more to Winchester than that. The town has had a rich history since before the Revolutionary War. The cabin used by George Washington when he was helping protect the frontier is located in Winchester's Old Town district. During the Civil War, the town changed hands many times; several battles were fought here. Novelist Willa Cather was born nearby in 1873 and lived her first nine years in the area. Country-music star Patsy Cline—real name Virginia Patterson Hensley—was born here, too.

The Amherst Diner is a little place about three miles off I-81 with most of what you'd expect in a diner—lots of stainless-steel cooking equipment behind the counter, stools, booths and breakfast any time of the day.

But there's one thing missing, and a few others added. The missing commodity—which you won't really miss at all—is the smell of grease and/or cigarette smoke. Smoking is not allowed inside. The extras include nice lamps, flowered valances on the windows, well-dusted miniblinds and a dried flower arrangement in a clay pot on every table. The place is attractive, neat, clean, friendly and busy.

At breakfast, real potatoes and fresh sausage are accompanied by well-buttered toast—and, in case you haven't guessed, there's real butter on the toast. The hot cakes come with syrup or gravy. And you can order sausage, fried ham or bacon in your omelet.

More than two dozen lunch options are listed, among them beef barbecue, hamburgers and a variety of sandwiches, including a crab cake sandwich and an oyster sandwich. The "Mexican Hot Dog" comes with a spiced hamburger concoction on top. The "lite" eater can order pineapple or peaches with cottage cheese.

Quite a few fish entrees are available for dinner, among them a haddock fillet, shrimp in a basket, crab cakes, a seafood platter and flounder stuffed with crabmeat. Strip steak, fried chicken, veal cutlets, grilled pork chops and country ham are also available. All dinners come with two vegetables, hot rolls and coffee or tea.

Cork Street Tavern

8 WEST CORK STREET / WINCHESTER, VA 22601
(540) 667-3777

Style	Pub
Meals	Lunch and dinner, seven days a week
Price Range	Inexpensive/Moderate
Superlatives	Ribs, split pea soup
Extras	Full bar

This brick building in the historic district dates back to the 1830s, but Cork Street itself was named way back in 1759, before the steam engine was invented or Hawaii was discovered.

When Prohibition was repealed in 1932, it spelled opportunity to two men, who opened a small beer parlor called The Rustic Tavern. The building has changed hands a number of times since then but is once again owned by two men, Anthony Andriola and Joel Smith. They have expanded to the property next door, constructing a new building and an outdoor patio on the site where Polly's Taxi stood for 30 years. In fact, Polly's old sign hangs above the new bar.

The first thing you'll notice upon entering the historic tavern is the well-used stone fireplace with trophies on the mantle. There are no baseball or soccer players on these trophies, but rather pigs—shiny, gold-toned pigs representing awards for the tavern's ribs. The tavern's ceilings are low and have recessed lighting. There's lots of wood. The dining room off the bar area is cream and tan above and below a chair rail. Dark green trim provides contrast, and hunt prints break up the wall space.

Appetizers, salads, sandwiches and burgers are served at lunchtime. An interesting salad is the tomato stuffed with shrimp or tuna salad and served with cottage cheese and a hard-boiled egg. The split pea soup is great. The "Tortilla Club" and the "Turkey Reuben" offer something a little different.

With all those trophies on the premises, it would be silly not to try the ribs. But if you prefer eating with a fork, there are plenty of entrees—steaks,

Cork Street Tavern

shrimp, chicken, broiled trout, catfish and crab cakes, among others. Specialties include "Tequila Chicken," "Shrimp Pasta Aristotle" and "West Side Pasta," which includes hot sausage, artichoke hearts, onions, peppers and spices.

Pies like pecan, peanut butter and Kentucky Derby are available for dessert, as is cheesecake.

In keeping with the original beer-parlor theme, Cork Street Tavern carries a wide range of beers—on tap, domestic, imported, microbrewery beers, premium and nonalcoholic varieties. The tavern claims that its "Cork Street Coffee" is the most stolen recipe in town. It's a combination of spiced rum, Bailey's, Frangelico, coffee and whipped cream.

The Cork Street Tavern T-shirts and sweatshirts worn by the servers are available for purchase.

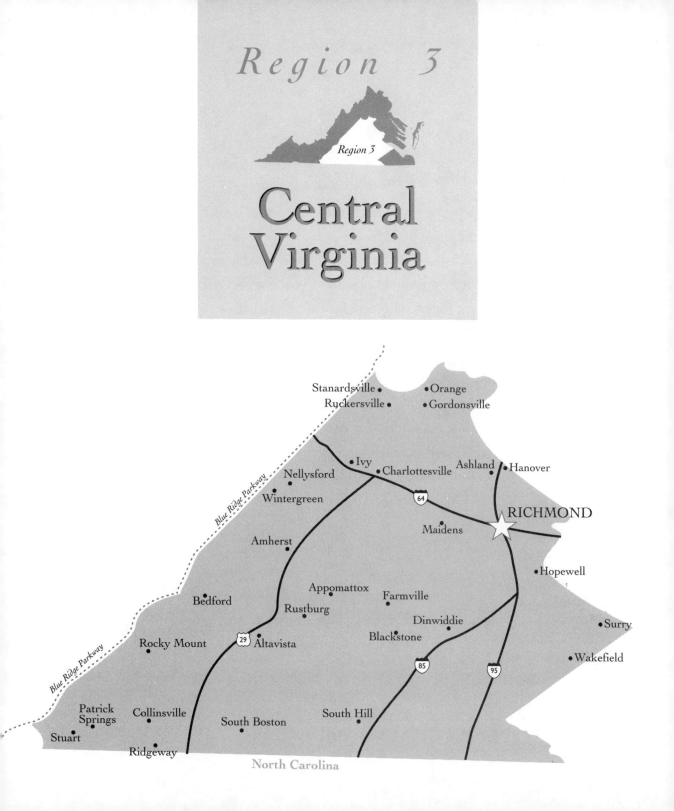

Region 3

Region 3

Central Virginia

Stanardsville • • Orange
Ruckersville • • Gordonsville

Blue Ridge Parkway

• Ivy
Nellysford • • Charlottesville Ashland • • Hanover

Wintergreen

64

★ **RICHMOND**

Maidens •

Amherst •

• Hopewell

Appomattox •
Bedford • Farmville •

Rustburg • Dinwiddie •
29 Blackstone • • Surry

Rocky Mount • Altavista
85 • Wakefield

95

Blue Ridge Parkway

Patrick Springs • Collinsville • South Hill •

Stuart • South Boston •

Ridgeway •

North Carolina

From the peanut farms and cotton fields in
the southeast to the furniture and textile factories in the
southwest to Thomas Jefferson's beloved homes in
Poplar Forest and Charlottesville, this region is more
diverse in geography and industry than
any other in the state.

Buggs Island Lake, which straddles the North Carolina
border, Smith Mountain Lake in the western part of the
region, Lake Anna in the north and the James River
offer a plethora of watersports and some great fishing.
Crabtree Falls in Nelson County is the highest water-
fall in the eastern United States.

The land is gently rolling, the people are friendly and
the area is rich in history. Winery tours, horseback
riding, antiquing, biking, golfing and rock climbing are
but a few of the activities to be enjoyed in the heart of
the Commonwealth.

Mayo River Seafood

STUART

Mayo River Seafood

VA 8 AND U.S. 58 / STUART, VA 24171
(540) 694-4854

Style	Family-style
Meals	Dinner, Wednesday through Sunday
Price Range	Inexpensive/Moderate
Superlative	Large portions, mahi-mahi

At last count, if 40 people move to town, Stuart will top 1,000 in population. This small community 15 miles off the Blue Ridge Parkway is the county seat of Patrick County. It was called Taylorsville for 50-odd years before being renamed for Confederate general J. E. B. Stuart in 1884. Stuart was born near here in 1833.

It's rare for a restaurant manager to insist that I eat something I haven't ordered, but Skip Sharp of Mayo River Seafood was bent on my trying the mahi-mahi. I consented only when he agreed that the piece he brought would be no bigger than half a graham cracker. The next time I go, I can promise you I'll order it without anyone's insistence. I expected it to be fried, but it was broiled, delicate and flavorful.

This restaurant seats more than 100 in its front and back rooms. The front room is the nonsmoking area. The back room overlooks the woods and the river and extends out over the water. The benches and chairs are all heavy pine wood. The place is predominantly gray with mauve trim and thick ropes over the chair rail and around the marvelous mural in the hall. The new exterior on two sides of the building provides an enclosed hallway so the doors don't open to the elements. Porthole windows enhance the restaurant's nautical theme.

On the Friday evening when I visited, there seemed to be as many people ordering at the takeout window as eating in. The servings are plentiful. You can place a half-order if you don't care for a humongous meal. Almost any kind of fish you'd want is here—perch, snapper, trout, shrimp, oysters, whitefish, flounder and more, along with several combinations. Platters come with your choice of potato, slaw and hush puppies. The carnivores in your crowd can order char-broiled steak or a combination of steak and either shrimp, scallops or crab legs.

The desserts include cheesecake and pies like apple, pecan and lemon meringue.

Convenient to the Blue Ridge Parkway, Mayo River Seafood is a casual, friendly, small-town sort of a place.

Ruby's Kitchen

U.S. 58 / PATRICK SPRINGS, VA 24133
(540) 694-3651

Style	Family-style
Meals	Breakfast, lunch and dinner, Monday through Saturday
Price Range	Inexpensive
Superlatives	Nice building, lasagna, beef tips

As soon as we started into Patrick Springs, a no-traffic-light spot in the road with a population measured in hundreds, my husband, John, said, "I'll look for a restaurant here."

In typical wifely fashion, I responded, "You don't seriously think there's a restaurant here, do you?"

Less than a mile down the road, we came across a new, attractive building with cedar siding, a red tin roof and rockers on the front porch. The sign out front said Ruby's Kitchen.

This restaurant doubles as a community gathering place. Soon after the closing of Ruby Shuff's first eatery—located next door—community pressure started to build for her to open again. You see, the seniors pop in here on Friday and Saturday nights to eat, listen to music and socialize.

The new building opened in July 1996. Once again, local folks have a place to go on weekend nights.

The colors are predominantly cream and burgundy. There are 11 booths and nine tables for four. The booth seats are dark green and the chairs burgundy in the dining room on the left and light oak in the room to the right.

The colorful breakfast menu will help you wake up. It describes "Ruby's Omelet," which comes stuffed with bacon, green peppers, onions, tomatoes and cheese. Biscuits, eggs, grits, hash browns and pancakes are also available.

Lunch sandwiches include a BLT, toasted or grilled ham and cheese, barbecue, chicken and flounder. Cheeseburgers, bacon burgers, double burgers, "Super Burgers" and "Ruby's Burgers" are offered. The "Country Boy Special" consists of a bowl of beans, slaw and hush puppies or cornbread.

Dinner plates come with two vegetables from the hot bar or slaw and french fries. If you don't select the hamburger steak, chicken tenders, barbecue, chicken fillet or flounder, then you can get the food bar alone (or the food and salad bars) and just help yourself.

The desserts are all homemade. The "French Strawberry Pie" is a cheesecake-style dessert. Chocolate cake, German chocolate pie, bread pudding and banana pudding may also be available.

I like surprises, and as you can tell from the above account, Ruby's was indeed a surprise. And a nice one at that.

Mackie's

U.S. 220 / COLLINSVILLE, VA 24078
(540) 647-3138

Style	Family-style
Meals	Breakfast and lunch, seven days a week; dinner, Tuesday through Saturday

Price Range	Inexpensive
Superlatives	Daily specials, buffet, Key lime cake
Extras	Full bar

*C*ollinsville received its name when the post office opened in 1945. The name comes from the Collins Company, a local firm that made flashlights. Collinsville is adjacent to Martinsville, famous for its speedway. Both towns are in Henry County, named for Patrick Henry.

Sputnik was the first thing that came to mind when I saw the chandeliers at Mackie's. From a ball in the center, numerous pipes extend about 18 inches to a candelabra bulb at the end. These have to be the most interesting light fixtures I've ever seen.

Otherwise, Mackie's is a very normal-looking restaurant. Out front are rockers facing the parking lot and an antique 10-cent Coke machine. Inside, you'll find a 35-cent cigarette machine. Neither is stocked, so don't bother grabbing your quarters and dimes.

The big stone fireplace on the left wall has a Robert E. Lee print over it. The walls are cinder blocks painted a cream color. The big windows at the front have plaid valances, and the tables have plastic tablecloths. The chairs are vinyl upholstered. There's another dining room off the hallway in the back.

This is the first place I've come across that goes out of state for its ham. Missouri country ham is part of the "Something Not to Miss Out On" breakfast. The "Smoke House Special" breakfast features smoked sausage patties. Almost anything you could want for breakfast is offered. Things like grilled chicken, tenderloin, cottage cheese and pineapple are available in addition to more traditional fare.

I didn't partake of the buffet on the Friday afternoon I visited, but I couldn't help noticing how good it looked. The salad greens looked crisp, and the fried chicken pieces were large and golden colored. Hamburgers, hot dogs, sandwiches and french fries are available, as is a food bar. Mackie's always offers a "lite" lunch item like grilled or stewed chicken, baked flounder or hot or cold broiled popcorn shrimp.

All the desserts are homemade, and someone here knows something about making cake. The Key lime cake has a wonderfully coarse texture, the kind you get from mixing the batter by hand.

Mackie's opened in 1981. Patricia Webb says the best thing about the place is that most of the food is homemade. You can take her word for it. She's been a cook here since the beginning.

Mackie's

Stoney Mountain Tavern & Deli

Stoney Mountain Tavern & Deli

705 VIRGINIA AVENUE / COLLINSVILLE, VA 24078
(540) 647-4544

Style	Pub
Meals	Lunch, Monday through Saturday; dinner, Friday and Saturday
Price Range	Inexpensive/Moderate
Superlatives	Fresh-squeezed "Lemon-Limeade," healthy food
Extras	Full bar

Gloria Keen and Tami Stone, an energetic mother-daughter team, are responsible for this cozy eatery.

Tami said the building has had as many as 20 restaurants in it over the years. "It seemed like there was a jinx on it, but if you drop around here at lunchtime, you'll see we've taken the jinx out," she said.

The exterior is gray stone and the interior a classy mix of black and white, burgundy and gray. The sof-

fit with recessed lighting over the rich-grained wooden bar and the track lights in the ceiling lend contemporary touches. The stone fireplace adds warmth.

Tami has a local health-food store, in which she opened a small deli a few years back. It grew so quickly that in December 1996, she and Gloria moved here and opened for dinner on Friday and Saturday nights.

Tami still has the health-food store, and her mom owns The Country Basket Flowers & Gifts. But neither business takes away from their devotion to the freshly prepared, home-cooked food served at Stoney Mountain.

The lunch salads include tuna salad and chicken salad. You can order them to accompany a sandwich or as a plate-size entree. The "Sample Platter" is a medley of all the restaurant's cold salads, served with a homemade muffin and fresh fruit. Two homemade soups are prepared daily, and there's a fresh fruit platter with cottage cheese. Sandwich lovers can choose from among ham, roast beef, smoked turkey breast, turkey and pastrami, corned beef and others.

Many of the dinners and sauces are prepared from Tami's grandmother's recipes. Though the menu is changed frequently, fresh salmon and king crab legs are always available. Rotating entrees include lasagna, baked stuffed chicken breast, grilled shrimp over pasta and a combination steamed platter with mussels, shrimp and king crab legs.

Blender drinks called "Smoothies" are concocted of frozen yogurt, protein powder and a variety of fruit juices.

Despite the fact that Stoney Mountain seats around

130 people, it exudes a cozy atmosphere. Add to that a healthy, homemade meal and some fresh-squeezed "Lemon-Limeade" and you have the makings of an excellent dining experience.

Clarence's

Clarence's

U.S. 220 / RIDGEWAY, VA 24148
(540) 956-3400

Style	Family-style
Meals	Breakfast, lunch and dinner, seven days a week
Price Range	Inexpensive/Moderate
Superlatives	Clean atmosphere, all-you-can-eat fish on Friday, "Pineapple Cheesecake"

*H*ere's a place with a good reputation far and wide — well, at least 50 miles to the north. All the way down U.S. 220, Clarence's was mentioned to me by regular folks and by restaurant owners as well.

This restaurant was opened by Clarence Pickurel in 1971. The big windows on the front and sides allow natural light into the cream and lavender dining areas. The vinyl chairs and booths are aqua. It's an unusual color scheme, but it's quite pleasant, especially with the prints of flowers and English-style cottages on the wall. Two private rooms with a single table in each are available for those who want to be away from the crowd. On the left in the back is a counter with five stools, a nice option for solo travelers.

Those who can't abide grits with their breakfast — that's us folks born north of the Mason-Dixon line — can get fried apples or hash browns with their eggs and breakfast meat. Brains and eggs, hot cakes, French toast, oatmeal and all kinds of biscuits are also served.

Among the popular items at dinner are the "Chef's Specialties," which include a minced barbecue platter, chicken, chicken livers and center-cut pork chops. The steaks are cut and prepared in the kitchen. Clarence's claims every bite to be tender, moist and delicious, though the menu is clear on one thing: "Not responsible for well-done steaks." The fresh seafood comes with a baked potato or french fries, hush puppies and slaw or a tossed salad. Golden oysters, frog legs, Gulf shrimp, catfish and lobster are among the options.

The menu suggests that customers "ask about our delicious desserts," and indeed you should. The "Pineapple Cheesecake" is very popular. The other options include cherry pie and apple pie.

Don't give up if you're heading down U.S. 220 to eat here. It's an easy five miles past Martinsville in a stone building on the right.

Billy's Steakhouse

Billy's Steakhouse

3102 HALIFAX ROAD / SOUTH BOSTON, VA 24592
(804) 572-6662

Style	Family-style
Meals	Dinner, Tuesday through Sunday
Price Range	Moderate
Superlatives	Old music, rib-eye steaks, shrimp cocktails
Extras	Full bar

When Boston, Massachusetts, was closed by the British because of the Boston Tea Party, Virginians passed a resolution of support for the New Englanders and named two settlements Boston. When this city was chartered in 1796, it was called South Boston to avoid confusion with the Boston in Culpeper County. Located on the Dan River and incorporated in 1884, South Boston is one of the country's leading tobacco markets.

When the Thomas Long Steak House opened in a South Boston strip mall in 1976, there were three things on the menu: shrimp cocktails, rib-eye steaks and cheesecake.

Soon thereafter, a high-school kid named Billy McGhee started working there. (Don't mix him up with the one Janis Joplin made famous. That was Bobby.) Billy kept his job weekends and summers through his college years. In 1988, when Long was ready to sell the business, it seemed natural that Billy and his wife, Dawn, should buy it. Billy changed the name. A year later, he moved the restaurant into a freestanding log building on the edge of the parking lot.

The wood interior with mauve accents and soft ceiling lights sets a casual tone in the two dining rooms, which can seat 160 people. Musical hits from the 1940s through the 1970s play continuously in the background.

Though Billy's Steakhouse is definitely not an Italian restaurant, garlic bread is served with every meal. In addition to the soup and salad bar, diners may frequent the restaurant's cheese bar. Shrimp cocktails and rib-eye steaks still command center stage on the menu, but the entrees now include New York strip, filet mignon, prime rib, seafood platters, hot or cold shrimp and chicken. Baked potatoes or steak fries come with the meals.

Cheesecake with or without cherry topping is still tops for dessert. The other choices are hot fudge cake and vanilla ice cream with chocolate sauce.

El Ranchito

SOUTH BOSTON

El Ranchito

1633 SEYMOUR DRIVE
SOUTH BOSTON, VA 24592
(804) 572-2225

Style	Mexican
Meals	Lunch and dinner, seven days a week
Price Range	Inexpensive/Moderate
Superlatives	Superclean atmosphere, "Fajitas Texans," soft or fried chimichangas
Extras	Full bar

I noticed the attractive sign and the entrance before asking anyone in town about the local restaurants. When El Ranchito was mentioned a couple of times, I was only too happy to backtrack and pay it a visit.

Since the Agurees family has opened just three of these restaurants in Virginia, El Ranchito doesn't qualify as a chain. In my view, having three restaurants merely implies that someone is doing something right. The family's other restaurants are in Martinsville and Collinsville.

Inside the South Boston restaurant, fancy sombreros and serapes provide brilliant splashes of color on the walls. Gold-framed mirrors make an already large dining area seem even more spacious.

There are 37 entree choices here. Since the manager mentioned that the "Fajitas Texans" and the chimichangas are very popular, I figured they'd be a good place to start. The fajitas are made with shrimp, chicken, steak, bell peppers, onions, guacamole and fried beans. The chimichangas, which can be ordered soft or fried, consist of two flour tortillas filled with beef tips and fried beans and topped with lettuce, tomatoes, sour cream, nacho cheese and guacamole. If you're the kind of person who's bored with just one entree, then you might find one of the 25 combination plates more suitable.

The Agurees family wants its customers at El Ranchito not only to enjoy their meal but to understand the dos and don'ts of eating Mexican food as well. In fact, there's a helpful clarification inside the menu: "It is absolutely correct to eat tacos, tostadas or tortillas with your fingers."

That's always nice to know.

SOUTH HILL

Kahill's

1799 NORTH MECKLENBERG AVENUE
SOUTH HILL, VA 23950
(804) 447-6941

Style	Pub
Meals	Breakfast, lunch and dinner, seven days a week
Price Range	Moderate
Superlatives	Seafood and steak specials, 22-ounce prime rib
Extras	Full bar

Kahill's

*I*n the days when South Hill was known by one of its early names—Ridgefork or Binford's Tavern—financiers purchased 56 acres around the local railroad depot and laid out a circular town one and a quarter miles in diameter. It was incorporated as South Hill in 1901 and was one of only three circular municipalities in the United States as late as 1958. It has since been reconfigured. Today, fishing events are so popular in this area that South Hill has been referred to as "Tournament Town."

Located at Exit 15 off I-85, Kahill's is a former country store and rental house that has been transformed into an English-style pub and restaurant. Tom Flowers, the owner, opened the place in 1991.

The bar sports some old signs, a large Clint Eastwood poster and banners from the University of Virginia and Virginia Tech. The neat, rustic dining room features an eclectic mix of antiques from Tom's father's collection, things Tom has picked up and items brought in by patrons. Paintings by local artists adorn the walls and are for sale at reasonable prices. The wood-pegged floors and the log walls below the chair rail enhance the warmth of the place. In nice weather, the large outdoor patio is open.

Kahill's offers comprehensive meals three times a day.

You can select the "Cowboy Chili Breakfast," eggs Benedict, a breakfast burrito or an omelet stuffed with your choice of cheese, crabmeat, chili, smoked salmon, salsa or a number of other things. Cereal, grits, hash browns and pancakes are also offered.

Great sandwiches, burgers and pasta selections are available at lunch. Reubens, steak sandwiches, pastrami sandwiches, knockwurst, Italian chicken and smoked turkey are among the favorites. There are also plenty of salads to choose from, as well as a vegetable plate, which consists of your choice of four vegetables.

Most of the dinner appetizers feature something from the sea. Crab-stuffed mushroom caps, "Scallops Tova" and deep-fried crab balls are among the choices. The entrees include a variety of veal, pork, fowl, pasta and seafood dishes.

Business has been good here, as evidenced by the addition of 75 seats in 1996. The place can now accommodate 150. Guests can join the crowd around the bar or take a quiet place in the dining room.

Boon Street Cafe - its first location in Boones Mill

Boon Street Cafe

18027 VIRGIL GOODE HIGHWAY (U.S. 220)
ROCKY MOUNT, VA 24151
(540) 483-2311

Style	Cafe
Meals	Late breakfast, lunch and dinner, Tuesday through Saturday
Price Range	Inexpensive
Superlatives	Meat loaf, Italian food
Extras	Wine and beer

Rocky Mount is the county seat of Franklin County, where Booker T. Washington was born into slavery in 1856. It was in recognition of his love of learning that he took the name Booker when he was freed at the end of the Civil War. Booker T. Washington National Monument is located near Rocky Mount.

The town is home to the Boon Street Cafe, a little restaurant that started in April 1995 just a hop, skip and jump across the river in Boones Mill. It moved to its current site in Rocky Mount—a brick building on the southbound side of U.S. 220—on July 1, 1997, so it could triple its dining space.

Stepbrothers Frank Maisenhelder and Tony Staite moved to this area from Philadelphia in the mid-1990s for "low taxes and country living," as they put it. Tony's sister, Tina Baker, who helps in the kitchen and waited on my table, moved here from Texas even more recently than that. The couple at the table next to mine relocated from Alaska for the same reasons Frank and Tony did. Sounds like this area should grace the cover of one of those retirement magazines.

If you're a late riser, the Boon Street Cafe is a great bet for breakfast, since it starts serving biscuits, omelets, eggs, French toast, pancakes, bacon and sausage at 10 A.M.

Hamburgers, BLTs, tuna salad and chicken nuggets are among the popular items at lunch. The specials might be hot roast beef and a seafood platter.

The stepbrothers' Italian heritage is reflected in the dinner menu, which includes spaghetti with either oil and garlic, marinara sauce, meatballs or Italian sausage. Linguine with clam sauce or shrimp sauce is also offered. If you're not in the mood for Italian food, then try baked fish, breaded shrimp, steak, pork chops or chicken. These dinner plates are accompanied by salad, a roll, two vegetables and the dessert of the day.

The etchings on the walls are for sale. They're done by Dr. Van Name, an 85-year-old retired physician. The good doctor says he's "anything but an artist. I don't do anything original. The kind of work I do is really documentary." Maybe so, since he draws local historical scenes and sailing vessels from the 1920s and the 1940s. But he's wrong about one thing: he definitely qualifies as an artist. Staite explained that the Boon Street Cafe sells the etchings as a favor, not for a commission. I like that.

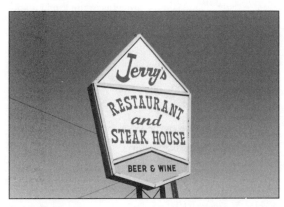

Jerry's Steak House

ROCKY MOUNT

Jerry's Steak House
U.S. 220 / ROCKY MOUNT, VA 24151
(540) 483-2070

Style	Family-style
Meals	Lunch, Monday through Friday; dinner, Monday through Saturday
Price Range	Inexpensive/Moderate
Superlatives	Homemade food, liver and onions
Extras	Wine and beer

*I*n the year 1964, Beatlemania swept the nation, my brother Bobby and Bill Clinton graduated from high school (in different parts of the country) and 21-year-old Jerry Leonard began delivering bread to a Dairy Queen in Martinsville.

The DQ owner loved to complain about his partner, Jerry noticed. Soon thereafter, the bread man became the new partner. That partnership, like the one before it, didn't last, but Jerry found he liked the restaurant business enough to persevere. In 1967, he opened the Redwood Steakhouse on U.S. 220. Ten years later, he moved to his current location about a mile north of Rocky Mount and renamed his restaurant Jerry's.

The small eating area to the right can accommodate a couple dozen folks and the middle room where you enter the restaurant another dozen; both rooms are wood paneled and have booths. At least 75 or 80 guests can sit in the comfortable wallpapered room to the left.

Lots of people know lots of people here, and that's a tribute to Jerry's food. He figures that less than 5 percent of his business comes from travelers. "It's the unofficial Democratic headquarters," he jests, referring to the victory parties held here for his friend W. Q. Overton, the longtime sheriff.

The inexpensive lunch specials are a great deal. Our waitress stressed that almost everything that can be made on the premises is. She recommended the liver and onions. My husband, John, eats anything, so he took her recommendation. I ordered broiled flounder, along with macaroni and cheese and peach cobbler for my "vegetables." Sandwiches, burgers and salads are available, too.

Sirloin steak and surf and turf are among the house specialties. Fresh seafood like deviled crabs, crab cakes, oysters, shrimp and a seafood platter are offered. You can also order spaghetti, chicken, ham steak and beef tips. All dinners come with a salad, a vegetable and hot bread.

All the pies are made by Jerry's wife.

Jerry's is a comfortable place where the waitresses are efficient and pleasant. And it really doesn't matter if you're a Democrat or a Republican. Everyone is greeted with the same friendliness.

Betty's Kitchen

ALTAVISTA

Betty's Kitchen
534 MAIN STREET / ALTAVISTA, VA 24517
(804) 369-5363

Style	Home-style
Meals	Breakfast, lunch and dinner, Monday through Saturday
Price Range	Inexpensive
Superlatives	Nostalgic atmosphere, antiques, cobbler

*M*eaning "high view" in Spanish, Altavista was the first town organized in Campbell County. It was chartered in 1907 by the Lane brothers, whose cedar chests are known around the world. Today, the Lane Company employs more than 1,000 people at its local plant.

What is now one of Altavista's favorite places to eat and catch up on town news started a little more than 10 years ago as a fancy establishment with linens, burnt-orange paint and small brass chandeliers. After a couple of struggling years, the restaurant was taken over by Richard and Sandra Mattox, who immediately took off the linens and put in some booths. Their son Todd happened to visit a similar restaurant in another state that had antiques on the walls. He suggested that his dad's antique sign collection might be interesting in the restaurant.

Today, those signs cover most of the wall space. High shelves hold dozens of antique tins. Guests immediately notice the couple of old gas pumps some 10 feet tall. Old violins sit on a shelf over the door. A working traffic light complete with its *Walk* buzzer is in the far corner.

There's a feeling here that you've stepped back in time. And that's just fine when it comes to the food, which is simple, everyday fare.

Breakfast is a well-rounded meal of ham, bacon or sausage, eggs, home fries, apples, tomatoes and homemade biscuits or toast. Of course, you can also order pancakes, waffles, French toast, cereal, breakfast sandwiches and biscuits.

Lunch is equally simple: sandwiches, burgers, salads, homemade soup in winter.

The dinner plates number 25. They run the gamut from baked fish and salmon cakes to chicken livers, pork chops and country-style steak. Mashed potatoes and gravy come with some entrees; two vegetables come with most everything. The Saturday-night specials are prime rib and rib-eye steak.

If you're on the go, call in your order for pickup. If you're not in a hurry, you can sit back and enjoy looking at signs advertising things that never hit the big time: Nichol Kola, Frosty Root Beer, Suncrest and Double Cola. After eating, you can meander on down a couple of doors to the owner's antique shop and browse some more.

The Home Place

14712 SPRING CREEK ROAD
DINWIDDIE, VA 23841
(804) 469-9596

Style	Family-style
Meals	Breakfast, lunch and dinner, seven days a week; Sunday brunch
Price Range	Inexpensive/Moderate
Superlatives	Setting, apple pie, ribs, prime rib
Extras	Wine and beer

Formed in 1752, Dinwiddie County was named for Robert Dinwiddie, deputy to the royal governor and the earl of Albemarle. The county seat was at Dinwiddie Courthouse; the name was shortened to Dinwiddie somewhere along the line. Pamplin Park Civil War Site, located in Dinwiddie County, preserves the scene of the battle fought here on April 2, 1865. The site includes Tudor Hall, a plantation home built around 1812 that has been renovated to reflect its days as the headquarters of Confederate general Samuel McGowan.

The Home Place is one of those tucked-away spots you might not find on your own, although it's just a few miles from Exit 53 off I-85 and a few hundred feet from U.S. 1. Your clue to turn off U.S. 1 is a little blue sign appropriately marked "Food." You'll be on a gravel road bounded by trees. The sign at the parking lot is a little more descriptive: "The Home Place Restaurant. Thanks for not giving up."

Owners William and Ethel Daniel live on the property. They've operated the restaurant since 1986 in a converted barn built by Ethel's parents in 1922.

The big, old wagon near the entrance overflows with colorful chrysanthemums and pumpkins in the fall. The brown-painted barnboard walls in the dining room feature old-fashioned wall lights akin to railroad lamps. Tables next to large picture windows opposite the front door overlook a small, peaceful, spring-fed lake you won't see until you're inside. Of course, you may have noticed the ducks and geese waddling about the grounds on your way in.

If you're here for breakfast, you can choose from among fresh eggs, Virginia country ham, sausage, bacon, homemade buttermilk biscuits, red-eye gravy and pancakes.

For lunch, there's homemade soup, salads, onion rings, cheese sticks and sandwiches.

You can order big-city stuff at dinnertime—shrimp

cocktails, Delmonico steak, prime rib, beef or pork ribs, country-cured ham and a number of seafood entrees, including homemade crab cakes.

The biscuits and pies are homemade from Mrs. Daniel's own recipes.

The restaurant's brochure says you'll find The Home Place "a refreshing change from the ordinary." And indeed you will.

The Virginia Diner

WAKEFIELD

The Virginia Diner

U.S. 460 / WAKEFIELD, VA 23888
(757) 899-3106

Style	Family-style
Meals	Breakfast, lunch and dinner, seven days a week
Price Range	Inexpensive/Moderate
Superlatives	Peanut soup, peanut pie
Extras	Wine and beer

*T*here's no traffic light in this town, so be alert. You'll see stores and gas stations on both sides of U.S. 460 for a short distance, then you'll be back in the peanut fields. This is the heart of peanut country. The town was named by Mrs. Billy Mahone for *The Vicar of Wakefield*, the classic Oliver Goldsmith novel. The wife of the president of the Norfolk and Western Railway, Mrs. Mahone was allowed to name some of the rail stops.

Started in a refurbished railroad car in 1929, The Virginia Diner has grown steadily thanks to its reputation for down-home cooking. Various dining rooms were added to the little train car for nearly 60 years, until it finally became necessary to replace the old with the new. At that point, the Galloway family, which has owned the restaurant since 1976, built a very large diner on the same land.

Big windows fill the place with natural light, and the red-and-white-checked tablecloths and bentwood chairs lend a country feeling. The aroma of peanuts from the gift and gourmet shop right inside the front door pervades the place. In fact, the diner is often referred to as the "Peanut Capital of the World" for once having served peanuts instead of after-dinner mints. The diner's flourishing mail-order business now ships peanuts around the world.

Breakfast is typical Southern fare. The menu lists 10 complete breakfasts numbered for convenience of ordering. For example, number six is an omelet with baked Virginia ham and cheese, served with grits or hash browns and hot buttered toast or homemade biscuits. Number nine, pan-fried salt herring with hash browns and cornbread, is available October through March.

Ham sandwiches, four-ounce crab cakes and

barbecue served with a special sauce are on the lunch menu. The entrees include ham, chicken and dumplings, country-fried steak, soft-shell crabs and a crab cake dinner.

Southerners have a broad spectrum of what they consider vegetables. Here, spoon bread, macaroni and cheese and applesauce are listed among the vegetable choices. But if you're serious about your vegetables and about being Southern, you can order black-eyed peas, turnip greens, candied yams or green beans.

At The Virginia Diner, it's possible to begin and end your meal with the peanut theme, starting with peanut soup and finishing with peanut pie.

Surrey House

SURRY

Surrey House
VA 31 / SURRY, VA 23883
(800) 200-4977 OR (804) 294-3389

Style	Family-style
Meals	Breakfast, lunch and dinner, seven days a week
Price Range	Inexpensive/Moderate
Superlatives	Ham, peanut soup, "Peanut Raisin Pie"
Extras	Wine and beer

After settling Jamestown on the northern side of the James River, some colonists decided they wanted to live on the southern side. They called their settlement Surrey, after the English county of the same name, which lies across the Thames River from London. At some point, a clerical error dropped the *e* from the names of the Virginia county and town, which have been written as Surry ever since.

The Surrey House, however, uses the original spelling. It's one of those places that takes you back in time—not too far, just to the fifties.

Established in 1954, the Surrey House is a classic example of that era's roadside restaurants with motel units. Don't change your watch to match the big clock out front, which ticks to the beat of its own drummer. You'll soon see that at the speed the hands on the western side of the clock are moving, 24 hours would pass in less than an hour. But that's all part of the charm.

The restaurant has an unusual V-shaped counter and 10 stools right inside the front door. To the left and right are knotty-pine dining areas with royal-blue linens. Between the booths and tables, 120 people can be seated.

The Surrey House serves Virginia cuisine under the watchful eye of Mike Stevens, who purchased the business in 1993. Located just a quarter-mile down the road are the S. Wallace Edwards & Sons smokehouses, which have been curing award-winning hams for three generations. It's no surprise, then, that many of the menu items at the Surrey House feature ham. For example, you can order a Virginia ham dinner, a ham steak, ham croquettes or ham with a quarter-chicken. There's a sandwich of Edwards ham and Swiss cheese stacked on rye. The chili is garnished with small slices of fresh ham laid neatly across the top under grated cheese.

Other entrees come from the water. The James River, located just a couple of miles away, opens into Chesapeake Bay, from whence come the makings of crab cakes and various seafood dinners.

Among the desserts the Surrey House is most proud of are its world-famous "Peanut Raisin Pie," its freshly made cobblers and its "Sweet Potato Pudding."

HOPEWELL

Ginny's Cafe

222 EAST BROADWAY / HOPEWELL, VA 23860
(804) 458-1401

Style	Cafe
Meals	Breakfast and lunch, Monday through Saturday
Price Range	Inexpensive
Superlatives	Chicken salad, "Piña Colada Pie"

*T*he small port city of Hopewell gained a piece of history in 1923 when it annexed the town of City Point—alternately known as Bermuda City or Charles City Point. City Point was where Ulysses S. Grant

and his Union army kept their headquarters and supply base during the siege of Petersburg in 1864 and 1865. Today, Hopewell's Crescent Hills neighborhood boasts one of the nation's largest concentrations of Sears and Roebuck mail-order houses, 44 of which can be seen on the Hopewell Driving Tour.

Terri Steve Vaughan of Ginny's Cafe is a former high-school teacher. She reached a point in her career of teaching psychology and sociology when she thought, "If I find something better, I'll do it." Running a small cafe was on her list of "something better," so when Ginny's came up for sale, she bought it.

In case you're wondering about the name, there really never was a Ginny. The place was called the Broadway Cafe for years; the Broadway is still in operation elsewhere in town. A succeeding owner chose to name the place Ginny's, though no one knows why. Terri didn't see a need to change it, so Ginny's it remains.

The cafe has windows facing the street, cream walls, slate-blue trim and room for 68 people. There are a few prints on the walls and mauve banquet chairs at the tables.

Omelets, scrambled eggs, ham rolls, biscuits, bagels and bacon are served for breakfast.

The lunch menu distinguishes between "Sandwiches" and "BIG Sandwiches," both of which come with chips and a pickle. The "Sandwiches" include burgers, BLTs, barbecue sandwiches and egg salad sandwiches. Subs, clubs, fried chicken sandwiches, fish sandwiches and double cheeseburgers qualify as "BIG Sandwiches." The chicken salad is made from scratch. Ginny's also offers a chef's salad, tuna salad, potato salad and pasta salad. The daily specials are the most popular choices at lunch—things like chicken casserole, stuffed peppers and meatloaf.

"Piña Colada Pie" is an uncommon—and uncommonly good—dessert. There's also apple pie, Key lime pie and "Peaches and Cream Pie."

Terri and her staff can spot newcomers instantly, since they know all their regular customers by name. They're hometown friendly to everyone. Terri has published a cookbook called *Southern Styles by Ginny's Cafe*. All in all, she's happy with her career move.

Blackstone's Restaurant on Main

123 SOUTH MAIN STREET
BLACKSTONE, VA 23824
(804) 292-5697

Style	Family-style
Meals	Breakfast and lunch, Tuesday through Sunday; dinner, Tuesday through Saturday
Price Range	Inexpensive/Moderate
Superlatives	French dip, crab legs, steaks

*O*nce upon a time, there were two taverns at the settlement that later became Blackstone. In those days, the place was called Blacks and Whites, as one of the taverns was run by a Mr. Schwartz (*schwarz* is German for black) and the other by a Mr. White. The current name may have been adopted to honor Mr. Schwartz. Others say it honors Sir William

Blackstone, the famous British jurist. Blackstone has close to 4,000 residents today, making it the largest town in Nottoway County.

Blackstone's Restaurant on Main is a clean, bright, contemporary kind of place. According to manager Ann Weiss, the space was totally renovated before the July 1996 restaurant opening. It's green and white with white stucco walls and a dark green print border around the middle. Old photographs of the town hang on the walls, as do impressionist posters and a few framed prints. Most of the tables are green with white chairs, though a few are wrought iron with matching chairs.

At breakfast, you can pick up pastries to take out or eat in, or you can sit right down and have a "Gravy Delight," a "Hungry Man Special" or a stack of pancakes. The omelets come with home fries or grits and toast or biscuits.

For lunch, there are cold sandwiches, hot sandwiches and light selections. The first category includes chicken salad, egg salad and fresh albacore tuna. My French dip sandwich was marvelous—the beef good and plentiful, the bread soft and tasty, the *jus* served in a deep cup about half full and the sandwich still dry when it reached the table. A stuffed tomato, a chicken or tuna cold plate, a veggie platter and a ground sirloin plate are among the light choices.

Dinner entrees come with soup or salad, a twice-baked potato, a vegetable and homemade rolls. T-bone and New York strip are among the steaks and fried butterfly shrimp, fresh marinated tuna steaks and breaded oysters among the seafood options. If you can't decide between beef and fish, you can get filet mignon with either crab legs or shrimp. Ham steaks, chicken kabobs and grilled pork chops are also available.

The desserts include cheesecake, pineapple upside-down cake, and fresh fruit pies like apple and cherry.

Blackstone's Restaurant on Main is making its mark by making everything from scratch with fresh ingredients.

Mitchell's
103 SOUTH MAIN STREET
BLACKSTONE, VA 23824
(804) 292-4100

Style	Pub
Meals	Breakfast, lunch and dinner, seven days a week
Price Range	Inexpensive/Moderate
Superlatives	Chicken, gyros
Extras	Full bar

*T*here's an interesting contrast in decorating in this former five-and-dime.

The booths are old and high backed. There are two bars, located in the back on the left and right. The tables are topped with cedar wood.

Then there are the pretty, heart-shaped baskets with silk roses and ribbons along the walls up front, a homespun touch added by one of Mitchell's regular customers. Tall plants—real ones—stand in the front windows. Variegated philodendrons weave their way across the front ledges.

Eggs, biscuits and hot cakes are available at breakfast.

At lunch, you can order sandwiches and burgers. Fried chicken and rotisserie chicken are big sellers. There are lots of boxes and buckets to go.

Dinner is a more comprehensive event, with appetizers, salads, "Stella's Greek Menu" and house specialties. Stella is owner Gus Mitchell's mother. Her Greek salads, gyros and steak sandwiches are very popular. The house specialties are surf and turf and "Fin-'n'-Feather." There are additional menu sections for beef, seafood, poultry and pork. You can order such items as Delmonico steak, a seafood platter, a sliced turkey dinner, a country ham steak (which translates to salt-cured) or a Virginia ham steak (which translates to sugar-cured).

You shouldn't be surprised to see baklava on the dessert menu here. If that's a little rich, you can try rice pudding or pie. Or you can stick with something really simple, like soft-serve ice cream.

Slaw's
U.S. 460 BUSINESS / BLACKSTONE, VA 23824
(804) 292-3252

Style	Home-style
Meals	Lunch and dinner, Wednesday through Monday
Price Range	Inexpensive
Superlatives	Brunswick stew, homemade pies
Extras	Wine and beer

Charlie Wootten graduated from Virginia Tech in 1972 with a degree in agriculture education, then served four years in the United States Air Force. When his time was up, he figured he'd stick with something he knew, and he knew the restaurant business. He returned to Blackstone and his family's restaurant.

Slaw's was started by a man named Slaw in 1934. Charlie's father used to tell Mr. Slaw, "If you ever want to sell, I want to buy." So in 1950, Mr. Slaw made a phone call, and Mr. Wootten bought himself an eating spot.

For a time, the restaurant coexisted with a sporting-goods store. As the years rolled by, major retailers began selling the same fishing rods and outdoor equipment Mr. Wootten carried. In 1988, he gave up the store and converted it to a banquet room.

The dining room has a homey atmosphere, thanks to its pine paneling and fruit-print tablecloths. There are eight booths, six stools at a counter and seats for nearly 40 at the tables, not counting the banquet room.

Charlie gets over to his alma mater for only one football game each season, but he hears all about the team from fans who stop on their way between Blacksburg and the Virginia Beach, Norfolk, Newport News area. Many of those going to the football games buy Slaw's Brunswick stew and homemade pie for their tailgate parties.

If you come for lunch, you might try the chicken salad, the minced or sliced pork barbecue, a hamburger and gravy, a double-decker cheeseburger or country-fried steak. Children have five choices, all of which come with french fries and applesauce.

Dinners are served with two vegetables and hot bread. Among the entrees are Slaw's specialty—fried chicken livers—as well as baked ham, country ham, fried chicken, sirloin steak, fried oysters, a seafood combo and fillet of ocean trout.

And what does Charlie bring along on his annual trek to see the Hokies play? He packs a tailgate picnic of chicken, ham biscuits and homemade pie—chocolate chess, lemon chess, coconut custard or apple. Or maybe sweet potato. Charlie digs the sweet potatoes from his own garden for this one.

FARMVILLE

Charleys Waterfront Cafe

201B MILL STREET / FARMVILLE, VA 23903
(804) 392-1566

Style	Casual nice
Meals	Lunch, Monday through Saturday; dinner, seven days a week; Sunday brunch
Price Range	Inexpensive/Moderate
Superlatives	Rustic atmosphere, "Peppercorn Filet Madeira"
Extras	Full bar

Though Farmville doesn't have the most exciting name in the world, most visitors are pleasantly surprised by this friendly, active, interesting town along the Appomattox River. Founded in 1798, Farmville has a nice blend of retirees, working folks and stu-

Charleys Waterfront Cafe

dents at Hampden-Sydney College and Longwood College.

Charleys Waterfront Cafe is located in a former tobacco warehouse more than a century and a quarter old. It was the first restaurant mentioned by everyone I surveyed in and out of the shops and offices along Main Street.

It's like a very large fern bar—lots of brass and cedar and plants with little white lights strung in them. Small copper hanging lamps illuminate the spacious dining areas. If the weather is agreeable, guests can dine at wrought-iron tables with dark green umbrellas on a patio overlooking the river. The whole place exudes a classy rustic atmosphere.

The sandwiches come with a dill spear and french fries. Charleys offers some interesting variations on common things. The "Black and Bleu Chicken Sandwich" is blackened chicken, melted bleu cheese, lettuce and tomato on an onion roll. The "Philly Pizza Steak Sandwich" includes roast beef, mozzarella cheese, grilled onion, sauteed mushrooms and

marinara sauce. The burgers weigh in at half a pound. Seasonally, you can find baked Brie, char-broiled swordfish and other items of interest.

Roasted red pepper and crab soup, beef and bean chili and French onion soup are offered. The dinner menu is changed four times a year, so you may not always find the "Outer Banks Crab Cakes," the grilled tuna and the "Big Steak"—a one-pound Delmonico. Greek shrimp and linguine, twice-baked potatoes, stuffed shells, a quiche of the day and chicken fixed a number of ways are pretty constant on the menu. The "Peppercorn Filet Madeira" is rolled in cracked peppercorns and finished with a smooth Madeira sauce.

There's another Charleys—called Charleys Stony Point Cafe—on Stony Point Road in Richmond. Once affiliated with the chain of the same name, these two restaurants are now independent. In fact, the name Charleys—with or without the apostrophe, and spelled *-eys* or *-ies* at the end—is supposedly the most popular restaurant name in the country.

FARMVILLE
Cheese & Company
214 NORTH MAIN STREET / FARMVILLE, VA 23901
(804) 392-5559

Style	Cafe
Meals	Lunch, Monday through Saturday
Price Range	Inexpensive
Superlatives	Eclairs, chicken salad
Extras	Wine and beer

*L*ook carefully for this narrow storefront on Main

Street. The front half of the space is a gift shop that offers greeting cards, paper products, baskets, lamps, rugs, gourmet food packages and dishes. The cafe is nestled in the back—five small tables that can seat four people each. An open staircase rises to the second floor, where there are three more tables overlooking the entire enterprise below. A big chandelier commands attention in the center.

Everything is prepared by hand in a tiny kitchen partitioned off in the center of the shop. Several of the sandwiches are named for current or former employees. "Tony's Tangy Turkey" is a combination of turkey, pepper jack cheese, salsa, sprouts and tomato on a toasted homemade roll. The "Deco Stacy" is smoked turkey, melted cheddar, lettuce, tomato and onion on a bagel.

"We hire many students from Longwood and Hampden-Sydney Colleges," explained owner Sherry Martin. "If one of them has a sandwich idea, we give it a try. It if sells well, it becomes part of the menu and is named for the student."

One of the most popular sandwiches is the "Good & Healthy Plus": muenster cheese, tomato, sprouts and turkey on pumpernickel bread.

An often-ordered salad is "Linda's Famous Chicken Salad." Regular and fat-free dressings are available.

Martin has had the gift shop—named The Finer Nest—for a dozen years. She purchased Cheese & Company in 1995 and moved the gift shop to this downtown location.

She and her staff make custom party trays and gift baskets. And they coordinate private parties for 12 to 36 people at the shop or up to a few hundred at your place. They'll also make lunch to go—for one or for many.

Walker's Diner

Walker's Diner

307 NORTH MAIN STREET / FARMVILLE, VA 23901
(804) 392-4230

Style	Diner
Meals	Breakfast and lunch, Monday through Saturday
Price Range	Inexpensive
Superlatives	Old-fashioned diner atmosphere, corn pudding, fried chicken

*H*ere's a tiny place you shouldn't miss if you have an affection for old diners. The entire restaurant measures around 24 feet long and eight feet wide. That's total width—customer walking space, stools, counter, worker walking space, grills, dishes. Almost everything behind the counter is stainless steel. At the far end—which of course isn't very far—are big windows and wallpaper with a blue flower print.

Eggs, omelets, hot cakes, bacon, sugar-cured ham and a variety of other breakfast meats are offered. For the adventurous breakfast eater—or perhaps the person who needs to think hard during the day ahead—there are brains and eggs.

At lunch, sandwiches, burgers, beef stew, country ham, roast beef, breaded veal steak, salads and a vegetable plate are among the choices. Daily specials are also offered. The barbecue special and the corn pudding and fried chicken special are particularly popular among the Hampden-Sydney College crowd who drop in here for a bite. Turnip greens are on the vegetable list. All the hot sandwiches are served with creamed potatoes—that's mashed potatoes made with cream—and gravy.

The dessert list is short: homemade pie. Depending on when you get here, there might still be some apple, coconut, lemon chess, chocolate chess or sweet potato pie available.

Because this place is so small, you can expect any conversation to be overheard. The lady on the stool next to me passed along some information on restaurants she liked in other parts of the state. And she let me know that she often leaves her horse farm to drive to Farmville, her hometown, to stop in at Walker's.

Granny B's

APPOMATTOX

Granny B's

MAIN STREET / APPOMATTOX, VA 24522
(804) 352-2259

Style	Home-style
Meals	Breakfast, seven days a week; lunch and dinner, Monday through Saturday
Price Range	Inexpensive
Superlatives	Hamburger steak and gravy, roast beef, homemade pies
Extras	Beer

*F*ormerly known as Appomattox Court House, this is one of the most famous towns in Virginia. It was here on Sunday, April 9, 1865, that Robert E. Lee surrendered the Army of Northern Virginia to Ulysses

S. Grant at the home of Wilmer McLean. That historic event is remembered today at Appomattox Court House National Historical Park. Appomattox is also the birthplace of country and bluegrass great Joel Sweeney, the man who invented the banjo.

Located on Main Street in Appomattox is the restaurant known as Granny B's. Granny B, whose real name is Betty Drinkard, got her nickname from her first granddaughter, Mary Elizabeth, who wanted to distinguish between her two grandmothers, both of whom went by Granny.

In the early 1980s, Granny B was looking for something to do. "I started cooking at 13. Then I raised four kids. I figured I can't get a job raising someone else's kids, but I surely can feed them." So she opened her restaurant in 1984 because "cooking was something I knew how to do."

The crowd inside and the line out the door certainly affirm that. The small place with blue carpeting seats 48 people in booths and chairs. Antiques are all over the restaurant. Some belong to Betty, but many were given by customers. The most unusual antique came from customer Jack Baker. It's a rope device designed to drop onto the head of a railroad fireman when his coal train was about to enter a tunnel, thereby warning him to duck.

The "Country Boy Special" is among the breakfast choices at Granny B's. It includes two eggs, home fries, two strips of bacon, a sausage, a pancake and biscuits or toast. Waffles, eggs, steak, hot cakes, omelets and biscuits are also available.

At lunch, sandwiches can be ordered on homemade rolls. The lunch plates come with a meat, two vegetables, a homemade roll and coffee or tea.

Prime rib, rib-eye steak and filet mignon are on the dinner menu, as are roast beef, baked ham, country ham, grilled chicken, shrimp and fish. All meals come with a baked potato or french fries, salad and homemade rolls.

Now and again, Betty has thought about moving to a bigger place because of the lines out the door. But on second thought, she feels maybe the lines are good for business.

Jack's Place
U.S. 501 AT VA 24 / RUSTBURG, VA 24588
(804) 332-5491

Style	Family-style
Meals	Breakfast, lunch and dinner, Monday through Saturday
Price Range	Inexpensive
Superlatives	Squeaky-clean setting, chili, peach cobbler

The county seat of Campbell County, Rustburg was named for Jeremiah Rust, who donated land for the first local courthouse in 1780. The present courthouse was erected in 1848.

Opened in the late 1940s by Jack Puckett, Jack's Place has changed hands a few times. In the 1980s, it came into the possession of Maxine Morris. In the 1990s, it was taken over by her son Matthew and his wife, Stephanie.

The name has stayed the same through the changes in ownership. So has the collection of plates on the walls. There's a plate from Egypt, delivered by a friend of Matthew's. And there are plates representing at least half the 50 states, most of them brought in by customers. Unfortunately, some have been broken over the years.

Jack's is a small, uncrowded place. You may be surprised to learn that it seats 59. There are seven stools at a very wide counter, nine booths and a few tables. The walls are light-toned wood paneling with blue trim.

A favorite at breakfast is the French toast sticks, which are bite-size pieces of battered, deep-fried French bread.

Sandwiches, burgers, salad, chili and pinto beans are staples on the lunch menu. Jack's Place is one of few restaurants where you can still order a dish of corned beef hash.

Dinners include Delmonico steak, beef liver, breaded jumbo shrimp and a seafood platter. Baked okra and creamed potatoes are among the vegetables.

According to Nan Foster, who has worked at Jack's for 45 years—that's right, she started here at age 15— peach cobbler is the big dessert hit among customers. Jack's "just can't keep enough made," she said.

Matthew is a nut for cleanliness, and his restaurant routinely receives high marks from the health department. There's something reassuring about knowing that when you're visiting a restaurant for the first time.

Bedford Restaurant

U.S. 460 / BEDFORD, VA 24523
(540) 586-6575

Style	Family-style
Meals	Breakfast, lunch and dinner, seven days a week
Price Range	Inexpensive
Superlatives	Beef and pork barbecue, homemade pies

*F*ounded as the town of Liberty in 1728, Bedford has more than 200 structures in its historic district. Among the stately homes in the area is Thomas Jefferson's Poplar Forest. Jefferson's old home is appropriately named, as Bedford is the home of the largest yellow poplar tree in the world and the largest tree of any kind in Virginia.

The Bedford Restaurant is a small, tan building with dark brown trim on the northern side of U.S. 460 west of town. The parking lot is a gravel space whose size must have been planned for the 18-wheelers that pull in here. But don't let those big trucks intimidate you. There's some good barbecue to be had here. Pork and beef. Not to mention the homemade pies.

Clay and Kathy Pope bought the restaurant in 1984 and have elevated it from a rough beer joint to a good family restaurant. Actually, the Bedford Restaurant was originally a two-story building across the road. When U.S. 460 was widened to four lanes, the building was moved to its present location. The second story was later destroyed in a fire, and the Popes put on the present roof. There are 14 tables and one big booth inside.

Breakfast items include eggs, sausage, bacon, grits, biscuits, toast, tenderloin, country ham and pancakes. The restaurant makes fresh cinnamon rolls every morning.

The specialty here is pit-cooked barbecue, both pork and beef. It's available in sandwiches of two different sizes, with or without french fries and slaw. If you're on the go, you can buy barbecue by the pound.

Truckers are partial to the roast beef, mashed potatoes and gravy and the specials, which include spaghetti, country-style steak, baked ham, whiting fillet and meatloaf. Meals come with two vegetables, which are defined as everything from applesauce, cottage cheese, rice pudding and macaroni and cheese to pickled beets, okra, breaded squash, spinach and broccoli.

Couples really need to work as a team in these mom-and-pop places. Kathy and Clay do this right down to the pie making—she makes the crusts, he makes the fillings. Of course, the earlier you stop, the greater the selection. Pumpkin, apple, cherry, peach and butterscotch are among the favorite pies.

According to Clay, their Bedford Restaurant fills a need. He says it can be hard for travelers to find a place with "food like you cook at home." That's what he and Kathy serve, and that's why they're popular with folks near and far.

Stephen's Galley
1600 SHADY KNOLL AVENUE
BEDFORD, VA 24523
(540) 586-4198

Style	Casual nice
Meals	Dinner, seven days a week
Price Range	Moderate
Superlatives	Prime rib, catfish, fresh fish
Extras	Full bar

Gary McKinney and his father, the late Stephen McKinney, opened a small restaurant called Stephen's Galley at Smith Mountain Lake in the 1980s. They started this restaurant in Bedford in August 1993, naming it the same thing. They ran both for a while but eventually sold the lake restaurant. Many of the nautical items here in Bedford were picked up at flea markets and garage sales.

Stephen's is located in a brick building behind a Dairy Queen just east of town. Stepping inside is a nice surprise. There are a few booths to the right and dining rooms beyond. You'll also note a couple of portholes, some nice model ships and fishing-related prints. The linens are white and the napkins deep maroon.

You can start your meal with "Oyster Shooters," steamed shrimp, quesadillas or other appetizers. Soups and salads are also served.

Sandwiches and burgers are available at dinner. Seafood pasta, chicken Alfredo, spaghetti and chicken marinara are listed among the "Pastabilities." The prime rib is superb. Or you can try *steak au poivre*, beef stir-fry, filet mignon, New York strip steak, chicken cordon bleu, "Monterey Chicken" or "Chicken à la Stephen"—a chicken breast with vegetables served over rice pilaf. Southern-fried catfish, stuffed flounder and shrimp scampi are among the seafood options. All entrees come with a salad, hot bread and either rice, a baked potato or french fries.

For a small restaurant, Stephen's maintains an impressive wine list of more than four dozen selections from all over the world.

The restaurant's famous "Hot Fudge Dessert" combines chocolate cake, vanilla ice cream, hot fudge and whipped cream. The Key lime pie is great, too.

The Briar Patch
U.S. 29 BUSINESS / AMHERST, VA 24521
(804) 946-2249

Style	Pub
Meals	Breakfast, lunch and dinner, Monday through Saturday
Price Range	Inexpensive/Moderate
Superlatives	Cozy atmosphere, all-you-can-eat seafood on Tuesdays, prime rib on weekends
Extras	Full bar

*T*he town and county of Amherst were named for Jeffrey, Lord Amherst, a hero in the Battle of Ticonderoga during the French and Indian War. Jeffrey was subsequently appointed royal governor of Virginia, but he never came to fill the post, instead sending deputies to conduct his business.

If the wood interior, the thick wooden tables, the wood burning in the fireplace and the rather cozy layout of The Briar Patch don't remind you of a European pub, the lively crowd might.

Set on the highway just south of town, The Briar Patch was purchased by Joanie Lingerfelt in the mid-1980s. It was built in 1948—the same year Joanie was born. She figures the name came from the college yearbook of the same title at Sweet Briar College, located just up the road.

The words at the beginning of the menu make you feel good about coming in: "Congratulations on your discerning taste, good looks, charming personality and appreciation of the finer things in life. We make every effort to prepare each of our dishes to order; therefore, we are not a fast food restaurant. During peak hours, it may take a little longer. So relax, have a drink, visit and enjoy!"

Among the sandwiches served at lunch are burgers, a Reuben, a Monte Cristo, a French dip

The Briar Patch

and a Philly-style steak and cheese. The "Sweet Briar Special" is a warmed onion dill roll stuffed with chicken salad and served with steamed broccoli. (The warmed onion dill roll has another role on the appetizer list, where it's offered with homemade spinach dip on top and fresh veggies around it.) The "Veggie Cheese Melt" is sliced tomatoes, mushrooms, grilled peppers, onions, cheese and a special sauce on rye bread. Salads, homemade soups, chili and pizza are also offered.

The dinner choices include rib-eye steak, stuffed flounder, beef liver, chicken livers and half a dozen seafood platters. Among the light entrees are nachos, seafood pasta, crab-stuffed mushrooms, quesadillas and grilled chicken breast.

Almost all of The Briar Parch's business comes from repeat patrons—so I guess if you stop here once, you'll just have to stop again if you want to fit in.

Tanglewood Ordinary

VA 6 / MAIDENS, VA 23102
(804) 784-7011

Style	Family-style
Meals	Dinner, Wednesday through Sunday
Price Range	Inexpensive
Superlatives	Country ham, fried chicken
Extras	Wine and beer

*Y*ou'll find Tanglewood Ordinary in a building that has previously served as a country store and a gas station. The name Tanglewood supposedly came from all the wood tangled on the property when it was cleared for building.

Jim and Anne Hardwick opened their restaurant in 1986. Jim consulted his dictionary and found one of the meanings of the word *ordinary* to be "a meal served at a fixed price." Since that was his and Anne's plan, naming the place Tanglewood Ordinary seemed logical.

The structure is log on the outside and log on the inside. It stands along Va. 6 about 16 miles west of Parham Road. Green-and-white-checked vinyl tablecloths cover the tables in the center of the large dining area. A small room in the back has lots of little windowpanes looking out over fields and more than 40 *Saturday Evening Post* covers from 1913 through the 1960s. You'll find bluegrass or country music playing in the background.

On Wednesdays, beverages and desserts are included in the meal price. The offerings includes shrimp, catfish, scallops, slaw, green beans, potatoes, cornbread and hush puppies. You receive one serving of the entree and can have seconds on the vegetables.

Other evenings, you can choose from country ham, fried chicken, beef stew and other traditional American fare.

Though Tanglewood Ordinary looks rustic and has an old-timey flair, you can find it on the World Wide Web at www.ordinary.com, and you can send along an e-mail message to tw@ordinary.com.

Houndstooth Cafe

U.S. 301 / HANOVER, VA 23069
(804) 537-5404

Style	Cafe
Meals	Lunch and dinner, Tuesday through Saturday
Price Range	Moderate
Superlatives	Fresh seafood, barbecue
Extras	Wine and beer

*H*anover County is noted for its native sons. Patrick Henry was born here in 1736 and Henry Clay in 1777.

Another local event took place in 1933. No, it wasn't on a par with the repeal of Prohibition or the launching of FDR's New Deal, which also took place that year. The event was the construction of a small country store with gas pumps on U.S. 301 at the intersection with Va. 54.

By the time Bob Cunningham started Houndstooth Cafe in 1988, the old country store had been vacant for a decade. Now, it's bright, clean and friendly. The burgundy valances on the windows, the hunt prints, the brass candelabra chandeliers and the black and white floor tiles contribute to the casual atmosphere.

The appetizers are the same for lunch and dinner—seafood soup, a soup du jour, "Wing Dings," crab puffs, fried veggies, mozzarella sticks. The lunch entrees include barbecue—beef, chicken or pork—and char-broiled chopped steak. Among the hot sandwiches are burgers, a barbecue sandwich, a crab cake sandwich, a steak and cheese sub and grilled cheese. The cold sandwiches are sliced turkey, chicken salad and a variety of clubs. Spinach salad, chef's salad and a chicken salad plate are among the salad options.

Fresh seafood is the specialty here. In fact, it's so fresh that it's not even printed on the menu, as Cunningham is never positive what he's going to offer. A marker board lists seafood appetizers and entrees each day. It may include flounder, tuna, salmon, rockfish, scallops, oysters or catfish. The flounder may be stuffed with crab, the catfish served with oyster stuffing—the options are countless. Stable dinner items include barbecue, surf and turf, crab cakes and baby back ribs. All come with two vegetables and your choice of rolls or hush puppies. Among the vegetables are boiled potatoes, baked beans, applesauce, macaroni salad and french fries. The "Houndstooth Feast for Four" is a whole barbecued pork butt with three vegetables, hush puppies and iced tea or coffee.

For dessert, the homemade brownies are served with ice cream and hot fudge sauce. The "Houndstooth Derby Pie" is hard to resist, as are the homemade apple pie and the cheesecake.

Bob has created an attractive eatery noted for its great barbecue and fresh seafood. I want to return here for two reasons: the beef barbecue and the intriguing antique shop across the street called Two Frogs on a Bike, which was closed the day I visited.

Homemades by Suzanne

102 NORTH RAILROAD AVENUE
ASHLAND, VA 23005
(804) 798-8331

Style	Cafe
Meals	Breakfast and lunch, Monday through Saturday
Price Range	Inexpensive
Superlatives	Cream puffs, "Strawberry Lemonade"

Homemades by Suzanne

*F*or many years, this community was merely a fueling stop for trains. That was until 1848, when the president of the railroad line bought 155 acres with mineral springs and built a health spa and a ballroom. Some folks came to dance, others to take the waters; all came on his trains. In 1855, after the spa had closed, the villagers renamed their community Ashland, after Henry Clay's Kentucky estate. Today, Ashland is best known as the home of Randolph-Macon College. Railroad Avenue still straddles the train tracks. Visitors find it exciting to see and hear trains right in the middle of their shopping and other activities.

It's hard to put a single superlative on Homemades by Suzanne. Suzanne Wolstenholme has created a highly successful baking, cooking and catering business with homemade everything.

She started the cafe in 1981 because she was by her own admission "the world's worst secretary." She expanded her operation in 1990, opening another shop on weekdays in downtown Richmond.

Homemades by Suzanne is blue and white and has old-fashioned globes hanging from a white tin ceiling. The partition behind the counter has a mural painted on it—an attractive door, windows with lace curtains, geraniums, hollyhocks, ivy, a pigeon on a coach light. The kitchen is located behind this and continues into the back of the building. Patrons are seated at three booths and seven wooden tables.

Before you sit down for the first time, you must

wander down the left side of the room, where glass display cases are filled with muffins, cookies, cakes, pies, salads and everything else that's available here. Then you must go to the drink containers in the front and get some of Suzanne's refreshing "Strawberry Lemonade." Now you may sit down.

If you've come for breakfast, consider the sliced country ham and cheese on a homemade roll, served with lettuce, tomato and fresh fruit. Egg salad and bacon on a croissant is another option. The fruit pastries, sweet rolls, jumbo muffins and freshly baked croissants with jam are also tempting.

Side salads number almost a dozen—11, to be exact. Among them are a green pea and cheddar salad, a baby shell macaroni salad, a marinated artichoke salad, and a Waldorf salad. Sandwiches come with lettuce and tomato and may be ordered on a homemade white roll or a wheat roll. Shrimp salad, country ham, seafood salad, sliced ham, roasted turkey and the "Hanover Club" are among the sandwich options.

The desserts here are phenomenal. The cream puffs come filled with Suzanne's own custard, made with real whipped cream and drizzled with chocolate. Among the homemade pies are Key lime, pecan, apple, peach and chocolate chess. Chocolate chip cookies, sugar cookies, peanut butter cookies and oatmeal-butterscotch cookies are also offered. Other options include mini-cheesecakes, chocolate pecan brownies, carrot layer cake and big macaroons dipped in chocolate. I suspect all of these are wonderful, because they look fabulous and because so many people recommend Homemades by Suzanne.

The Ironhorse

ASHLAND

The Ironhorse
100 SOUTH RAILROAD AVENUE
ASHLAND, VA 23005
(804) 752-6410

Style	Casual nice
Meals	Lunch, Monday through Friday; dinner, Tuesday through Saturday
Price Range	Moderate/Expensive
Superlatives	"Cajun Barbecued Shrimp," Caesar salad
Extras	Full bar

*Y*ou might think the name Ironhorse was chosen because of the railroad tracks and the daily trains running down the center of Railroad Avenue. But according to the owner, Texas native Mimi Siff, the name was actually taken from a 1960s television series called *Ironhorse*, a Western in which the star, Dale Robertson, would hook up his railroad car to a train and travel around doing good.

Constructed in 1900, the building operated as the D. B. Cox Department Store for six decades. For three more decades, it was home to a variety of stores and offices. The restaurant opened its doors on April 4, 1991.

The building's status as a former department store explains the huge windows and the wide ledges inside, where many a mannequin must have stood. That space now holds a few plants and antiques.

The overall color scheme is peach, cream and teal. The place has high tin ceilings and lots of natural light. The bar, located to the right, has a piano, a mounted moose head and several tables with captain's chairs. To the left is a large, comfortably uncrowded dining room that seats close to 100. The tabletops are dressed up for dinner with double linens. The photos and prints on the walls relate to the understated railroad theme.

Burgers and sandwiches like roast beef, grilled chicken breast, Smithfield ham, tuna melt and a Reuben are available at lunch. The Ironhorse's signature sandwiches are named for "Hall of Fame People," who are loosely defined as those who are "in a rut or [who have] provided some extraordinary service to the Ironhorse, or both." The burger with bacon, cheese and pesto is called the "Ned Stiles" simply because he comes in a couple times each week and orders one. The "Sheila Hunter" is named for Mimi's good friend. The chicken and cheese quesadillas are named for the landlord, Art McKinney, who kept asking for something Mexican on the menu. Such items as noodles with spicy tomato sauce, chicken salad and tuna salad

are also offered. Side orders include pinto beans, grilled potatoes and potato chips.

The dinner appetizers include pepper-crusted smoked salmon, "Quail Tortellini," sauteed wild mushrooms in a puff pastry and the very popular "Cajun Barbecued Shrimp." Three salads are offered. The entrees range from "Crawfish Etouffée" and stuffed leg of lamb to "Veal and Artichoke Ragout" and garlic-roasted quail. For the unadventurous, there's filet mignon, rib-eye steak and grilled pork loin.

All the desserts are made from scratch. Two of the most popular are the Key lime pie and the chocolate truffle cake.

ASHLAND

The Smokey Pig

212 SOUTH WASHINGTON HIGHWAY (U.S. 1)
ASHLAND, VA 23005
(804) 798-4590

Style	Family-style
Meals	Lunch and dinner, Tuesday through Sunday
Price Range	Inexpensive/Moderate
Superlatives	Pig collection, barbecue, homemade pies
Extras	Full bar

Saying there are a few pigs here is like saying there are a few government offices in Northern Virginia.

First, you'll see the restaurant sign with the pig on it. Then you'll turn into the parking lot at the "Pig In" sign. You'll see more pigs on shelves behind glass inside the front door. Porcelain pigs, plastic

The Smokey Pig

pie. On Thursday, it's "Chef's Choice." On Friday, it's a seafood potato—a baked potato smothered with a thick Mornay sauce to which seafood has been added.

Daily dinner specials are also offered.

The most popular dessert is the homemade brownie with ice cream and hot fudge.

The bar is inconspicuously located at the back of the center dining room. Its stained-glass hanging lamps flank a sign reading, appropriately enough, "Live well, laugh often, love much."

pigs, glass pigs, piggy-bank pigs. Depending on where you're seated, you'll view more pigs. Ceramic ones, metal ones, wooden ones, stuffed ones. Mobiles of pigs, photos of pigs, prints of pigs.

It's all nicely done, however, in three dining rooms with blue-and-white-checked tablecloths, sconces and ceiling lights. The atmosphere is casual, warm and friendly. The waitresses all seem to enjoy serving their customers, which was especially nice on the dark, rainy afternoon when I visited.

The building has housed a variety of stores and restaurants since opening in 1927 as a general store with overnight rooms upstairs. This Smokey Pig opened in the fall of 1978. A second one opened recently in Short Pump.

Of course, barbecue is the specialty here. Pork, chicken or beef. Chopped or sliced. On a bun or not. As a sandwich or a meal.

Other lunch offerings include homemade soups, salads, sandwiches and burgers. The lunch special for Tuesday is meat loaf. On Wednesday, it's chicken pot

WINTERGREEN

The Copper Mine

WINTERGREEN RESORT
VA 664 / WINTERGREEN, VA 22958
(804) 325-2200

Style	Fine dining
Meals	Breakfast and dinner, seven days a week
Price Range	Moderate/Expensive
Superlative	*Steak au poivre*, rack of lamb, "Bourbon Pecan Pie"
Extras	Full bar

*I*f you've never been to the Wintergreen Resort, you're in for a special surprise. The Mountain Inn, the main building here, is a rustic contemporary structure with great wooden beams and lots of native stone. Attached to it is the restaurant known as The Copper Mine. The whole place is friendly. In fact, one of the waitresses even invited me into the kitchen to try the daily specials with the staff.

The decor is teal, cream and black. The dining areas ramble around corners and at angles to one another. Altogether, the restaurant seats around 140. Windows form one wall overlooking the Blue Ridge Mountains, and there's patio dining outside for around 28 guests. Each table has a small oil lamp and fresh flowers.

The breakfast menu offers an enticing list of fresh fruits, cereal, pastries and entrees. French toast with Canadian bacon, toasted pecan hot cakes, Belgian waffles, omelets and eggs Benedict are among the choices. The "Miner's Breakfast" consists of a layered dish of potatoes, Canadian bacon and cheddar cheese topped with two eggs cooked your way.

The dinner appetizers include wild mushroom strudel and crabmeat and shrimp ravioli. French onion soup and seafood chowder are always available. Among the seafood entrees, you're likely to find swordfish with black bean and red pepper relish and rainbow trout accompanied by pecan-pear salsa. The grilled entrees include filet mignon and tenderloin of pork. The Copper Mine's signature dishes are *steak au poivre* with a brandied cream sauce and Châteaubriand for two. According to chef Scott Estelle, a Culinary Institute of America graduate, the "Rack of Lamb Persille" is very popular.

My waitress recommended "Pineapple Bananas Foster" for dessert. "Bourbon Pecan Pie" is also a good choice.

You don't have to go hungry around here at lunch just because The Copper Mine isn't open. There are a couple of lunch spots—the Garden Terrace and Cooper's Vantage—that offer their patrons panoramic views of the mountains. And there's a watering hole on the golf course that serves salads and sandwiches.

Bistro 151
VA 151 / NELLYSFORD, VA 22958
(804) 361-1463

Style	Pub
Meals	Lunch and dinner, Tuesday through Sunday
Price Range	Inexpensive/Moderate
Superlatives	Contemporary decor, hand-tossed gourmet pizzas
Extras	Full bar

The little town of Nellysford doesn't have a traffic light, but it does have friendly people and beautiful mountain scenery. This is apple country, as is obvious each fall, when pick-your-own-apples signs are posted and apple festivals and apple butter–making events are held. The area also hosts the Eastern Primitive Rendezvous, a nationally renowned commemoration of frontier history, skills and activities.

One usually thinks of the words *crisp* and *white* as going together, but Bistro 151 has what can fairly be described as crisp black decor, with gray and white accents. The bar is in the center, and dining areas are on both sides. Though the place has a capacity of around 100 people, it's decidedly cozy.

The restaurant opened on May 11, 1996, the brainstorm of two hairdressers, a Miami entrepreneur and a writer. According to Joni Voss, one of the hairdressers, the four just wanted to offer a dining experience that's "a little different." They also have live entertainment on weekends. Several black-and-white photographs of musicians hang over the bar, and a grand piano used in the 1984 Olympics resides in one dining area.

Gourmet pizzas have taken off in popularity here, with white ones outnumbering red ones on the menu. Among the white pizzas are the "Maine Event," which features lobster and scallions; the "Dutch Treat," which has Gouda, bacon and caramelized onion; and the "Surf and Turf," which includes prime rib and shrimp. The red pizzas include the "Bistro Beast," with pepperoni, onion, sausage, bell pepper and mushrooms; the "Magnum P.I.," with ham and pineapple; and the "Shoots 'n' Roots," which is vegetarian. Philly cheese steak, French dip and a veggie pita are some of the sandwiches. Fish and chips, stuffed shells and linguine and meatballs are also on the menu.

The evening appetizers include stuffed potato skins, blackened shrimp cocktails and a nightly special. Onion soup is offered, as are a house salad and a Caesar. The entrees include "Shrimp on Fire," salmon with avocado, eggplant Parmesan, trout, steak and "Chicken Bistro."

The restaurant justly describes its desserts as "delicious and decadent."

Don't leave the kids at home just because this is a tavern. Above all, it's a classy place, and it has a kids' menu.

Having visited all the restaurants in the area, I'd say the owners of Bistro 151 have accomplished in a very nice way their goal of offering something "a little different."

Duner's

U.S. 250 / IVY, VA 22945
(804) 293-8352

Style	Casual nice
Meals	Dinner, seven days a week; Sunday brunch
Price Range	Moderate
Superlatives	Fish, sweetbreads, local game and poultry
Extras	Full bar

*T*his town is named for the native evergreen ground cover growing along the banks of Ivy Creek. The plant in question is really kalmia, but it looks a lot like ivy, so Ivy it is. Meriwether Lewis, the explorer best known for his expedition with William Clark

Duner's

between 1804 and 1806, was born here in 1774.

Around Ivy, as on highways all over the state, you'll find 1950s motor courts in various states of disrepair. Duner's is the restaurant part of one of these now-defunct enterprises. The part that was once a motor court has been tastefully renovated into offices.

The restaurant is doing well under owner Bob Caldwell. He worked here as a cook in the mid-1980s, then bought the place in 1988.

The square, brick building has a row of newspaper boxes in front but is otherwise pretty basic. Inside, it's casually comfortable. A side room has deep red wallpaper, while the main dining room has cream walls and few decorations. Copper pot collections are displayed on two walls. There are close to 80 seats in the two dining rooms and several stools at the bar. Though the mural behind the bar seems a little out of place, it definitely adds an element of interest. It's an island scene with palms, a beach and hula dancers. It was put here by the previous owner, a Turkish fellow whose nickname was Duner.

The menu changes every day. Soups like lentil and cream of asparagus may be available. The appetizers might include crayfish in puff pastry, veal and green peppercorn pâté and warm white-bean and sausage salad.

Caldwell said he is especially picky about buying and preparing fish and about purchasing poultry, rabbit or other game locally. Rockfish baked with oysters and served with champagne cream sauce might be an option, as might pan-fried mountain trout with caramelized onions, mushrooms and tarragon. Most all the entrees come with a unique sauce or demi-glace. A dried cherry and rosemary demi-glace tops the grilled pork loin chops, and a ginger and onion cream sauce dresses up the marinated grilled flank steak.

The vegetarian choice might be eggplant and mushrooms in phyllo pastry. The pasta selections might include sauteed shrimp, tomatoes, olives, artichoke hearts, roasted red pepper and spinach over linguine, topped with feta cheese.

A couple of sandwiches are also offered.

Desserts like "Pumpkin Crunch Torte," "New Orleans Bread Pudding" and "Chocolate Soufflé Cake" are baked daily.

If you make a Sunday brunch excursion here, you can enjoy traditional brunch cuisine—egg dishes, omelets, sticky buns, French toast—or you can make it a sandwich event or a dinner-type meal.

C & O

515 EAST WATER STREET
CHARLOTTESVILLE, VA 22902
(804) 971-7044

Style	Pub
Meals	Lunch, Monday through Friday; dinner, seven days a week
Price Range	Moderate
Superlatives	Rustic atmosphere, baked salmon, crème caramel
Extras	Full bar

*N*amed for Charlotte, the wife of King George III,

this once-small town is now a bustling city of around 40,000. While it exceeds the population ceiling that I established for this book, I've included Charlottesville because of its popularity as a place of culture, education and history. And, conveniently enough, there may be more restaurants per square mile here than anywhere else in the state. Given the many eateries recommended to me by locals and travelers, it was no small task to narrow the field to those I've included.

If your first visit to the C & O takes place after dark, don't let the old Pepsi sign with the hole in it or the warehouse appearance put you off. This place was once a greasy spoon and a boardinghouse for railroad workers—which is pretty much what it still looks like after dark in winter. But the C & O is a nice restaurant now. In fact, it was recommended to me more often than any other place in Charlottesville.

If you sit downstairs, it may seem like you've descended a lot farther than you have. I thought I'd gone into a basement, only to find I was really at street level. The thick wooden bar has an aquarium at one end. A floor-to-ceiling brick wall with shelves stands behind the bar. The walls have a mix of posters, old prints and newspaper articles, most of them slightly askew. With just 22 dining seats, this is an intimate room.

Another 18 or so guests can be seated on the main floor, where you entered. On special occasions, the floor above the main floor is opened for another couple dozen folks.

There's no money wasted on a fancy menu. It's handwritten, copied and folded in half.

On the night I visited, the soups were vegetable and New England clam chowder. Among the appetizers were artichoke pâté and chicken liver mousse. Bread comes with your dinner, but if for some reason you're not ordering dinner, order bread anyway. It's wonderful, warm and slightly yeasty—bigger than a dinner roll, smaller than a loaf.

Vegetable stir-fry, scallops, rainbow trout, veal liver, lamb loin and Cornish game hens are among the entrees.

Though I didn't have room for dessert, the pastry chef told me that the crème caramel is very popular. I'll save room next time.

CHARLOTTESVILLE

Lakeside Restaurant & Gallery

1 BOAR'S HEAD PLACE
CHARLOTTESVILLE, VA 22905
(804) 972-7715

Style	Casual nice
Meals	Lunch, Monday through Friday; dinner, Tuesday through Saturday
Price Range	Moderate
Superlatives	Seafood, pasta salads
Extras	Full bar

*F*rom the outside looking in—well, you can't look in, because this ultramodern, three-story glass rectangle reflects you and your surroundings in green tones. Situated at the end of a large man-made pond, the building commands attention because it's the most

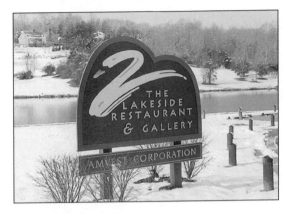

Lakeside Restaurant & Gallery

futuristic construction in a neighborhood that includes the upscale Boar's Head Inn & Sports Club across the street and Colonial-style homes on gently rolling terrain.

But on the inside looking out—that's a different story. The downstairs is a casual, 40-seat restaurant with white-painted brick walls, round tables and comfortable, heavy chairs. Patrons can view the water stretching in front of them and the gentle landscape beyond. The water is soothing whether or not the fountain in the center is working. Swans, ducks and geese lazily paddle around the pond or waddle on the shore. The Lakeside doubles in size when another 40 or so seats are placed around umbrella-topped tables outside.

The building's primary tenant is the Amvest Corporation, a holding company for several mining firms. The glass structure was built around 1986, and the Lakeside opened to the public for lunch five years later. In the fall of 1996, it began offering dinner five nights a week.

Executive chef Marc Ford labels his cuisine "California French"—which, he points out, includes a wide range of presentations. "California is sort of a melting pot of much of the world," he said. Ford also creates many entrees with the Virginia palate in mind.

The menu changes frequently. The sandwiches might include Parmesan chicken, the "Santa Fe" (which includes turkey, Jack cheese and peppers) and a grilled chicken and bacon croissant. A healthy turkey burger is offered, as are salads and vegetable dishes.

The dozen or so dinner entrees include breast of duck, jambalaya, sauteed lamb, quail and grilled salmon. They all come with soup or a house salad.

Paintings by local artists hang on the walls and are for sale. The art is rotated every month or two. Usually, one artist is featured at a time.

This is a peaceful, pretty place with a lovely pond and creative cuisine.

CHARLOTTESVILLE

métropolitain

214 WEST WATER STREET
CHARLOTTESVILLE, VA 22902
(804) 977-1043

Style	Casual nice
Meals	Dinner, seven days a week
Price Range	Moderate/Expensive
Superlatives	Presentation, shrimp cakes
Extras	Full bar

*E*ntering *métropolitain* is a little like taking that final walk to board an airplane. You're in a channel not much wider than those expandable tunnels, except here you can see into dining rooms on both sides.

At the end of your walk, you step into a bold, ultramodern space. A stainless-steel cooking area is straight ahead behind a high counter. The spacious, uncrowded dining areas feature unusual *objets d'art*. The bright yellow wall along the back adds a dramatic touch to a decor that's otherwise black and white. There's piped music, but it's drowned out most of the time by the sizzling activity in the kitchen.

The restaurant is the brainchild of two chefs—one from West Virginia and the other from France—who met while working together years ago at a restaurant outside Charlottesville.

The menu changes daily. The food matches the decor in that it's out of the ordinary. Appetizers include "Potato and Black Truffle Soup," a consommé of wild mushrooms with salmon ravioli, "Rabbit Quesadillas" and shrimp cakes with Thai sauce. There's "Seaweed Salad" for the daring and a simple salad for the unadventurous.

A vegetarian entree is offered. Fish selections—such as cornmeal-dusted rockfish and red snapper with whipped purple potatoes—outnumber beef entrees.

Save room—in both your stomach and your wallet—for dessert. The "Chocolate, Chocolate, Chocolate and Chocolate" dessert features four very rich confections huddled in the center of a 15-inch plate, covered with chocolate and raspberry sauce and then dusted with confectioners' sugar. It's fabulous. The

blackberry crisp with "Honey Lavender Ice Cream" is also wonderful, though the presentation isn't quite so dramatic.

As you might imagine, the *métropolitain*'s wine cellar stocks fine Scotch, wine and champagne, mostly from France and California. A couple of Virginia wines also grace the list. A reserve wine list is available for the asking.

The Boar's Head Inn—location of Old Mill Dining Room

CHARLOTTESVILLE

Old Mill Dining Room

BOAR'S HEAD INN / U.S. 250
CHARLOTTESVILLE, VA 22901
(800) 476-1988

Style	Resort
Meals	Breakfast, lunch and dinner, seven days a week
Price Range	Moderate/Expensive
Superlatives	"Bison Carpaccio," pork loin, grits
Extras	Full bar

A blue boar's head has symbolized good food and warm hospitality for centuries. The Boar's Head Inn delivers on both counts. It's a luxurious resort setting with sports facilities.

The Old Mill, the main dining room at the Boar's Head Inn, was built in 1834 and operated as a gristmill for many years. Burned during the Civil War, it was spared major damage thanks to superior construction and a heavy rain. The building was disassembled in the early 1960s and reconstructed to take its place at the Boar's Head Inn. Fieldstones from the foundation were used to build the fireplace, and wood from the grain bins was used as paneling. The wrought-iron chandeliers, the green and white linens, the fresh flowers and the classy silverware all evoke a warm, rustic elegance.

Traditional fare—eggs, breakfast meats, salads and sandwiches—are offered at breakfast and lunch.

Dinner is when you'll find innovative cuisine. The menu changes daily, and the staff uses local produce and meat as much as possible.

The soups may include black bean, French onion and sweet corn and lobster chowder. Pepper-seared bison and smoked salmon with mushrooms, spinach and mascarpone might be on the appetizer list. A classic Caesar and roasted quail with dried black figs on warm spinach are two of the salads that might be offered.

The Old Mill is best known for creative entrees such as cider-marinated pork loin with stone-ground grits. Or you can order the ever-popular rack of lamb, broiled salmon or pan-seared tuna. At the bottom of the menu is a chef's selection—perhaps pan-seared striped bass and grilled jumbo shrimp with a green peppercorn velouté served over a rice medley with lump crab.

All the expectations one has when dining at a four-diamond resort are met in the Old Mill Dining Room—lovely atmosphere, excellent service, attractive presentation and delicious food.

Rococo's

VILLAGE GREEN SHOPPING CENTER
2001 COMMONWEALTH DRIVE
CHARLOTTESVILLE, VA 22901
(804) 971-7371

Style	Italian
Meals	Lunch, Monday through Friday; dinner, seven days a week; Sunday brunch
Price Range	Moderate
Superlatives	Decor, homemade pasta, mesquite-grilled entrees

Contemporary and *intimate* don't always go together, but Rococo's has managed to seamlessly blend the two. Located off the beaten path in this chronically congested town, it's a local refuge with an air of romance.

Rococo's opened in 1989 on the upper floor of the two-story space it now occupies. Its contemporary appeal comes not only from its colors—white trim, taupe walls and coral-colored square columns—but also from the sharp angles of the walls, the partitions, the coffee station and even the staircase. The arch-topped windows in one dining room have mirrors in the panes, an effect that expands the visual sense.

The lower level was acquired around 1994. A hole was cut in the upper floor and the staircase set in. Paisley bench fabric, a classy bar and orange-hued tabletops are features of the rectangular downstairs room. Artwork exhibited by local artists and employees is for sale.

Rococo's pizza is popular with the lunch crowd. Some 40 toppings are available. The crusts are homemade; small pizzas may be ordered with a whole-wheat crust. Several white pizzas are offered. Calzones are also on the lunch menu.

The antipasto appetizer changes daily, as do the two soups, one of which is always vegetarian. The handmade ravioli also changes daily, but there always is one. There's lots of pasta, much of it dressed up. "Tortellini Bellisima" is a house specialty.

At Sunday brunch, the emphasis is as much on traditional brunch fare as on Italian food. Eggs, French toast, crepes and a small filet mignon are offered. On the Italian side are a country frittata, "Pumpkin Tortellini," a couple kinds of lasagna, a gnocchi of the day, linguine and handmade ravioli.

This is a nice place whose success in this out-of-the-way little shopping strip is a testimonial to its food, service and atmosphere.

Silver Thatch Inn

CHARLOTTESVILLE

Silver Thatch Inn

3001 HOLLYMEAD DRIVE
CHARLOTTESVILLE, VA 22901
(804) 978-4686

Style	Fine dining
Meals	Dinner, Tuesday through Saturday
Price Range	Expensive
Superlatives	Salmon, game in season
Extras	Full bar

During the Revolutionary War, Hessian soldiers captured at the Battle of Saratoga were marched from New York to Virginia. In 1780, they built a two-story log cabin here. That cabin is now known as the Hessian Room at the Silver Thatch Inn.

The middle of the inn was built in 1812 and the final wing in 1937. A small cottage with four of the seven overnight guest rooms was constructed in 1984. The inn has since been featured in several magazines, newspapers and books.

The Silver Thatch exudes an old-time warmth. The

rich interior colors are called "Colony Red" and "Valley Forge Green." The dining rooms are predominately cream and green with white linens, candlelight and a few sconces. There are seats for around 60. The tables are numbered for logistical purposes. Ironically, table 13 is unofficially referred to as "the Engagement Table." According to Vince and Rita Scoffone, the owners of the inn since 1992, more couples have gotten engaged while seated at this table than any other. It could be the window. Or possibly there's just some challenge in defying superstitious numbers.

Only lodging guests can partake of freshly baked muffins, cereals, fresh fruit and hot coffee and tea at breakfast. But dinner is open to the public.

The appetizers may include mussels steamed in lemon grass and Virginia lump crab. A soup du jour is offered.

Modern American cuisine—grilled meat and fish with healthy sauces—is the focus here. Salmon is the Silver Thatch's signature dish, prepared and served in a variety of innovative ways. Venison, rabbit, antelope and other game are offered in season. Fresh catch, duck breast and a vegetarian special are also available. The filet mignon comes with a demi-glace of Scotch, tarragon and green peppercorns. The roasted pork tenderloin is served on a mess of greens with grits, sweet potatoes and red-eye gravy.

The Scoffones extend the kind of greeting that makes you feel like you've entered a circle of old, familiar friends.

The Inwood

U.S. 15 / GORDONSVILLE, VA 22942
(540) 832-3411

Style	Family-style
Meals	Breakfast, lunch and dinner, seven days a week
Price Range	Inexpensive/Moderate
Superlatives	Burgers, steaks, pies
Extras	Full bar

This community got its start in 1787, when Nathaniel Gordon opened a tavern for travelers going over the Blue Ridge Mountains. The Exchange Hotel, a local landmark, was built in 1860 and within a few years was being used as a Civil War hospital. It stands today as a fine example of Greek Revival architecture.

Local resident Pamela Watson started her career in the restaurant business in the late 1950s, when she was given a Coke crate to stand on so she could wash the dishes. She was not yet 10 years old. A little more than three decades later, she bought The Inwood from her father.

The family operation doesn't stop with father and daughter. Currently, Pamela's three daughters, a sister and a niece work at the restaurant. She's not sure where the name Inwood came from, but she's never considered changing it because, as she says, "it works."

The Inwood occupies a brick building with light-grained wood paneling on the top of the interior walls and pine on the lower half. Tan miniblinds and dark green print valances decorate the large front windows.

There are 18 booths, eight chairs at the counter and a couple of tables.

The breakfasts here range from inexpensive selections to a deluxe combination that includes a country ham steak with eggs, potatoes and biscuits.

Lunch features a variety of burgers and sandwiches. The ground chuck is purchased fresh every day, and the burgers are hand-pattied in the kitchen. Fish and chips, chicken and chips, country ham, sliced turkey, barbecue and a breaded veal cutlet are also offered. Beer-battered onion rings are a popular side order.

There are more than two dozen dinner entrees. According to Pamela, The Inwood's steaks are excellent. She offers only two—New York strip and sirloin. Both are cut on the premises. Broiled swordfish, cod fillet, crab cakes, fried scallops and stuffed flounder are a few of the seafood selections. Chicken tenderloin, pork chops, veal parmigiana, spaghetti and a fish and chicken combination plate are also offered. For lighter fare, you can order just the soup and salad bar.

The restaurant's cream pies are made in the kitchen. Depending on the day's demand, you may have a choice of coconut, chocolate, butterscotch or banana. As for me, I'll take the homemade strawberry pie.

Toliver House

Toliver House
209 NORTH MAIN STREET
GORDONSVILLE, VA 22942
(540) 832-3485

Style	Family-style
Meals	Lunch, Tuesday through Saturday; dinner, Thursday through Sunday; Sunday brunch
Price Range	Moderate
Superlatives	"The Toliver," fried chicken, international prix fixe dinners
Extras	Full bar

Constructed around 1870, the building that is now home to the Toliver House served as a private residence, a general store and a nursing home prior to opening as an eatery. Husband-and-wife team Mike

DeCanio and Pat O'Rourke started the restaurant. Ten years later, Gary Johnson and Jim Reber came on board. The restaurant's name is a version of the surname found on the first recorded deed for the property.

There are three dining rooms in the slate-blue house. One is cream and dark green with burgundy chairs and a fruit-and-vine border around the walls. Another has light-colored paneling, mauve and cream linens and captain's chairs. Lace curtains, sconces, tall plants in the corners and prints on the walls add inviting touches.

Gary and Jim are from Wisconsin, which explains the Wisconsin bratwurst sandwich, one of the Toliver House's most popular lunch selections. The lunch appetizers include breaded mushrooms, hush puppies and jalapeño peppers stuffed with cheese and served with ranch dressing. French onion soup, a soup du jour, chili and Brunswick stew are offered, as are an Italian salad, a Caesar salad, a Greek salad and a chef's salad. Burgers and deli sandwiches are also available. The crab cake served on a toasted bun is nearly as popular as the Wisconsin bratwurst sandwich.

The dinner entrees—named for Virginia places like Richmond, Hampton and Smithfield—include rib-eye steak, grilled swordfish, breast of chicken and pork tenderloin cutlets. The restaurant's signature dish, "The Toliver," is shrimp stuffed with lobster, then broiled. The "Gordonsville Sunday Fried Chicken Dinner" showcases fried chicken the way it was prepared in the old days. Fresh whole chickens are cut in the kitchen, hand-dipped, fried golden and served with mashed potatoes, gravy, buttermilk biscuits and a country vegetable.

Each month, the Toliver House selects an ethnic theme and creates a four-course prix fixe dinner. Everyone agrees it's a great way to "travel" on a budget. Russia, England, Germany and Asia have been featured, as has Native American cuisine.

ORANGE

Firehouse
Cafe & Market

137 WEST MAIN STREET / ORANGE, VA 22960
(540) 672-9001

Style	Cafe
Meals	Breakfast and lunch, Monday through Saturday; dinner, Friday and Saturday; Sunday brunch
Price Range	Inexpensive/Moderate
Superlatives	Burritos, chicken salad
Extras	Wine and beer

*H*istory-rich Orange County was named for William, prince of Orange, in 1734. The first local courthouse was built in the 1750s. Robert E. Lee worshiped at St. Thomas's Church, which also happens to be the only surviving example of Thomas Jefferson's church architecture. Presidents James Madison and Zachary Taylor were both born in Orange County. Madison's home, Montpelier, is a National Historic Landmark. The James Madison Museum commemorates the man and his life.

The town of Orange is home to the Firehouse Cafe

Firehouse Cafe & Market

& Market, a big place with high ceilings, concrete walls and plenty of space to park a few trucks—or ten times as many diners. The walls probably weren't painted peach when this structure was built by the Orange Volunteer Fire Company in 1938. On second thought, in a town called Orange, maybe they were. The building was vacant in 1990 when Dornin Formwalt and Marty Van Santvoord leased it to open a cafe and market.

Big windows with dark green awnings are at the front of the cafe. Three plants at least six feet tall and a rack of Virginia wines are about the only decorations. A few art pieces hang behind the counter and are available for purchase. The one that caught my eye was a huge painting of a pasta-filled colander with steam rising and water pouring out the holes—definitely the only painting of a colander I've ever seen.

The day I visited, there was a mix of people in the lunch crowd, some in suits, others in sweats, a few in jeans. Takeout customers seemed to equal sit-down diners.

Salads, salad plates, a quiche of the day, a quesadilla of the day, homemade burritos and a plethora of deli sandwiches are available at lunch. The deli sandwiches come with your choice of mayonnaise, mustard, onions, cheese, lettuce, tomato, sprouts and hot peppers on either bread, a roll or a pita. Specialty sandwiches include a Reuben, a BLT and a turkey club. The "Smoked Firebird" is a grilled sandwich of smoked turkey, smoked Gouda, tomato, onion and mustard or mayo on sourdough. Prosciutto and melted Brie on a baguette is another popular choice.

The dinner menu changes with the seasons. The spring menu, for example, might offer filet mignon, broiled marinated salmon, grilled chicken breast stuffed with mozzarella and New Orleans–style fried shrimp. Health-conscious diners might choose the tomato basil fettuccine or the "Indian Vegetable Round," which includes pita wedges, yogurt, chutney and couscous.

Those who come for Sunday brunch can select from among an omelet du jour, French toast, eggs Benedict, steak and eggs, salads, quiche and a sandwich or two.

The Firehouse Cafe carries a nice selection of beers, ales, stouts, specialty brews and Virginia wines.

Morgan's

182 BYRD STREET / ORANGE, VA 22960
(540) 672-0800

Morgan's

Style	Family-style
Meals	Lunch and dinner, Tuesday through Saturday
Price Range	Inexpensive
Superlatives	"Virginia's Best Baked Potato Soup," seafood, pasta
Extras	Full bar

When Rich Baker was working for the Marriott in Washington D.C., he hired a lady named Laurie to supervise the outdoor cafe. Rich and Laurie worked well together. So well, in fact, that they were married a few years later.

They started their own restaurant in February 1997. According to Rich, one of their goals was this: "We wanted to create a restaurant that we could afford to eat at on a weekly basis." They named it for their young daughter, Morgan.

The building, a former residence, was renovated in the 1970s. There are three dining rooms. The one in the front is separated from the one in the back by the bar, which has a gracefully curved counter to match the curve of the grand piano located nearby. Down a short hall is another dining room that has become popular for local meetings and events. Dark green napkins sit on attractive multicolored vinyl tablecloths. There are candles on the tables in the evening. Light jazz can be heard in the background. The music goes a little more upbeat after 9 P.M.

The lunch offerings include a variety of salads, appetizers, sandwiches, burgers and potatoes. "Virginia's Best Baked Potato Soup" and North Carolina–style pulled pork barbecue top the popularity chart.

Dinner includes some pasta dishes, New York strip steak, "Chicken Blue Ridge" (Morgan's version of chicken cordon bleu), blackened prime rib and other entrees.

Morgan's is a casual, friendly, affordable restaurant. Rich and Laurie seem to have achieved their other goal as well: creating a comfortable place to go no matter what your mood.

Willow Grove Inn

U.S. 15 / ORANGE, VA 22979
(800) WG9-1778

Style	Casual nice
Meals	Dinner, Tuesday through Sunday in summer and Thursday through Sunday in winter; Sunday brunch year-round
Price Range	Expensive
Superlatives	Smoked trout cakes with horseradish cream
Extras	Full bar

Willow Grove is a majestic plantation house in the rolling Virginia countryside just north of Orange on the western side of U.S. 15. The original frame structure was built in 1778, and a brick addition was constructed in 1820.

Husband and wife team Richard Brown and Angela Mulloy acquired the property in 1987. Since then, they've made great strides in restoring it. The former schoolhouse outbuilding, for example, is now a small, sweet, two-story guest room. Angela is a purist. Her philosophy is that if she can't get the right people to do restoration work that has historical integrity, things wait. And there's always work to be done on buildings of this vintage. She's patiently biding her time.

Meanwhile, down in the kitchen, chef Douglas Gibson is contributing his culinary talents to the region's epicurean history. He calls it "New Virginia cuisine," but it's not all that different from what was served on the Virginia plantations of old.

Angela and Doug have researched the plantation period extensively with respect to food and culinary traditions. Willow Grove has its own herb garden and some fruit trees, and Doug has cultivated relationships with local suppliers of produce, fish and game.

Dinner is a three-course affair. To whet your appetite, the first course might be quail glazed with bourbon and molasses. Salads comprise the second course. Your entree might be grilled tenderloin of beef accompanied by roasted garlic mashed potatoes and Jack Daniel's sauce. Or it might be pecan-crusted Virginia trout with wild mushrooms. Or grapevine-smoked chicken served with forest mushrooms.

Clark's Tavern, located on the first floor, is a cozy, rustic place with a brick floor and brick walls painted dark green. It doubles as a breakfast room for overnight guests. Soup, salad, sandwiches and entrees are also offered here. The "Rustic Pizza" is an interesting combination of Virginia ham, bourbon-glazed red onions, roasted bell peppers and mozzarella on a cornmeal-dusted crust.

Plantation history may be the theme here, but Richard and Angela also have a foot in the 21st century. Their e-mail address is wginn@gemlink.com. You can reach their Web site at http://www.willowgroveinn.com.

Blue Ridge Cafe
U.S. 29 / RUCKERSVILLE, VA 22968
(804) 985-3633

Style	Casual nice
Meals	Lunch, Monday through Saturday; dinner, seven days a week; Sunday brunch
Price Range	Moderate
Superlatives	Simple good cooking
Extras	Wine and beer

There are those who dream of doing things and those who do things. Chef Shawn B. Hayes falls in the latter group. In fact, he reached one of his personal goals early in 1996: to have his own business by age 30.

A graduate of the Culinary Institute of America,

Blue Ridge Cafe

Chicken teriyaki, prime rib, "Swordfish Sherando" and "Pasta Thai Juan" are some of the dinner entrees.

Sunday brunch is an all-you-can-eat continental buffet with an entree. You can choose to take your meal with or without champagne. Salmon cakes, eggs Benedict, a "Chef's Omelet" and a "Chef's Brunch Special" are some of the entrees from which to choose.

Although I couldn't pinpoint Hayes on a specialty item, his pastries definitely qualify. In fact, his original idea was to open a pastry and confection shop. I, for one, am glad he expanded his idea and opened the Blue Ridge Cafe. This is a nice place.

Hayes worked in restaurants in the Washington, D.C., area before moving to Charlottesville, where his wife, Rita, was living. He has a simple philosophy: to serve good food in healthy portions in a clean, inviting atmosphere.

The restaurant is on one end of an attractive yellow building. The contemporary interior is primarily black and white with track lighting on the ceiling and small white lights around the windows and the tops of the walls. A bar on the right has five tall chairs. The front dining room seats 32, and there's room for 20 or more in a dining area down a hallway. At the time of this writing, plans included a banquet room behind this second dining area.

The salads include a grilled blackened shrimp salad and a spinach salad with chicken tenders. Sandwiches come with chips or fries, and burgers are accompanied by fries and slaw. A stir-fry du jour, beer-battered fish, pasta primavera and vegetable quesadillas are also available.

The Lafayette

U.S. 33 / STANARDSVILLE, VA 22973
(804) 985-6345

Style	Casual nice
Meals	Lunch, Tuesday through Saturday; dinner, Tuesday through Sunday; Sunday brunch
Price Range	Moderate
Superlatives	Mountain trout, bison specials, "Kahlua Cake"
Extras	Full bar

*O*nce upon a time, there was a Beatles concert and the tickets cost $4.75. It's true. The date was August 18, 1966, some 11 days before the group's final concert. You can see a ticket from the August 18 Suffolk Downs show at The Beatles Museum in the heart of Stanardsville. Rare recordings, memorabilia, photo-

The Lafayette

graphs and videos are featured in this, the only registered Beatles museum in the country.

Stanardsville is also home to The Lafayette Hotel, whose rich history of serving travelers has been revived by three enterprising young men.

Whitt Ledford and Nick Spencer met while working at a resort in the area. Whitt lived in Stanardsville and drove by The Lafayette each day going to work. "Someone ought to do something with this building," he often thought.

When the opportunity presented itself, Whitt was there. Nick had by then moved to Monterey, California, but he returned to Stanardsville, and the two started a massive renovation with the help of Daniel Huff, a public relations and marketing guy. Today, the trio operates a bed and breakfast inn and a res-

taurant on the premises. Nick is the chef.

The restaurant has two inviting dining rooms with tall windows and old-fashioned chandeliers. The tables have dark green napkins and fresh flowers.

The soup du jour might be split pea. The appetizer of roasted garlic—a big, baked garlic clove you spread on little bread pieces—is interesting, though it's definitely not something to eat before meeting your future in-laws. Among the salads are a house salad, a Caesar salad, a spinach salad and the "Marquis Salad," which comes with smoked bacon, tomato, cheese, sweet peppers, tart apples and grilled chicken breast. The sandwiches offered at lunch include grilled chicken, barbecued pork, grilled veggies and London broil. Salmon cakes and vegetarian lasagna are also available.

The dinner menu is a creative mix of regional cuisines. The mountain trout comes with cheese herb grits, which are loved by those who don't even care for grits in general. The bison specials are popular, as are nightly specials like pan-seared mahi-mahi with pineapple salsa and grilled chicken breast with light garlic cream sauce and apple compote.

A lady at the table next to mine recommended the "Kahlua Cake" for dessert. The presentation, flavor, texture and taste put this cake in the highest echelon. It was fabulous.

Count me among those who are glad that this Federal-style hotel building with large columns, porches and triple-brick, 15-inch-thick walls is once again a dining and lodging landmark.

Skipper's Cafe

64 FORD AVENUE
STANARDSVILLE, VA 22973
(804) 985-7706

Style	Home-style
Meals	Breakfast and dinner, Tuesday through Saturday; lunch, Tuesday through Sunday. The restaurant is closed the third Sunday of each month.
Price Range	Inexpensive/Moderate
Superlatives	Chicken stir-fry, hamburger steaks
Extras	Wine and beer

*L*ike Loretta Lynn, Ann Toms is a coal miner's daughter. The oldest of seven children, she looked after her siblings and "sort of ran the household" while her dad was working. He therefore nicknamed her "Skipper." The yellow rose in the logo is her favorite flower.

Having a restaurant was the dream of Ann's husband, Jim. A native of Waynesboro, he learned to cook as a teenager at a Howard Johnson's on Afton Mountain. They met when he was employed in food service at a nearby school and she was the school nurse. They bought the restaurant in September 1996 and opened it under its present name after a lot of cleaning and remodeling. Ann still works full-time as a registered nurse.

Skipper's is closed the third Sunday of the month so Jim and Ann can help out at the local firehouse breakfast. It's "a way to give something to the community," said Ann.

The restaurant is predominantly red and white with hanging lamps and recessed ceiling lights. The room in the front has seven counter stools, four booths and three small tables. Another dining room seats 50 or so.

At breakfast, you'll encounter choices like "The Works," "The Quickie," "The Country Gentleman," "The Foreign Exchange" and "Uncle Flap Jack," all of which are variations on pancakes, French toast, eggs, breakfast meats, fried potatoes and coffee. Coffee is included in the price of all breakfasts.

Burgers, sandwiches, subs, chicken nuggets and barbecue top the lunch menu. Among the old-time favorites are hamburger steak, country-style steak and liver and onions, which are served with mashed potatoes, a vegetable and rolls.

Shrimp cocktails, Buffalo wings and cheese sticks are popular appetizers at dinner. Sandwiches and burgers are on the menu. One of the favorite entrees is the chicken stir-fry. Other dinners include filet mignon, T-bone steak, Virginia ham, pork chops, pit-cooked beef, flounder, catfish and crab cakes. The seafood platter has shrimp, a crab cake, catfish and flounder.

The desserts are baked in the kitchen. The most popular is the hot fudge brownie. Skipper's is one of the few places where you can get a milk shake made the old-fashioned way with old-fashioned equipment. Lots of folks drop in just for a shake.

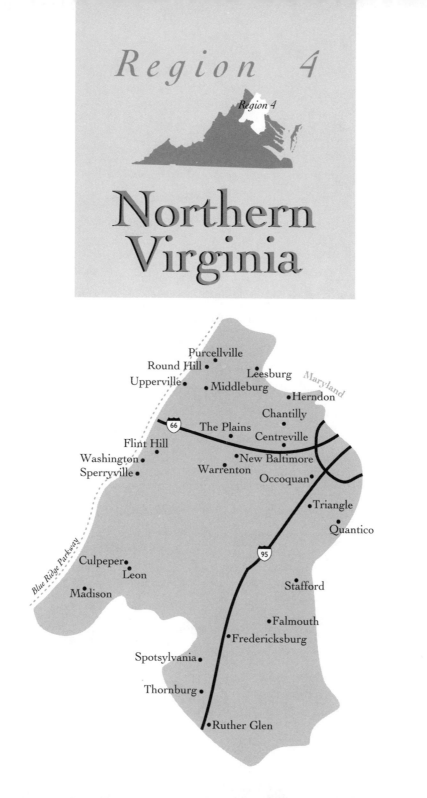

Region 4

Region 4

Northern Virginia

Purcellville
Round Hill
Upperville
Leesburg
Maryland
Middleburg
Herndon
Chantilly
The Plains
Centreville
Flint Hill
Washington
New Baltimore
Sperryville
Warrenton
Occoquan
Triangle
Quantico
Blue Ridge Parkway
Culpeper
Leon
Stafford
Madison
Falmouth
Fredericksburg
Spotsylvania
Thornburg
Ruther Glen

66

95

This is the region where historical tradition and contemporary living—and horses—exist in harmony. The verdant countryside is one of gentleman's farms, split-rail fences, wildflowers—and horses.

This is Virginia's hunt country. Steeplechases and fox hunts are regular weekend events, and horse breeding, training, riding and showing are a way of life. Gift shops, restaurants, country inns and boutiques exhibit or stock all kinds of horse-related items.

History abounds in small towns well endowed with old homes, picket fences, stone walls and cobblestone streets. But contemporary times are nowhere more evident than in the angular architecture of the corporate and government offices that have crept west of the nation's capital.

The towns are charming. The shops are delightful. The countryside beckons. This is one of those rare growth-oriented regions that is conscientiously preserving its past.

RUTHER GLEN

The Feed Lot Restaurant

VA 207 / RUTHER GLEN, VA 22546
(804) 633-5732

Style	Home-style
Meals	Lunch, Tuesday through Friday and Sunday; dinner, Tuesday through Sunday
Price Range	Inexpensive/Moderate
Superlatives	Farm antiques, beef, homemade pies
Extras	Full bar

I was driving west on Va. 207, also known as Roger Clark Boulevard, when The Feed Lot Restaurant popped up in the middle of nowhere. Actually, it's just a few miles east of Exit 114 off I-95. It's a mighty big building with dining space all across the front half and a large room with a stage in the back. An aerobics class was going on in the back room when I stopped in.

Most of the antiques on display are farm related, and all belong to the Upshaw family. Dorothy Campbell Upshaw's parents opened Campbell's Country Club here in 1947. It had nothing to do with golf. It was a nightclub with country music and dancing. After the club evolved into a restaurant, it needed a new name. Since the building was once used to raise hogs, "The Pig Parlor" was tossed around, but "The Feed Lot" seemed more appealing. I tend to agree. The Campbell's Country Club sign is still out front.

Among the antiques from the family home and out-buildings are photographs of a great-grandmother and an aunt, an old pump organ and a Victor junior cookstove.

Dorothy now runs the restaurant with her two sons, Buck and Spike, who are also responsible for operating the 800-acre family farm. Though the pigs are gone, cattle are now raised here—thus the wonderful beef.

Among the sandwiches served at lunch are burgers, pork barbecue, chicken breast, hot Italian sausage, grilled cheese, ham and cheese, a steak sub and chicken salad. In keeping with The Feed Lot's policy of offering affordable food to a patron base that is mostly local, each of the four side orders—french fries, onion rings, slaw and hush puppies—is less than a dollar.

Steaks (T-bone, rib-eye, country-fried and chopped), fried chicken, grilled pork chops, breaded veal Parmesan and surf and turf are offered at dinner. These come with two vegetables and hot rolls. The seafood offerings—among them crab cakes, fried flounder, clams and fantail shrimp—are served with slaw, french fries and hush puppies.

The homemade pies include chocolate chip and coconut. There's also ice cream and cake.

The Feed Lot is a folksy place. Nothing fancy. Just some hardworking farm folks trying to bring you a good, hot, homemade meal.

Olde Mudd Tavern

Olde Mudd Tavern

U.S. 1 AT VA 606 / THORNBURG, VA 22565
(540) 582-5250

Style	Fine dining
Meals	Dinner, Wednesday through Sunday
Price Range	Moderate
Superlatives	Cozy atmosphere, costumed waitresses, bread baskets, "Olde Tavern Mixed Grill"
Extras	Full bar

*T*he Thornburg area saw quite a bit of Civil War activity. Stonewall Jackson died just a few miles to the east in May 1863.

And though it's not always clear what's fact and what's fiction, there's also a good deal of history connected to the Olde Mudd Tavern. It's believed that James Mudd and several of his brothers came to America from England around 1665. A couple of the brothers settled in Maryland and the others in Virginia. James started an oxcart stop at what is now Thornburg. In time, the oxcart stop grew into a tav-ern made of wood and mud. The building was destroyed by fire during the Civil War, after which a second tavern was built of fieldstone. The fieldstone structure was eventually torn down to make way for a new road. The current restaurant is located in what was once a residence on the property.

The first dining room inside the door is predominantly white and has ivy and grape clusters draped over trellises. The other dining rooms are cream with blue trim. All the tables have double tablecloths, small oil lamps and fresh flowers. The menu is printed on parchment-style paper and comes rolled and tied with a silver band.

Dinner starts with a bread basket of the tavern's signature baked goods—cornbread, raisin muffins, sweet potato biscuits. The appetizers include shrimp, homemade crab chowder, baked stuffed clams and fresh fruit and assorted cheese. The "Tavern Platter" is an assortment of hot hors d'oeuvres.

If you're in the mood for seafood, you can try the broiled lobster tails, the catch of the day or baked rainbow trout stuffed with seafood dressing. The breast of chicken is stuffed with ham and cheddar cheese and comes with wild rice on the side. The roast duckling comes with a brandy and orange sauce. Filet mignon and prime rib are available. New York strip steak can be ordered sliced and served with garlic butter or broiled and served with mushroom caps.

The homemade desserts may include strawberry crepes and the popular "Mudd Pie"—vanilla ice cream whipped with Kahlua and served in a chocolate cookie crust with real whipped cream on top.

Courthouse Cafe

SPOTSYLVANIA

Courthouse Cafe

8955 COURTHOUSE ROAD
SPOTSYLVANIA, VA 22553
(540) 582-3302

Style	Home-style
Meals	Breakfast and lunch, seven days a week; dinner, Monday through Saturday
Price Range	Inexpensive
Superlatives	"Salt Fish Breakfast," meatloaf, bread pudding
Extras	Wine and beer

*T*he road sign reads *Spotsylvania C.H.* As is the case with several other Virginia towns whose names have evolved over the years, the *C.H.* stands for *Court House*. This area is best known as the site of the Battle of Spotsylvania Court House, which took place north of town near what is now Va. 613. Here in May 1864, Union and Confederate troops battled for two weeks—sometimes for as much as 20 hours a day—

in some of the most dramatic hand-to-hand combat of the Civil War. Today, the National Park Service maintains more than 5,000 acres for those who wish to learn about the battle.

At the Courthouse Cafe in Spotsylvania, most folks know each other. They arrive in work clothes, uniforms or jeans—it doesn't matter. Conversations go on between patrons and waitresses, from booth to booth and even across the high front counter.

Andy and Kelli Blevins opened this restaurant in 1994, after it had been closed for about 15 years. Kelli operates a school for children, and Andy—a former cop in Washington, D.C.—caters food to almost 100 pupils each weekday.

The seats in the Courthouse Cafe are bright vinyl. Burgundy cafe curtains on brass rods are mounted halfway up the windows. The stained-glass hanging lamps add touches of color. Everything here is very casual—except for the cleaning team. When I visited around 7:30 P.M.—which was toward the end of the cafe's 14-hour day—everything was exceptionally clean.

In the morning, you can get your eggs with anything from bacon, fried bologna or scrapple to corned beef hash, grilled pork chops or jalapeño smoked sausage. And all the combinations come with home fries, grits or fried apples. The "Salt Fish Breakfast" features herring that's been cleaned, filleted and cured in salt before being soaked, breaded, frozen and deep-fried. It's served with home fries, sliced tomatoes and corn cakes.

Lunch is simple—a fresh soup each day, homemade

chili, salads, burgers, sandwiches and subs. You may order breakfast fare at lunch, or you can select fried chicken, grilled pork chops, a fish fillet, corned beef hash or sirloin steak.

The homemade meatloaf is popular at dinner, as is the hamburger steak dinner and the spaghetti and meatballs. Other choices include lasagna, turkey, liver and onions, veal Parmesan and a char-broiled New York strip.

When it's time for dessert, the Courthouse Cafe's bread pudding ranks high on the popularity chart.

Olde Towne
Steak & Seafood

1612 CAROLINE STREET
FREDERICKSBURG, VA 22401
(540) 371-8020

Style	Family-style
Meals	Dinner, Tuesday through Sunday
Price Range	Moderate/Expansive
Superlatives	Prime rib, prime rib, prime rib
Extras	Full bar

*S*ome of America's most famous names are associated with Fredericksburg: Captain John Smith landed here in 1608; George Washington lived in the area from 1739 until his marriage in 1759; James Monroe had a law office here. But it is for the Battle of Fredericksburg, which took place on December 13, 1862, that the town is best known. Today, Fredericksburg's 40-block National Historic District showcases hundreds of buildings from the 18th and 19th centuries.

You can't mention Fredericksburg restaurants without hearing about Old Towne. The prime rib is described as "this thick" (picture a thumb and index finger held two inches apart) and "this big" (picture a medium-size platter).

In a brick building set back from the street, Greg and Hyon Harding have brought the concept of hands-on ownership to its height. Hyon is in the restaurant each evening greeting and seating guests and making sure everyone is content with their dinner. Greg has his hands full in the kitchen cooking the prime rib for which Olde Towne is so well known.

The interior is brick and wood. Captain's chairs surround tables topped with mauve-colored vinyl and oil votive candles. Artificial plants hang in copper pots and kettles. It's very crowded; wait staff and guests have to go sideways between tables. The servers wear tuxedo-style uniforms. Everyone is helpful, efficient, busy and attentive.

Your meal begins with homemade crab soup or lobster bisque, smoked trout or smoked salmon, a stuffed oyster or clams on the half shell.

Various seafood options are offered—broiled flounder stuffed with crabmeat, broiled scallops and "Salmon Old Towne," which comes with shrimp, crabmeat and Bearnaise sauce. Or you might enjoy stuffed lobster or lobster tail. If you love surf and turf, you can select the fillet of beef paired with lobster tail or stuffed shrimp or the New York strip steak paired with six ounces or nine ounces of lobster tail.

The famous prime rib comes in 12- and 16-ounce portions and the filet mignon in eight- and 12-ounce portions. New York strip and Delmonico steaks are also on the menu.

Oh, and there's one lonely chicken entree, an eight-ounce breast with Cajun spices, topped with a couple of shrimp, some crabmeat and Bearnaise sauce.

Olde Towne's signature dessert is a hollowed-out orange filled with orange sherbet and topped with triple sec, crushed almonds and a cherry. It's tricky to eat, as the orange turns easily under the pressure of a spoon. But there's no denying it's light and unique.

Sammy T's

Sammy T's

801 CAROLINE STREET
FREDERICKSBURG, VA 22401
(540) 371-2008

Style	Pub
Meals	Breakfast, lunch and dinner, seven days a week. Sammy T's is closed during breakfast hours one Monday per month.
Price Range	Inexpensive
Superlatives	"The Jordan," black bean cakes
Extras	Full bar

*O*wners Sammy T. and Sylvia "Sibby" Emory bought this building in 1980, some 176 years after it was built as an auction house and store. It's also been used as a post office, a residence, a gas station, and an auto supply store. Sammy T. is a geography professor at Mary Washington College. Sibby was a teacher, a manufacturer's rep and a shopkeeper before helping launch this casual, popular dining spot.

The old tin ceiling has been painted a terra-cotta color. The 14 booths are made of heavy, thick wood.

Breakfast is traditional—eggs and toast, corned beef hash, sausage gravy over a homemade biscuit, pancakes, French toast, fresh fruit. I'm partial to the waffles with bananas, strawberries and nuts. I even talked them into some whipped cream on top. That way, I figured I'd hit four food groups during breakfast.

The two most popular items at lunch are "The Jordan" and black bean cakes. "The Jordan" is a half pita stuffed with spinach, cucumbers, tomatoes, sprouts and tabouli. The black bean cakes are deep-fried beans, wheat germ, lettuce, tomato and red onion in a pita, served with a side of hot sauce. Lots of the sandwiches come in pita bread. The "Swiss Pig" is ham, Swiss cheese, lettuce and tomato on toast. Most of the stuff is health oriented—falafel, an avocado melt, a bean-and-grain burger—but look closely and you'll find a hamburger, a grilled cheese and a club sandwich. As you might expect, there's quite a selection of salads, served with homemade dressing and bread. French fries, onion rings and baked potatoes are also available.

The dinner entrees include chicken Parmesan, vegetarian lasagna, stuffed potatoes, quesadillas, bean burritos, omelets and a stir-fry of broccoli, mushrooms, green peppers and red onions.

Apple crisp, lemon chess pie, pecan pie, chocolate mousse or a fresh fruit cup can complete any meal nicely.

Smythe's Cottage

FREDERICKSBURG

Smythe's Cottage
303 FAUQUIER STREET
FREDERICKSBURG, VA 22401
(540) 373-1645

Style	Casual nice
Meals	Lunch and dinner, Wednesday through Monday
Price Range	Moderate
Superlatives	Neat little historic house, chicken pot pie, roast pork
Extras	Full bar

*I*n this 160-year-old former blacksmith shop hangs an upside-down portrait of Ulysses S. Grant that was noted in a 1984 issue of *National Geographic*. It seems that the founder of the restaurant, Joyce Ackerman, had a great-great-grandfather who was hung by his thumbs during a Civil War interrogation. The best retaliation she could think of was not only to hang Grant—a well-known bourbon imbiber—upside down but also to place him across from the bar, facing the bourbon but out of reach.

The little house is neatly framed with a picket fence. Floors of brick and old wood, farm antiques, hanging lanterns, an old wood stove, homemade print valances and matching menu covers give the place a rustic feel. The pen-and-ink drawings hanging in the dining rooms are the work of waiter and artist Jim Fracks. Splashes of elegance include soft classical music and waiters in formal attire. There's dining inside and out, with room for a little more than 50 when all the tables are set.

Lonnie Williams, a former chef at the Pentagon and at George Mason University, bought the restaurant in 1987. Now, his daughter Jessica Herring does the cooking, having learned well from her father. Williams fills the top management slot.

Smythe's Cottage serves an upscale version of

Southern and Virginia cuisine. Peanut soup is a staple, as are such items as chicken pot pie, ham biscuits, ginger beef and roast pork with spiced apples.

Lunch is a simple affair. Soup, salads, a quiche of the day, biscuits and sandwiches are offered. The sandwiches—sliced breast of turkey, ham and Swiss, roast beef, tuna salad and chicken salad among them—can be ordered half or whole or as a soup-and-sandwich combination.

Dinner entrees like "Turkey Shortcake" (sliced turkey served on cornbread with a cheddar cheese sauce), "Braised Brace of Quail" (served with a bourbon sauce, which I guess Grant would've liked) and "Trout Boil" (rainbow trout poached with vegetables) caught my eye. All entrees come with soup or salad, a vegetable and freshly baked bread. Children under 10 receive a half portion for half price.

Paradise Diner

268 WARRENTON ROAD (U.S. 17)
FALMOUTH, VA 22405
(540) 372-2013

Style	Diner
Meals	Breakfast, lunch and dinner, Tuesday through Sunday
Price Range	Inexpensive/Moderate
Superlatives	Greek omelets, chicken kabobs, stuffed shrimp
Extras	Full bar

*F*almouth was founded in 1728. During the Civil War, Walt Whitman and Clara Barton worked side by side here, treating wounded soldiers at Chatham, a Georgian-style mansion now operated by the National Park Service. Another local attraction is Belmont, the estate of painter Gari Melchers. Some of Melchers's works are displayed in the stone studio on the property.

The Paradise Diner is located on U.S. 17 about a mile north of the U.S. 1 junction. Formerly a bar, the building is a white-brick place with statues of Greek gods and a flagpole flying the United States and Virginia flags. Inside, you'll find more statues, along with lots of mirrors, artificial plants and silk flowers. The booth seats and chairs are a gold color. At each booth is a "Wall-O-Matic" music selector for the jukebox.

At age 15, owner Jimmy Zotos traveled alone from Greece to the United States and started working as a dishwasher in the Baltimore area. From there, he moved from restaurant to restaurant, learning everything. The Paradise Diner is his third restaurant.

Paradise Diner

While this diner offers American, Italian and Greek cuisine, Greek is definitely the strong suit. In the morning, the Greek omelet—fresh eggs, gyro meat, onions, mushrooms, tomatoes, green peppers and feta cheese—is featured. If that's not your style, then there are hot cakes, chipped beef and waffles.

At lunch, the sandwiches run the gamut from roast beef, pastrami, tuna salad and chicken salad to hamburgers and subs. The "Paradise Special" has two pieces of French toast with bacon, turkey, cheese and tomato, all grilled and served with french fries or onion rings. A barbecue platter is also offered.

Dinner entrees include steaks, beef liver, lamb chops, pork chops, spaghetti and lasagna. The shrimp is stuffed with crabmeat and served with Bearnaise sauce. The Greek influence is felt in the souvlaki, gyros, moussaka and shish kabobs. A popular dish is the chicken kabob—green peppers, tomatoes, onions and chicken served on rice with chicken gravy.

The Paradise Diner has no trouble at all selling dessert. Knowing that people eat with their eyes, Jimmy has strategically placed a tall, rotating dessert display right inside the front door. It's the first thing you see, and you're not likely to forget it. The desserts aren't made *at* the restaurant, but they are made *for* the restaurant, and every one of them looks scrumptious.

If you're seated in the dining room on the right next to the inside wall, you'll find yourself next to another dessert display. This is the kind of place where it's tough to skip dessert even when you know you should.

Beulah's Madison Cafeteria & Restaurant

Beulah's Madison Cafeteria & Restaurant

MAIN STREET AT WASHINGTON STREET
MADISON, VA 22727
(540) 948-7131

Style	Home-style
Meals	Breakfast, lunch and dinner, Monday through Saturday
Price Range	Inexpensive
Superlatives	Macaroni and cheese, apple dumplings

*M*adison County was settled by German Lutherans. The first public school in the state was started around

1896 in one of their churches. Both the town and the county were named for James Madison, whose family owned property here. Two dozen 19th-century buildings stand in Madison today.

Beulah's Madison Cafeteria is one of the folksiest places in the state. Simple and underdecorated, it's a former gas station. In fact, the original door to the service bay now separates two dining areas. Wagon-wheel hanging lamps illuminate the rooms. Vinyl chairs, plastic tablecloths and an artificial plant in a clay pot on each table set the stage for your meal.

A daily lunch special includes a meat of the day, two vegetables, bread and a drink. From the menu, you can order such things as a burger, a BLT, a grilled cheese, crab cakes or roast beef with gravy and mashed potatoes. The children's portion of the menu has four items. There's also a section that features healthy food like grilled chicken, a chicken salad plate and a tuna salad plate, each served with a choice of vegetables.

Dinner at Beulah's features a food bar with vegetables, salad and bread, which you may visit with any entree order. Hot roast beef, pork chops, fried oysters, crab cakes, veal cutlets and a dozen other items are available.

The people here couldn't be friendlier. Owner Beulah Cason dusted the flour off her hands and took time out from making biscuits to visit my table. She's a Madison native who worked for two decades in this restaurant in the days when it was called Rixey's. She bought the place in 1980 and renamed it.

I adhere strictly to a policy of not accepting free meals, but I do have a teapot-shaped magnet with a small calendar attached to it on my refrigerator. The red teapot is emblazoned *Beulah's Madison Cafeteria & Restaurant, Beulah Cason, Proprietor*, and includes the phone number and town. She insisted and I accepted. That's small-town folksy.

MADISON

Pig 'N Steak
WASHINGTON STREET
MADISON, VA 22727
(540) 948-3130

Style	Home-style
Meals	Lunch and dinner, seven days a week
Price Range	Inexpensive
Superlatives	Pork barbecue, ribs, fresh steaks
Extras	Full bar

*I*t's hard to find pulled, pit-cooked barbecue that my husband, John, and I don't like. It seems, though, that the fancier the place, the worse the barbecue.

Pig 'N Steak isn't very fancy, but, as the rule cited above might lead you to suspect, the barbecue is very good. Eating here may be a high-cholesterol experience, as someone in the area suggested to me, but who wants to live without one on occasion?

The restaurant building was once a turkey farm. Inside, there's a bar to the left and a sign for those in bad need of civilizing: "No street shoes allowed on bar." You'll note the airplane made from Budweiser cans by some patron. Straight ahead and to the right are wooden tables and vinyl chairs. In the back is a

Pig 'N Steak

on what's currently available. But rest assured that they're always fresh and never frozen.

As with most serious barbecue places, you can carry Pig 'N Steak's barbecue away by the pound.

If you're a local resident, consider these folks for hosting a catered pig roast. My fond memories of pig roasts go all the way back to the mountains of Colorado, but that's another story.

glorious mural of horses by local artist Diane Perl. She finished and signed it in 1987. Down a short hallway at the back is a new banquet room nicely done in dark green and white.

Naturally, I'm going to suggest the barbecue sandwich for lunch, along with a small basket of french fries. (If you love fries and can eat a mound about the size of a football, order the small basket. Someone back in the kitchen has a generous conception of *small* when it comes to fries.) You can also get a cheeseburger, a chicken sandwich, a BLT loaded with bacon, a hot dog or a rib-eye steak sandwich. Potato salad and macaroni salad are available some of the time.

The barbecue platters are especially popular at dinner. They come with your choice of two items from among fries, slaw and baked beans. The hickory-smoked ribs have been cooked a minimum of 12 hours. The "Mountaineer Platter" comes with fries, slaw and a half-pound hamburger with all the trimmings. There are also two chicken options. And as its name suggests, Pig 'N Steak is known for its steaks. They're not listed on the menu, because the selection depends

Prince Michel

U.S. 29 / LEON, VA 22725
(800) 800-WINE

Style	Fine dining
Meals	Lunch, Thursday through Sunday; dinner, Thursday through Saturday
Price Range	Expensive
Superlatives	Atmosphere, wine, cuisine
Extras	A full bar is on the premises. The winery is open every day except major holidays.

*L*ike lots of places in Virginia, this town is so small that it has only a post office and a handful of houses. But a governor was born in the area. James Lawson Kemper was born near Leon in 1823 and moved his family to a Greek Revival home here in 1865.

Prince Michel Winery, owned by Jean Leducq of France, is located in an attractive brick building on the western side of U.S. 29 a few miles north of Madison. The restaurant was established in 1992 for this stated purpose: "To offer one of life's great pleasures:

the enjoyment of great wines with outstanding food."

To this end, a downstairs room has been tastefully converted to a classy dining area with the atmosphere of a Paris cafe. Awnings, trellises and shutters frame trompe l'oeil murals of Bordeaux and set the stage for executive chef Alain Lecomte's innovative cuisine. You won't be surprised to find fine silverware and exquisite china and crystal here. The white director's chairs with sage-green canvas add a casual touch. Overall, the atmosphere is elegant but not at all stuffy.

The winner of some impressive awards in France, Alain blends regional foods with classic French dishes. Lunch and dinner include a first course, a main course, a salad and dessert.

The menu changes constantly, as Alain uses only fresh ingredients. The lunch appetizers might be sliced duck breast with peaches or scallops and jumbo shrimp. For the main course, patrons might enjoy such things as grilled rack of veal, Châteaubriand or a veal sweetbreads and chicken combination. In the French tradition, the salad follows the main course, and dessert is served with coffee or tea. The crème brûlée is a popular dessert choice, as is "Bavarois aux Framboises" (raspberry mousse).

Several selections are offered for each dinner course. Among the main-course options are things like lamb medallions perfumed with garden herbs and red snapper on a spinach cushion. The desserts, which you order at the beginning of your meal, include creative sweets like "Charlotte au Grand Marnier," a ring of sponge cake filled with Grand Marnier mousse.

Prince Michel wines are available by the glass during lunch and dinner. Some patrons try one to complement each course. The maître d' is available to assist with wine selection.

Besides enjoying a leisurely dining experience, you should reserve time to visit the museum, view the video presentation, take the self-guided tour of the winery and browse the gift shop.

Visiting Prince Michel shouldn't be something you do on your way to something else. It is worthy of being a destination.

CULPEPER

Baby Jim's
701 NORTH MAIN STREET
CULPEPER, VA 22701
(540) 825-9212

Style	Snack bar
Meals	Breakfast, lunch and dinner, Monday through Saturday
Price Range	Inexpensive
Superlatives	Steak sandwiches, shrimp boxes, chicken boxes

Captain John Smith came to the site of Culpeper one year after the founding of Jamestown. The county was named for Lord Thomas Culpeper, the colonial governor from 1680 to 1683. The town was called Fairfax before Culpeper became the official name in 1870. Many Civil War battles were fought in and around the town, which was occupied by each side a number of times. One local farmer whose property was devastated is said to have remarked, "I hain't took

Baby Jim's

no sides in this yer rebellion, but I'll be dog-garned if both sides hain't took me."

Just in case you're not familiar with weekend fun in Culpeper, here's one popular activity: back your car in front of Baby Jim's and watch the traffic go by. If you can find a parking place, that is. This local landmark is especially popular after football games and on weekend nights. Its sign was refurbished a year or so back and is identical to the original one.

Collis Jenkins III runs the place, and he knows about things to do in Culpeper because he grew up here. Not just in town, but right here at Baby Jim's, which is built on the front of the family home. Baby Jim's was the first fast-food place in town when his dad opened it on March 7, 1947. Another eight years would pass before Ray Kroc opened his first McDonald's. Collis the third figures he'll stick around for a while even though operating this friendly, old-time snack bar doesn't let him get much use out of his

American University degree in real estate and urban development.

There are a few picnic tables on either side of the building and two windows inside to place your order. The interior is about the size of a house hallway, only a few feet longer.

Baby Jim's opens at 4:30 A.M. for the Washington, D.C., commuters who pop in for breakfast before joining the early rush that precedes the main rush hour. They leave with sausage and egg, ham and egg and bacon and egg sandwiches, hash browns and perhaps a biscuit or two. And most likely coffee.

Soup, beef stew, hamburgers, hot dogs, grilled ham and cheese sandwiches, egg sandwiches, ham salad, chicken salad and tuna salad are among the items offered throughout the remainder of the day. The steak sandwiches are especially good. Prices top out with the shrimp dinner.

There's a prominently placed sign here that reads, "No loud talking, no foul language," so be sure to mind your manners.

CULPEPER
Dee Dee's
502 NORTH MAIN STREET / CULPEPER, VA 22701
(540) 825-4700

Style	Family-style
Meals	Breakfast, lunch and dinner, seven days a week
Price Range	Inexpensive/Moderate
Superlatives	Comfortable setting, seafood, barbecue

Dee Dee's

$\mathcal{T}$he wooden tables and chairs, the bay windows, the antiques on the walls and the clocks with different times on them all contribute to the character of this comfortable, country place.

The tables, booths and chairs in the larger of the two dining rooms are made of a rich-grained oak that gives the room an appealing warmth. And if you've ever wondered about the claims of Miracle-Gro, your answer can be found in the trailing ivy and philodendron all around this room. In fact, it's challenging to try to find the pot where the plants originate. This is a great unsolicited advertisement for the plant product.

The smaller dining area to the left of the front door

has a nautical theme, with the proverbial nets, shells and portholes, as well as an aquarium with very large fish in it.

Originally a Gulf gas station, the building became the Ocean Deli, a carry-out seafood place, before opening as Dee Dee's in the early 1990s.

Breakfast can be ordered to eat in or take out. Steak, eggs, pancakes, omelets, sausage gravy, scrapple and French toast are among the items you might expect. But I do wonder how many orders Dee Dee's gets for the homemade oyster stew for breakfast.

Pork and beef barbecue sandwiches, burgers and subs are featured at lunch. "Appeteasers," salads and homemade soups—with *homemade* underlined—are also offered.

Fresh seafood and combination plates dominate the dinner menu. The fish—described on the menu as "whatever Pop caught today"—can be ordered deep-fried, broiled or stuffed with crab. Dee Dee's offers both Chesapeake blue and Alaskan crab. Shrimp, scallops, oysters, clams and a seafood casserole in a creamy cheese sauce are also available. Or you might try ribs, New York strip steak, spaghetti or one of the half-dozen or so seafood and barbecue combinations.

And whether you read it here or on the menu, you should know that the homemade strawberry shortcake is made fresh every day. There are other desserts, too, but I'd hold out for the shortcake.

It's About Thyme

It's About Thyme

128 EAST DAVIS STREET / CULPEPER, VA 22701
(540) 825-4264

Style	Casual nice
Meals	Lunch, Monday through Saturday; dinner, Tuesday through Saturday
Price Range	Moderate
Superlatives	Atmosphere, murals, bruschetta
Extras	Full bar

*T*his classy place with a striped awning out front rivals any big-city spot for atmosphere. From the dark green tin ceiling to the original murals on the walls to the wood floors, It's About Thyme evokes artistic elegance.

You don't have to know much about art to recognize the characters in the impressionist murals as adaptations of those in the best of Monet and Renoir. Owner and chef John Yarnell has a lengthy history of opening restaurants. For this, his most recent acquisition, he hired Italian artist Davide Rodoquino to create the unique floor-to-ceiling scenes.

The attractive etched globe lamps were custom-made for the building when it was renovated before Yarnell moved in. Each of the wooden tables has fresh flowers, a bottle of wine, sparkling crystal and fine silverware. Instrumental music sets the tone for Yarnell's European country cuisine.

For lunch, you can go with roasted peppers and artichoke hearts or a puff pastry sandwich. Bruschetta—a crusty bread topped with tomato, basil and garlic and then finished with Parmesan cheese—is also available, as are soups and salads. Main courses such as grilled tuna and pesto or chicken and dumplings are offered.

The dinner appetizers include portobello mushrooms and cold poached salmon. The soups might be cream of potato and turkey and pasta. For your entree, you might try scallops served the French way—with cream, brandy and mushrooms, topped with whipped potatoes. Roasted chicken, tuna fillets and roasted pork loin are often available. Items like beef kidney with white onions and red wine will please the restaurant's European clientele.

Fresh desserts like "Chocolate Ecstasy" and bread pudding are made daily.

At the time I visited and chatted with Yarnell, he had plans to open a smoking room upstairs and to add patio dining in the alley beside the entrance. After seeing his stylistic touches inside It's About Thyme, I'd guess that any alley he creates for dining will be quite inviting and romantic.

Durango's

2610 JEFFERSON DAVIS HIGHWAY (U.S. 1)
STAFFORD, VA 22554
(540) 720-6315

Style	Family-style
Meals	Lunch and dinner, seven days a week
Price Range	Moderate
Superlatives	Prime rib, baby back ribs
Extras	Full bar

Stafford County and the town of Stafford were named for Staffordshire, England. Just north of town is a marker noting an Indian trail that became a frontier road in 1664. More than 100 years later, George Washington traveled this road on his way to Yorktown.

Steve Estes is a native Californian who just likes steakhouses a lot. He worked in restaurants while attending Embry-Riddle University in Florida, then put in a few years with a couple of chain restaurants. He was working for an independent place when a Golden Corral restaurant closed on U.S. 1 just south of Fredericksburg. Steve consulted an atlas for a Western-sounding name, found the town of Durango in southern Colorado, and started his own Western-style steakhouse in the old Golden Corral in 1992.

Four years later, he constructed this new building on U.S. 1 just north of Stafford. It was decorated by his wife, Keri, and his mother, Sally Estes. It's very clean and very Western, with lots of wood, country-and-western music and Western prints.

The lunch plates include your choice of meat, two fresh vegetables and freshly baked bread. There are more than a dozen meat choices, like "Rodeo Riblets," teriyaki steak, beef tips, catfish, shrimp, a chicken breast and pork chops. Among the dozen vegetable choices are baby carrots, baked potatoes, mashed potatoes, sweet potatoes, stewed tomatoes and rice and gravy. Burgers, chili dogs, roast beef sandwiches and chicken sandwiches are also offered. You can choose from among several appetizers, soups, salads and pasta dishes.

Dinner features lots of beef, of course. Prime rib, filet mignon and steaks are offered, as are ribs, chops and combination specials like filet mignon and lobster, filet mignon and shrimp and steak and lobster. Value is emphasized in Durango's inexpensive "Lighter Side" meals, for which you may select one meat and two vegetables; bread comes with your meal.

Durango's desserts, appropriately called "Fantastic Finishes," include cherry cobbler, "Snickers Cheesecake," "Strawberry Labamba" and "Brownie Bottom Pie."

The Log Cabin

1749 JEFFERSON DAVIS HIGHWAY (U.S. 1)
STAFFORD, VA 22554
(540) 659-5067

Style	Casual nice
Meals	Dinner, seven days a week
Price Range	Moderate/Expensive
Superlatives	Crab, Cajun pasta dishes
Extras	Full bar

*B*esides being a charming log structure, The Log Cabin is one of the few old restaurants that have survived along U.S. 1, which used to be one of the main arteries through the state.

Darrell and Tammy Mitchell have been operating The Log Cabin—formerly an Esso station and general store—since 1979. Darrell's grandfather purchased the place in 1941, primarily for use as a dance hall. Darrell's dad, George "Slug" Summerfield Mitchell, also ran it as a bar and dance hall. His was one of the first places in the area to offer pizza. But it's Darrell and Tammy who are responsible for creating an elegant dining experience here.

The fireplace still burns real wood. The exquisite piano near the entrance dates from around 1890. The hanging lamps are definitely one of a kind. They're inverted peach baskets that Darrell bought and wired. The tablecloths are burgundy, and the chairs are basic black vinyl. The atmosphere is rustic and casual.

Crab is one of their specialties at The Log Cabin, and it comes many ways. Chef Mike Buttram, who's been here almost two decades, is emphatic that no fill-ers be added to the crabmeat. The restaurant's signature soup is a cream-based white crab with a hint of wine. The appetizers include a crabmeat cocktail. Crab cakes and a crab sampler are stable menu items.

Clams and spiced shrimp are popular among those who elect not to choose a crab appetizer.

Brazilian lobster tails and a lobster and steak combination are among the entrees. The "Northeast Feast" entree features a Maine lobster, Gulf shrimp, steamed clams and Alaskan snow crab legs. A couple of New Orleans dishes are offered—a three-seafood garlic fettuccine and shrimp Diane. The Norfolk-style seafood offerings include various combinations of crab, shrimp, lobster and scallops. Beef lovers can select filet mignon any night or prime rib on Friday and Saturday evenings.

The most popular dessert here is "Bourbon Street Crunch," a sweet variety of chocolate pie.

Command Post Pub

335 POTOMAC AVENUE / QUANTICO, VA 22134
(703) 640-6998

Style	Pub
Meals	Lunch and dinner, seven days a week
Price Range	Inexpensive/Moderate
Superlatives	Ribs, "Sgt. Major" sandwich
Extras	Full bar

*Y*ou'll enter the small town of Quantico by stopping at a little guard post, then driving three miles through the United States Marine Corps reservation. You'll bear left and cross some railroad tracks to reach the town's main street.

Besides being the tallest building in Quantico, the Command Post Pub is also the dressiest. Five flags wave out front. The facade is brick. Brass coach lights flank double oak doors.

When Albert Gasser bought the place in the late 1980s, it was a small, one-story, dark brown building with wood siding. His vision didn't end with the transformations he's brought to the facade and the first floor. His current plans include a banquet room on the second floor and rooftop dining on the third.

Inside the pub, there's a long bar to the left and a dining room to the right. The bar seats more than a dozen. The dining area has six booths and around 10 tables. Of course, there's all sorts of military memorabilia on the walls—posters, plaques, prints, framed medals.

The Command Post is known for its ribs—but they're not on the menu, so you'll have to ask for them.

Command Post Pub

The "Sgt. Major" sandwich is turkey with Swiss cheese and all the trimmings on white toast. Other sandwiches include an Italian hoagie, a patty melt, a club sandwich and hamburgers. Soup and chili are always available. You can get either with half a sandwich and a side order of fries, onion rings, slaw or potato salad.

One of the most popular items at dinner is the "Steamship," which is sliced beef served on a roll with *jus* and horseradish; a potato and salad come on the side. The Virginia ham is smothered in a spicy pineapple sauce, and the pork chops are covered with grilled onions. Fresh seafood is offered, as are spaghetti and lasagna.

You can then complete your meal with chocolate cheesecake or traditional cheesecake with blueberry or cherry topping.

TRIANGLE

The
Globe and Laurel

18418 JEFFERSON DAVIS HIGHWAY (U.S. 1)
TRIANGLE, VA 22172
(703) 221-5763

Style	Pub
Meals	Lunch, Monday through Friday; dinner, Monday through Saturday. The pub is closed on national holidays.
Price Range	Moderate
Superlatives	Military memorabilia, roast duckling à l'orange
Extras	Full bar

U.S. 1 meets two county roads at the entrance to the Marine Corps base at Quantico, forming the neat little triangle with flowers planted in it that gives this community its name. Otherwise, the town isn't much more than gas stations and a few motels and stores along U.S. 1.

Richard Spooner, a retired Marine Corps major, opened this restaurant in 1968. When asked why, he responded, "Oh, I think it's the dream of every marine to have a little bar to swap stories."

This may have been a little bar at one time, but it's evolved into a restaurant. It's a great place to swap stories, but it's also more than that. It's a veritable museum of patches, medals, swords, crests and other memorabilia from military units all over the world.

Dozens of little flags hang over the bar area. If Spooner knows in advance that foreign patrons are coming to dine, he sets the flag of their country with the United States flag on their table. He says they appreciate that, and I'm sure they do. Also, they might feel inclined to contribute something from their country to his collection of memorabilia.

Wooden tables are crowded in a room that can hold about 30, and a front dining room can seat another 30 or so. It's all very cozy and warm, and it's smoke-free.

There's a lot of consideration for fat intake here. The menu notes that there's only one gram of fat in the wheat bread (without butter) and two grams in the French onion soup (without croutons and cheese).

At lunch, the excellent salade niçoise has lettuce, tuna, egg, potato, artichoke hearts, hearts of palm, bell peppers, sliced mushrooms, capers and anchovies if you wish. The sandwiches include a meatball sub, ham and Swiss, a Reuben, a turkey club, steak, grilled chicken breast and barbecued beef. Each comes with the soup du jour or a garden salad.

Among the dinner entrees are a vegetarian platter, New York strip steak, char-broiled chicken, poached fillet of tilapia, salmon crowns stuffed with fresh vegetables, medallions of beef tenderloin, roast duckling à l'orange with Grand Marnier sauce and filet mignon with Bearnaise sauce.

Coffee, espresso, cappuccino and a nice selection of teas are offered.

Regardless of your interest in military history and memorabilia, this is a good place to find a warm welcome and get a good meal.

SPERRYVILLE

The Appetite Repair Shop

MAIN STREET / SPERRYVILLE, VA 22740
(540) 987-9533

Style	Family-style
Meals	Breakfast and lunch, seven days a week; dinner, Friday through Sunday in winter and Thursday through Sunday in summer
Price Range	Inexpensive
Superlatives	Auto theme, hamburgers, cookies
Extras	Wine and beer

*A*t a lecture on food service, I once heard John

Appetite Repair Shop

Schumacher, the owner and chef of Schumacher's New Prague Hotel in Minnesota, speak of the importance of having a theme and/or one or two signature dishes—something to set your establishment apart from others.

Gregg and Cindy Gillies understand that principle. They opened The Appetite Repair Shop more than a decade ago, making liberal use of an auto-repair theme in everything from the decor to the dishes on which their food is served.

Among the items on the walls are a German license plate sent by a visitor, a steering wheel from a Model T, a grill from a 1940 Ford truck, a hubcap from a Nash and Virginia license plates for every year from 1900 through 1974.

Patrons sit in car seats rather than chairs. The carpet looks like a two-lane highway. It was made by local resident Warren Darnell (who, by the way, also put carpets in the home of King Hussein of Jordan).

The servers are "technicians." To select a drink, you consult the section of the menu called the "Fluids Department." The "Parts Department" section lists fries, onion rings, crab cakes, cottage cheese and other extras. Chicken sandwiches come in "Two-Door," "Four-Door," "Sports Car," "Luxury" and "Thunderbird" varieties. The "Junk Yard" is a vegetarian stir-fry pita pocket. The "Solar Vehicle" is a veggie burger. Should you order a "Sub in a Hub," it will be served to you in a real hubcap. The "Master Mechanic" platters include roast beef with mashed potatoes and gravy, rib-eye steak, deep-fried catfish and crab cakes. The hamburger served here is from cattle raised by a local Mennonite farmer.

If you're not already wearing a spare tire (or even if you are), you might consider ordering one for dessert. The "Spare Tire" is your choice of ice cream between two cookies. Speaking of which, the cookies here are delectable—white chocolate macadamia nut, oatmeal raisin, chocolate chip, even a "Turtle Cookie." If I skip dinner, can I have one of each?

The cleanliness of the place won't surprise you once you learn of Cindy's stint with Dairy Queen. Her supervisor checked above and below every surface and ordered anything cleaned again that put a slight color on her white-gloved fingers.

Blue Moon Cafe

Try - next time
in Skyline

Blue Moon Cafe

U.S. 211 / SPERRYVILLE, VA 22740
(540) 987-3162

Style	Family-style
Meals	Lunch and dinner, Tuesday through Sunday
Price Range	Inexpensive/Moderate
Superlatives	Greek-style chicken, salmon
Extras	Full bar

I skipped this restaurant my first time through Sperryville because the sign says just "Pizza." But on the recommendation of a few folks, I gave it a second look. I found that although pizza is indeed on the menu, the Blue Moon Cafe is much more than a pizza place.

The building is a boxy, cinder-block affair, but owner John Loretto has put striped umbrellas on the picnic tables on the side deck and added a wooden fence around a grassy area next to that. Pretty flowers grow along the front. From a table on the deck, you can get a view of the cabbages, parsley and flowers growing in the back garden. You can also see a nearby baseball diamond. This is not some old, forgotten ball diamond. Well, old, maybe, but definitely not forgotten. At least not on Monday nights, when the cafe is closed and the Blue Moon softball team goes into action.

There's room for about 50 people inside the restaurant. The small stage in one corner is the focus of attention during open-mike night on Tuesdays. Most of the performers are musicians, but there are some storytellers and comics as well. A band plays on Saturday evenings.

White pizza, buffalo wings and red-pepper hummus are among the appetizers. Seven salads and a couple of soups—perhaps cracked crab soup and black bean and rice soup—are available. The sandwiches include burgers, garden burgers, teriyaki chicken, roast beef on an herb roll, stuffed pitas and a "Chef's Sandwich" of roast beef, turkey, chicken, bacon and Swiss cheese.

The dinner entrees include things like filet mignon, grilled game hen and salmon nestled in a pool of cucumber and dill sauce. Vegetarian entrees are available on request.

Spiced waffles with vanilla ice cream and caramel sauce are one of the dessert choices. "Old Rag Pie," named for Old Rag Mountain, a local landmark, is a chocolate chip, bourbon and walnut masterpiece.

Bleu Rock Inn

U.S. 221 / WASHINGTON, VA 22747
(800) 537-3652

Style	Fine dining
Meals	Dinner, Wednesday through Sunday; Sunday brunch
Price Range	Moderate/Expensive
Superlatives	Excellent view, French cuisine
Extras	Full bar

There are 28 towns named for our first president. Local residents claim this one is the original—witness the First Washington's Museum on Main Street. Washington is the county seat of Rappahannock County. Its streets are laid out just as they were surveyed more than 220 years ago.

The Bleu Rock Inn is the place to go if you consider a nice view an enrichment to your dining experience. I take that back. *Nice* is an understatement. The view of the tranquil countryside between Washington and Sperryville is superlative. Each of the three dining rooms faces west. Your eyes look out to a pond with swans, ducks and geese, to rolling fields, to Blue Rock Farm's vineyards and to the Blue Ridge Mountains beyond.

The Bleu Rock Inn is the restaurant and lodging part of the 80-acre Blue Rock Farm. Owners Bernard and Jean Campagne are from France. They've used the French spelling of *blue* in the inn's name, while the farm retains its English spelling.

If I were to spend three days here, I'd sit in a different dining room each day. All have double linens, nicely upholstered chairs and a fireplace. The main dining room is decorated in shades of blue, burgundy, pink and mauve. Murals have been painted on walls in the Garden Room. Blue and teal grape print fabric accents the windows in the Vineyard Room. Oh, and there's terrace dining outside. Make my reservation four days.

The place was originally a horse farm. Horses still graze on the property. The chef team, husband and wife Richard and Lynn Mahan, make creative use of the produce from the farm's orchard—nectarines, apples, peaches and apricots.

The appetizers might include smoked trout cakes, roasted goat cheese or a salad of calamari, mussels and lobster.

Bouillabaisse and "Alsatian Choucroute Garnie"—a medley of pheasant, roast pork, smoked sausage and grilled quail served with champagne apple sauerkraut—might be among the entrees. Roasted salmon, veal tenderloin, Maine sea scallops and grilled local free-range lamb loin come with various accompaniments like wild mushroom mashed potatoes and sweet red pepper risotto.

At Sunday brunch, you may order such things as a crabmeat and smoked chicken tart, grilled yellowfin tuna and "Bleu Rock Benedict." The latter incorporates beef or smoked salmon, sauteed tomato and a mustard hollandaise on an English muffin.

Key lime cake with strawberry sauce, "Three-Chocolate Terrine" or vanilla crème brûlée might follow your meal. And a night upstairs in one of five guest rooms might even follow your dessert.

Country Cafe

389-A MAIN STREET / WASHINGTON, VA 22747
(540) 675-1066

Style	Cafe
Meals	Breakfast and lunch, seven days a week; dinner, Monday through Saturday
Price Range	Inexpensive
Superlatives	Homemade coconut cake

On the left side of this former Ford dealership is the Country Cafe. On the right side is the local post office. The building was renovated in the 1970s. David Huff, who has lived in Rappahannock County all his life, bought the cafe in 1989. His objective: to serve good American food.

A few frying pans and coffeepots painted with country scenes hang on the walls or sit on ledges. The artist is Elizabeth Crusan of Harpers Ferry. David liked her work and bought a few pieces to decorate the cafe. Now, he allows her to have some of her pieces for sale here. A bulletin board with local business cards tacked to it contributes to the cafe's small-town atmosphere. A Great Majestic cookstove commands attention on one side of the room. There's space for 52 people.

Breakfast runs the gamut from biscuits, croissants and omelets to pancakes, waffles and "Baby Cakes." The latter are small pancakes popular with children and those who want light fare.

Soups, salads and sandwiches are offered at lunch. "Dave's Deluxe" is an eight-ounce sub with all the cheeses and meats on the premises. The "Vegetarian Delight" contains white cheeses and vegetables. The 16 lunch platters range from hot dogs, hamburgers and grilled turkey burgers to crab cakes and shrimp baskets, all of which come with a choice of two sides.

The dinner entrees are similar to the lunch platters, though there are additional choices like ham steak, pork chops, New York strip steak and grilled salmon steak.

Far and away the most popular dessert is the coconut cake, made right here by David's mom. Peanut butter pie, cheesecake, cobblers and brownies are also available. But best of all, they have cookies! It doesn't matter to me what kind. I've never met a cookie I didn't like.

The Inn at Little Washington

MIDDLE AND MAIN STREETS
WASHINGTON, VA 22747
(540) 675-3800

Style	Fine dining
Meals	Dinner, Wednesday through Monday year-round and Tuesday during May and October only. Reservations are required.
Price Range	Expensive
Superlatives	Lavish decor, artistic presentation
Extras	Full bar

Young people often struggle with what to do with themselves upon reaching adulthood. A common strategy is to go to college, travel in Europe and then get back to nature—live in the country somewhere, eat granola. And stall making a decision.

This was the route for Patrick O'Connell, co-owner and chef of The Inn at Little Washington. He thought he wanted to be an actor, so he studied drama in college. Then he went to Europe, then to rural life in the Shenandoah Valley.

Reinhardt Lynch, co-owner of the restaurant, dropped in on O'Connell one day. He loved the area so much that he's never left. Together, the two started a catering business. The complications of toting food over country roads gave way to the idea of having a restaurant—people would move to the food, instead of the other way around.

Thus, in the winter of 1978, The Inn at Little Washington opened in a converted garage. O'Connell and Lynch charged $4.95 for a roasted chicken dinner in those days.

There were many struggles the first few years, not uncommon for a small business. What is uncommon, however, is what O'Connell and Lynch have since created—a restaurant and inn consistently ranked at the top of the hospitality industry and known around the world.

Today, The Inn at Little Washington is lavishly decorated with plush carpets, fringed lamps, exquisite art, antiques and an interesting mix of fabrics and wall coverings. There's little solid color. The upholstery, the ceiling drapes, the pillows, the curtains and the valances all have stripes, flowers, geometric patterns or other prints. It doesn't match, but it works. Opulence abounds in the 12 guest rooms as well.

Dinner is an extravagant event. The presentations made the biggest impression on me. You'll be served edible art from hors d'oeuvres through dessert. O'Connell's aim is to pair tastes and textures, colors and contrasts that will appeal to the palate and be visually stimulating as well.

The menu changes all the time. Your entree will not necessarily be the main attraction. It's the innovative preparation and the accompaniments that place The Inn at Little Washington in a class of its own.

To say it's expensive is an understatement. But remember, dining out is a form of entertainment and a social excursion, not merely an exercise in nourishment. Here, you enjoy an artistic culinary event in luxurious surroundings. To quote local innkeeper Susan Longyear of Fairlea Farm Bed & Breakfast, O'Connell and Lynch "strive for perfection."

If you're interested in cooking well, you might consult *The Inn at Little Washington Cookbook*. The three-page introduction provides an excellent lesson on how to present food graciously and tastefully.

The Flint Hill Public House

U.S. 522 / FLINT HILL, VA 22627
(540) 675-1700

Style	Fine dining
Meals	Lunch, Monday, Tuesday and Thursday through Saturday; dinner, Thursday through Tuesday; Sunday brunch
Price Range	Moderate
Superlatives	Fresh meats and seafood, wine list
Extras	Full bar

John Pearson, a native of southern California, has been, in his words, a "kitchen rat" since age 17. "You name it, I've done it," he says of his restaurant experience. His wife, Denise, majored in nutrition at Louisiana Tech because she wanted to work in the food industry.

In 1991, John was working for a Washington, D.C., gourmet retailer and Denise was attending cooking school and still longing to be in the food business. He hired her. They began dating and got married in May 1994. A few months later, they started work as a chef team at The Flint Hill Public House. They purchased the business the following June, and that's where you'll find them today, making wholesome, tasty food in this rather impressive 1903 schoolhouse.

The flower gardens around the building are beautiful. The gently rolling terrain out back provides a tranquil setting for any meal. The herb and vegetable gardens bring fresh flavors and produce to your table.

If you prefer a light lunch, you can select soup alone or soup and a BLT or soup and salad. Sandwiches and burgers are available. The entrees might be broiled rainbow trout, grilled sirloin and eggplant Parmesan. An abbreviated wine and beer list accompanies the lunch menu. "Fred's Hard Cider," an apple brew made just down the road, is also offered.

The menu changes often. The evening appetizers might be a tomato-oregano tart and buttermilk-fried calamari. Atlantic halibut, grilled rockfish, oven-roasted chicken, beef tenderloin and jumbo lump crab cakes are popular entrees.

Wholesome breads—potato bread and sourdough bread among them—are made on the premises. All the desserts are also homemade. You might find hazelnut torte and cheesecake among the choices.

Sunday brunch entrees include things like French toast with fresh peaches and raspberries, a "Shenandoah Valley Breakfast" (scrambled eggs and grilled rainbow trout or eggs and country ham), a club sub and fish and chips.

Special "Vintner's Dinners" are held four times a year. These events feature winemakers and winery owners whose wines are paired with specially planned and prepared food selections.

The Flint Hill Public House offers a tranquil setting in a warm, hospitable, historic building. And don't forget those two overnight guest rooms away from it all.

FLINT HILL
Four & Twenty Blackbirds

U.S. 522 / FLINT HILL, VA 22623
(540) 675-1111

Style	Fine dining
Meals	Dinner, Wednesday through Saturday; Sunday brunch. Reservations are recommended.
Price Range	Moderate
Superlatives	Creative cuisine
Extras	Full bar

This small 1910 building has served as a carpentry shop, a real-estate office, a beauty shop and a general

Four & Twenty Blackbirds

store. It is now home to a cozy restaurant with an unusual name.

According to Vinnie DeLuise, who has owned the restaurant with his wife, Heidi Morf, since 1990, the couple was brainstorming names related to birds and nature when Four & Twenty Blackbirds was mentioned. "It was catchy and easy to remember," he said. And so it is.

The color scheme is bold—purple, dark green and pink. Linens, candles and a delightful assortment of bright, fresh flowers adorn each table. Between the upstairs and downstairs dining areas, the restaurant can seat around 54. There are bird prints on the walls and a wonderful aquarium near the kitchen. The corncob salt shakers and blackbird pepper shakers add a touch of whimsy. Soft music contributes to an intimate country atmosphere that is neither stiff nor pretentious but rather comfortable and comforting.

Vinnie describes the cuisine as "New American with ethnic twists." The menu changes all the time, so most anything mentioned here won't be available when you visit, but should rather serve as an idea of the food at Four & Twenty Blackbirds.

One appetizer that has appeared from time to time is oysters baked with Southwestern chili sauce and topped with crispy cornbread and cheese. Another is a steamed vegetable and mushroom dumpling with Oriental ginger plum sauce. Another is broiled sea scallops and sage cheddar cheese puffs.

Among the entrees, you might find grilled swordfish marinated in coconut milk and lime and served with fresh pineapple-mango chutney. Veal chops stuffed with Italian cheeses, a spicy Thai seafood stew and lightly smoked grilled chicken with an apricot mustard glaze have also graced the menu.

The desserts are made from scratch. Homemade cookies are sometimes available, usually as an aside to something else, like "Lemon Crème Caramel" with fresh strawberries.

At Four & Twenty Blackbirds, the gentle countryside, the quaint small town and the attractive little building create a perfect backdrop for Heidi's culinary talents.

WARRENTON

The Depot

65 SOUTH STREET / WARRENTON, VA 20186
(540) 347-1212

Style	Casual nice
Meals	Lunch, Tuesday through Saturday; dinner, Tuesday through Sunday. The restaurant is closed on Monday year-round and on Sunday during July and August.
Price Range	Inexpensive/Moderate
Superlatives	"Mnazzaleh," "Stolen Orange Cake"
Extras	Full bar

The Depot

*K*nown as Fauquier Court House when it was founded in 1760, this community was renamed Warrenton in honor of Dr. Joseph Warren, a man who helped Paul Revere begin his famous ride and who later died at the Battle of Bunker Hill. Today, one of Warrenton's attractions is the Old Jail Museum, located in one of the oldest jails in Virginia. The museum houses an interesting collection of Indian, Revolutionary War and Civil War artifacts.

One of the town's dining attractions is The Depot. There's something appealingly nostalgic about old train depots. The original exterior of this depot is now an inside wall. Train pictures and memorabilia are tastefully arranged on narrow ledges and shelves. The cozy room to the left has a bar and some high tables with tall chairs. The dining area in the back is a solarium-style room with a fireplace. Another dining room has a hunt theme and a fireplace. Patio dining in nice weather brings the seating to just under 80. Rumor has it that a park with railroad cars and grassy areas is to be created on the back border of the property.

Owner Karen Dorbayan grew up in the restaurant business. Her father, Charles Saah, started the Iron Gate Inn in Washington, D.C., in the 1950s. Many of Karen's recipes came from him. She and her former husband opened The Depot in 1976 with a focus on Mediterranean-American cuisine.

There's no printed menu, but the large marker board can easily be transported to your table so you can peruse it to your heart's content.

Lunch items include Cajun black bean soup, a Middle Eastern garden salad, a curried breast of chicken salad, a vegetable omelet and sandwiches.

The Depot's signature dish, "Mnazzaleh," is sauteed eggplant with ground lamb, onions and pine nuts. Roasted eggplant with grilled tomato is also available. Lamb is another specialty here. You might try the shank of lamb or the ground lamb stuffed into cabbage rolls.

Baklawa (spelled *baklava* most other places) is one of The Depot's most popular desserts. It's a delightful pastry with a taste of walnuts. But I suggest you try the "Stolen Orange Cake," which is wonderful.

WARRENTON

Fantastico

251 LEE HIGHWAY / WARRENTON, VA 20186
(540) 349-2575

Style	Italian
Meals	Lunch, Monday through Friday; dinner, Monday through Saturday
Price Range	Moderate
Superlatives	Homemade pasta, veal
Extras	Full bar

The Oderda family moved to the United States from Turin, Italy, in the 1980s. The parents came first and the grown children followed.

In 1989, the family opened Fantastico in an upscale shopping center at the intersection of U.S. 17 and U.S. 211. In 1998, the restaurant will be moving to a large stone building on the other side of the intersection. Plans call for a piano bar and overnight guest rooms on the second floor. According to daughter Paola Oderda, restaurant hours will be expanded to include Sunday.

The most important thing, of course, is that the northern Italian cuisine moves with the family. The menu items appear in Italian with English descriptions below. Grilled polenta with roasted bell peppers in a garlic sauce is one of the hot appetizers. The arugula, radicchio and fennel salad with shaved Parmesan cheese and the *"Insalata Giulio Cesare"* salad with croutons and Caesar dressing are popular. A soup of the day is offered, as is a traditional Italian mixed vegetable soup.

The numerous pasta entrees feature a wide variety of sauces and stuffings. There's red clam sauce, white clam sauce, pesto sauce, wine sauce and rosemary sauce. The ravioli is stuffed with meat and spinach, the manicotti with ricotta cheese and spinach. The beef entrees number two, the chicken entrees three and the veal entrees more than half a dozen. It's all very Italian.

When I dined here, the Oderdas were experimenting with some delectable desserts imported from Italy but were unsure of their appeal in the United States. For the time being, tiramisu and other fine desserts

made on the premises are sure to satisfy the after-dinner sweet tooth.

Most of the wines are Italian, but there's also one from Virginia—Naked Mountain Chardonnay. Two champagnes are from France, one from California and one—Champagne Brut-Barboursville—from Virginia.

WARRENTON

Napoleon's

67 WATERLOO STREET / WARRENTON, VA 20186
(540) 347-4300

Style	Casual nice
Meals	Lunch and dinner, seven days a week
Price Range	Inexpensive/Moderate
Superlatives	"French Connection," daily specials
Extras	Full bar

After I enjoyed a delightful lunch of "French Connection" and "Mahi-Mahi Creole," owner Philip Harway proudly gave me a tour of the building. And proud he should be.

When Harway bought the property in 1977, it was chopped into five cheap apartments. He opened Napoleon's the following year. Today, it's a spiffy eatery with casual dining in a solarium setting on the ground level and a tablecloth restaurant in the house proper upstairs.

Built in the 1830s, the Greek Revival structure has been home to an attorney, a judge, an artist, a writer and a general who served in both houses of Congress. It's now white with red shutters. The terrace outside

Napoleon's

the solarium is outfitted with yellow-and-white-striped umbrellas, while the outdoor garden dining area has green umbrellas. In the booth section, the seats are burgundy and the formica tables are coral. The atmosphere downstairs is upbeat, cheerful and noisy. The quieter, more traditional dining room upstairs has pink walls, burgundy linens and stemware.

The "French Connection" is a croissant filled with ham, Swiss cheese and cream cheese, baked and served with fruit. The "Mahi-Mahi Creole" is sauteed with peppers and onions and served over rice. The lunch specials vary. They may include chicken Caesar salad or a kielbasa sub. A menu item that sounds especially appealing is the "Smoked Duck Salad"—a Belgian endive salad with smoked duck, strawberries and citrus dressing. A quiche of the day is always available.

Lamb steak au jus, Thai chicken and shrimp, lasagna, salmon with salsa and seafood fettuccine are some of the dinner entrees. The "Tournedos Napoleon" are

sauteed tenderloin medallions topped with Madeira sauce, carrots, scallions and mushrooms.

Actually, most everything on the menu sounded good, right through to the white chocolate mousse in a chocolate cup, the "Frozen Lemon Zing" with raspberry sauce, the chocolate walnut cake and other sweet endings.

Café Rochambeau

Café Rochambeau
310 COMMERCE STREET / OCCOQUAN, VA 22125
(703) 494-1165

Style	Casual nice
Meals	Breakfast, lunch and dinner, seven days a week
Price Range	Moderate
Superlatives	French onion soup, Caesar salad
Extras	Full bar

*T*his village's name comes from an Indian word meaning "at the end of the water." Before 1800, there were sawmills, gristmills, storehouses and homes here. More recent times have dealt the community some blows, however. In 1916, the town was crippled by a major fire. Shortly after that, U.S. 1 bypassed Occoquan. In 1972 came Hurricane Agnes. But thanks to the same kind of spirit shown by the pioneers who shaped this place, the townsfolk have since rallied to restore Occoquan's status as a place that is quaint, pretty, charming, interesting and fun.

Visiting Café Rochambeau gave me a déjà vu feeling for a restaurant I know in Niagara Falls, New York. Perhaps it was the slight knoll and the architecture. Perhaps it was the spectacular flowers and shrubs.

The atmosphere here is delightfully bright and cheerful. The tables have fresh flowers, a wine-bottle oil lamp, double linens, white lace place mats and teal napkins. The front dining room is a pale clay color with green and peach valances. The room behind it has pinkish peach walls with painted vines and herb bouquets. The dining area to the left of the entrance has more of a European flavor. Some of the watercolor art and limited-edition prints on the walls are for sale.

Annie Dayries, once an interpreter at the French embassy, opened Café Rochambeau on another street in town in the early 1990s. In 1995, she moved to this former schoolhouse, residence and retail shop.

The menus are in French, with English translations below. You can start your day with a breakfast of crepes stuffed with Virginia ham and cheese, an omelet, quiche or grilled ham and cheese on three layers of French toast.

A medley of entrees and sandwiches is offered at lunch. Grilled salmon, a grilled vegetable plate and fettuccine are among the entrees and ham and Brie, smoked breast of turkey and homemade chicken salad among the sandwiches.

The dinner appetizers are wonderful, especially *"Le Gravlax"* (paper-thin Norwegian salmon marinated in dill, peppercorns, brown sugar and salt) and *"Le Brie Fondue"* (baked with applesauce and walnuts). If you're fond of lettuce, you'll love the house salad with its seven different varieties. The seafood selections might be a salmon fillet, twin fillets of trout, shrimp in a bourbon sauce and scallops. The chicken entree comes with raspberry sauce. Veal, lamb and beef dishes round out the menu.

Among the many desserts are three fabulous cakes—chocolate mousse cake, raspberry mousse cake and "White Chocolate Lemon Silk Cake." The last one gave me no sense of déjà vu. I've never seen it on a menu anywhere else.

OCCOQUAN

Sea Sea & Co.

201 MILL STREET / OCCOQUAN, VA 22125
(703) 494-1365

Style	Family-style
Meals	Lunch, Monday through Saturday; dinner, seven days a week; Sunday brunch
Price Range	Moderate
Superlatives	Crab cakes, "Apple Walnut Crunch"
Extras	Full bar

ere's a large, bright restaurant overlooking the Occoquan River. The theme is nautical. Small nautical flags on strings decorate the ceiling beams. The interior is predominantly blue and white, with lots of natural wood. There's also dining at tables on the patio, where you practically become part of the waterfront. A bridge is to the right, boats crowd a marina to the left and sea gulls are everywhere. In short, there's no mistaking that this is a seafood restaurant.

Since each order is prepared individually, the management requests customers' patience if they have to wait a bit. As it says right on the menu, "We assure you—it will be worth it." And indeed it is.

The lunch specialties include baked baby coho salmon, a fried clam platter and oysters. Among the many salad plates are crab salad, chilled spicy shrimp salad and tuna salad. There's also a "Chicken Salad Supreme," a spinach salad and a chef's salad. If you'd prefer to try the chicken salad or one of the seafood salads in a sandwich, it will come with lettuce on a fresh croissant. Other sandwiches include a Reuben, hamburgers, cod and hot ham and Swiss, all of which are served with french fries.

You have to be 21 years of age or older to order the "Oyster Shooter," an appetizer of freshly shucked oysters floating in vodka. A raw bar sampler, crab soup, crab puffs and oysters on the half shell are some of the other appetizers. The house specialties at dinner are grilled shrimp salad, grilled chicken salad and surf and turf—filet mignon and lobster tail. Rainbow trout amandine, stuffed shrimp and Cajun catfish are but a few of the selections from the sea. Other en-

trees include barbecued baby back ribs and marinated chicken breast.

You may end your meal with Key lime pie, strawberry shortcake or peanut butter pie, but I urge you to have Sea Sea & Co.'s most popular dessert—hot "Apple Walnut Crunch" with ice cream.

Toby's Cafe

Toby's Cafe
201 UNION STREET / OCCOQUAN, VA 22125
(703) 494-1317

Style	Cafe
Meals	Breakfast and lunch, seven days a week year-round; dinner, seven days a week during spring, summer and fall
Price Range	Inexpensive/Moderate
Superlatives	Homemade soups, pastries

his cute little cafe is tucked into the corner of a courtyard. There are about nine tables for two in the front room and another seven in the side room, with some pushed together to make space for four patrons.

The wooden picnic tables in the brick courtyard are great for warm-weather cafe dining. An element of class is added by the music from Stringfellows Folk Music, located next door. The speakers are small, but the sound is lovely.

Dale Hamburg brought a varied background (including some serious restaurant experience) when he took over Toby's in the fall of 1996. He graduated from Indiana University of Pennsylvania. (It took some time for me to get that right. The campus is in the town of Indiana, Pennsylvania—which, incidentally, is the hometown of actor Jimmy Stewart.) Dale majored in education and was a special-education teacher for a while. Then he was a retail buyer, and then he put in 11 years with Marriott and a few with the Olive Garden chain. He's pretty happy now being self-employed and managing his own place.

For breakfast, you can get an omelet or French toast, or you can stick to the gourmet muffins, scones and croissants.

All the lunch sandwiches are served on freshly baked French bread and come with homemade slaw. You can choose from among open-faced egg, smoked turkey, roast beef and cheddar, a "BLT Nouvelle," "Toby's Club" and others.

Toby's signature soup is a black bean and rice. The pasta dishes are popular at dinner. Among them are spinach fettuccine and the pasta of the day, which may be served with Alfredo, Florentine Alfredo or marinara sauce or with fresh basil and garlic in olive oil.

Flavored coffees and iced teas are a specialty here. The selection reads like a list of ice cream flavors—almond, apple, blackberry, chocolate, chocolate mint, pineapple, vanilla, pistachio, lemon. There are more than two dozen in all. Toby's also offers latte, cappuccino, mocha, hot chocolate and hot tea.

There's entertainment in the courtyard most summer weekend evenings. Dale says all the shops in the courtyard work together to make it an appealing off-the-beaten-path place to visit and relax.

Town 'N' Country Restaurant

Town 'N' Country Restaurant

U.S. 29 / NEW BALTIMORE, VA 20187
(540) 347-3614

Style	Home-style
Meals	Breakfast, lunch and dinner, seven days a week
Price Range	Inexpensive/Moderate
Superlatives	Greek salads, steak sandwiches
Extras	Full bar

*T*he restaurant industry has one of the highest turnover rates of any business. On occasion, it reaches as high as 300 percent per year!

Not so at the Town 'N' Country, located in New Baltimore a few miles north of Warrenton. I chatted with Linda Johnson, who's been here 30 years. The salad cook has been on the job 22 years, another cook 17 years and one of the night cooks 17 years also. Linda says that the low turnover contributes to the restaurant's consistency in food preparation.

This is a down-home kind of place built in the 1940s. You'll note the pine paneling, the red booth seats and the oldies playing on the radio.

Breakfast is superlative. The sausage is made in the kitchen, as is the gravy. The home fries are cut from real potatoes right on the premises. Country ham, hot cakes, omelets, rib-eye steaks and grits are some of what's available.

At lunch, you can get a crab cake sandwich, a hot turkey sandwich, a roast beef sandwich, a tuna salad sandwich or a chicken salad sandwich. A popular choice is the steak sandwich, which comes with on-ion rings. There are four triple-decker sandwiches to choose from, among them the "Gladiator"—corned beef, pastrami, lettuce and tomato. One of the three "Waist Watcher" selections combines shrimp, cottage cheese, tomato, half a peach and half a pear on let-tuce. Onion soup and the soup du jour are homemade.

At dinner, the early-bird specials include prime rib, fish and chips, eggplant parmigiana, cheese ravioli, fried clams and New York strip steak. Among the fa-vorites on the regular dinner menu are meatloaf, grilled ham steak and roast beef. Lasagna, chicken

cordon bleu, shrimp parmigiana and veal cutlets are among the continental specialties.

It's hard to skip dessert when there are so many choices. Cheesecake, mousse cake, carrot cake, apple pie, meringue pies, cobblers, bread pudding, rice pudding and a reduced-fat cherry pie are some of the offerings.

Hammer's Supper Club
NEWGATE SHOPPING CENTER
U.S. 29 AND VA 28
CENTREVILLE, VA 22020
(703) 631-8545

Style	Fine dining
Meals	Lunch and dinner, Tuesday through Saturday
Price Range	Moderate/Expensive
Superlatives	"Lobster Crab Cakes," salmon
Extras	Full bar

There was a lot of Civil War activity around here—namely, the two Battles of Manassas, which took place in 1861 and 1862. The place was almost obliterated in the first battle. One lone Methodist church survived intact. It saw use as a hospital before succumbing during the second battle. Originally known as Newgate, the town was renamed Centreville in 1792 for its location midway between Arlington and Warrenton. It's still a major crossroads where U.S. 29 and Va. 28 intersect.

Tucked into the corner of a shopping center,

Hammer's Supper Club is definitely worth seeking out. The dining room is creatively done in aqua, black and white. The etched glass between the booths has a muted Southwestern design and is lit from underneath by narrow fluorescent bulbs. The tables have linens, little oil lamps and fresh flowers. The walls are soft gray stucco with brass sconces. One wall is adjacent to the attractive bar and another opens to the dance floor.

Appetizers, soups and salads are the same at lunch and dinner. The "Lobster Crab Cakes" are a house specialty. Some of the other appetizers are broiled clams, baked Brie and stuffed mushroom caps. Crab and corn chowder is the restaurant's signature soup. Among the salad selections are a grilled beef tenderloin salad and a spicy chicken salad.

The "Lobster Crab Cakes" are also available in a sandwich, served with jalapeño mayonnaise. The "Jazzy Turkey" sandwich has turkey, Swiss cheese, sauerkraut and Thousand Island dressing on marble rye bread. Burgers, a chicken club, half a rack of baby back ribs and meatloaf are also offered at lunch. The potato chips are homemade.

Prime rib is available on Friday and Saturday nights. On other nights, you can select from a menu that includes spiced pork tenderloin, seafood linguine, lobster ravioli, veal chops, fresh catch and other enticing entrees.

The desserts are made on the premises. Chocolate torte with raspberries and "Chocolate Fudge Cheesecake" might be among the choices.

The entertainment at Hammer's varies. On Wednesday evenings, a jazz guitarist plays. If you visit on Thursday, Friday or Saturday evening, you may find a group performing.

At Hammer's, the atmosphere is romantic and intimate and the food excellent.

CENTREVILLE

Shark Club Billiards & Cafe

NEWGATE SHOPPING CENTER
U.S. 29 AND VA 28
CENTREVILLE, VA 22020
(703) 266-1888

Style	Cafe
Meals	Lunch, Monday through Saturday; dinner, seven days a week; Sunday brunch
Price Range	Inexpensive/Moderate
Superlatives	Pork chops, crab cakes, "Amaretto Tiramisu"
Extras	Full bar

*M*ore square footage is dedicated to pool tables than to the cafe here. But rest assured that John Tsiaoushis and his co-owners know what they're doing with space allocation. They operated another Shark Club in Falls Church for more than two years before opening this one in February 1997.

There are 27 pool tables on both sides of the large bar that lies straight ahead as you enter. The most popular games played here are one-pocket, nineball and eightball. On the left are floor-to-ceiling cigar humidor lockers—oak boxes with brass locks that are available for rent for several hundred dollars per year. Each box contains humidified air for keeping cigars fresh and moist. On the right is the cafe, a large, bright room with a tile floor and lots of windows. The walls are brick and the ceilings have black and mahogany fans. The glass partition separating the dining area from the billiards room is etched with sharks.

Of all the appetizers, the "Tenderloin en Casserole" sounded the most interesting. It features sliced pork tenderloin marinated in fine herbs and spices, then sauteed in lemon butter and white wine, then served "en casserole" with pita wedges. Other appetizers include shrimp scampi, spinach and artichoke dip and potato skins. Homemade soup and "Firehouse Chili" are available every day. The chef's salad, grilled chicken salad and Greek salad are offered in small and regular sizes.

Greek, Italian, steak and cheese and veal cutlet subs are popular at lunch, as are crab cake sandwiches, corned beef and Swiss sandwiches, turkey sandwiches, London broil sandwiches and chicken sandwiches. And though the Shark Club isn't open during normal breakfast hours, late risers can get eggs and omelets until midafternoon.

Dinner features a tender 20 ounces of pork chops lightly seasoned and char-broiled. Steak and onions, filet mignon, stuffed flounder, surf and turf and other entrees are also served.

"Amaretto Tiramisu" is the Shark Club's signature dessert. Consult your server about what else is available, as the selections change frequently.

Backyard Steakhouse

13999 METROTECH DRIVE / CHANTILLY, VA 20151
(703) 802-6400

Style	Family-style
Meals	Lunch and dinner, seven days a week
Price Range	Moderate
Superlatives	"Chili Mignon," steaks, ribs
Extras	Full bar

*C*hantilly, a crossroads in Fairfax County, was named by a member of the famous Lee family of Westmoreland County. Richard Bland Lee, the first man from Northern Virginia elected to Congress, lived in the historic home called Sully from 1795 to 1842. When Sully was scheduled for demolition to make way for the construction of Dulles International Airport, residents of Chantilly went into action to save it. The estate is now managed by the Fairfax County Park Authority.

The Backyard Steakhouse opened in October 1996 in a corner of the little shopping strip known—appropriately enough—as Sully Place. It was recommended to me by the men at the Chevrolet dealership on the other side of U.S. 50. Perhaps it's no coincidence that Robby Qreitem, who owns the restaurant with his brother Freddy, happens to drive a Chevrolet Blazer. He also runs a pretty good place to eat.

The brothers have overlooked nothing in creating a comfortable place to dine. The walls are dark green, the trim and railings bright white and the tables and chairs mahogany. A bar is a few steps higher than the dining room and is separated from it by a wall and a glass partition. The napkins—even at lunch—are cloth.

There's something for everyone at the midday meal. Potato skins, "Jalapeño Poppers," steamed spiced shrimp, quesadillas and "Texas Toothpicks"—thinly sliced onions dipped in seasoned batter and flash-fried—are a few of the appetizers. "Backyard Chili," a California salad and a Caesar salad are also offered. You can get a traditional hamburger, a turkey burger or a veggie burger. The sandwiches include North Carolina barbecue, Maryland crab cake, an "Arizona Chicken BLT," Cajun catfish, a Reuben and prime rib. If you have a big appetite, you might opt for the Backyard's signature "Chili Mignon"—beef tips with black bean chili served over cornbread and topped with cheese, diced tomatoes, onions and avocado.

Some of the most popular dinner entrees are shrimp scampi, pork chops, baby back ribs and "Blueberry Fried Chicken."

You can finish any of this with "Bananas Foster" or "Strawberries Romanoff."

THE PLAINS

Fiddler's Green
VA 626 / THE PLAINS, VA 20198
(540) 253-7022

Style	Fine dining
Meals	Lunch and dinner, Tuesday through Sunday
Price Range	Moderate
Superlatives	Roasted chicken breast, grilled salmon salad
Extras	Full bar

*T*he center of The Plains can be loosely placed at the intersection of Va. 55 and Va. 626, where you'll find a few neat shops, one of them called "Mainly in The Plains." North of the intersection on Va. 626, the beautiful flowers along a fence belong to Fiddler's Green.

There's not a hint of the country store or the convenience store that operated here from 1880 until recent years. The barn beams and the hand-stenciled

Fiddler's Green

curtains and valances add a country touch. The elegant appointments include Thomas Moser chairs handcrafted in Maine, white linen napkins and sconces. There's a pub with a slate floor downstairs. Patrons can enjoy patio dining in a pretty, shaded setting.

Owner Richard Squires describes the food as New American cuisine. Special appetizers and entrees are featured each month. The special appetizers one recent month included chilled seafood gazpacho and roasted plum tomatoes with fresh pesto. Pork loin chops with Hawaiian-style marinade and homemade angel hair with Prince Edward Island mussels were among the special entrees that same month.

Sandwiches like smoked ham with Vermont white cheddar and grilled rib-eye with herb butter are available at lunch, as are entrees like grilled rainbow trout and pasta shells with ham, mushrooms and cheese.

One popular dinner entree is the roasted chicken breast with two mustards and toasted shallots. Among the others choices are a mixed grill of quail and duck, baked stuffed rainbow trout and veal chops with red wine and rosemary.

The pastry chef at Fiddler's Green makes all sorts of delicious desserts, like tiramisu and crème brûlée. The ice cream served with the à la mode desserts is made on the premises. It's not listed separately on the menu, but perhaps if you ask nicely, you might be able to have a small dish.

The Rail Stop

The Rail Stop

MAIN STREET / THE PLAINS, VA 22171
(540) 253-5644

Style	Family-style
Meals	Breakfast and lunch, seven days a week; dinner, Wednesday through Sunday
Price Range	Inexpensive/Moderate
Superlatives	Omelets, Reubens, crab cakes
Extras	Wine and beer

*T*he Rail Stop is not a rail stop, and never was. Rather, it's a cozy and inviting restaurant stop.

Kevin Whitener, the owner, moved to the area from Maryland in the 1970s. His philosophy when he started The Rail Stop in 1982 was practical: "If I'm going to go broke, I'll go when I'm young." And here he is, working behind the counter in his own place, serving all kinds of folks—some in suits, some with kids, some on shopping sprees, others just meeting friends or getting a good meal.

There are five stools at the counter in the back. The guys seated there—boots resting on a railroad rail—all knew Kevin and each other. Must have been regulars. The Rail Stop has lots of wood, train memorabilia, some watercolor paintings and very clean windows. A miniature train track runs around the room high on the wall.

The "Morning Express" sandwiches can be ordered on an English muffin, a kaiser roll or your choice of bread. The "Conductor's Specials" cover the basics—eggs, biscuits and gravy, Belgian waffles—and big-ticket items like smoked or grilled pork chops and Delmonico steak.

At lunch, you can get a burger, a hot dog or a sandwich of liverwurst, bologna, turkey, tuna salad, chicken salad, corned beef, grilled bacon or ham and cheese. You get one side dish with the grilled or fried chicken, the barbecue, the fried cod and the eight-ounce cheeseburger.

The Rail Stop is leased in the evenings to Tom Kee, whose dinner appetizers include such items as a skewer of grilled shrimp and chicken, an antipasto plate and smoked salmon on a potato cake. Two of the salads are a grilled sirloin salad and an arugula salad, which includes grilled onions, shaved Parmesan and lemon vinaigrette. Angel hair with seafood and tomato is one of the light entrees. Fusilli pasta with pesto, potatoes and green beans is another. The main entrees include a seafood of the day, sauteed jumbo

shrimp, grilled loin of pork or lamb, a New York strip steak and a vegetarian plate.

The desserts change with the seasons. You might find creative sweets like a "Lime Curd Tartlet" and "Fresh Mango Crisp" among the selections.

1763 Inn

UPPERVILLE

1763 Inn

U.S. 50 / UPPERVILLE, VA 20184
(800) 669-1763

Style	German-American
Meals	Lunch, Saturday and Sunday; dinner, Wednesday through Sunday
Price Range	Moderate/Expensive
Superlatives	Wiener schnitzel, sauerbraten, "Hot Love" dessert
Extras	Full bar

*U*pperville could be called "Horseville" for its beautiful horse farms. Most of the goings-on here involve horses. For example, the Annual Stable Tour is held the last weekend in May and the Upperville Colt and Horse Show the first week in June.

The name this magnificent old inn bears today recalls its origin well over two centuries ago. The original section of the main house was built in 1763. The inn sits on 50 acres of rolling land and forest.

Purchased in 1970 by Uta and Don Kirchner, the property has been renovated into an elegant country inn. You'll find Oriental rugs, fine art, oak tables and chairs and lots of small brass animals. The 1763 Inn is a refined country manor where comfort and a casual atmosphere prevail. There are several dining areas, some overlooking the grounds and the pond behind the house, others more intimate rooms. All are cozy and inviting.

Bratwurst and sauerbraten are served at both lunch and dinner. Greek salad with ham, a grilled vegetable salad, a "Chef's Special Omelet" and grilled chicken are some of the other lunch offerings.

The dinner appetizers include a prosciutto platter for two, baked Brie and Hungarian goulash soup. The entrees range from German dishes to poached salmon and filet mignon.

"Hot Love" is a dessert of vanilla ice cream with hot raspberry sauce. Or you can choose classic Black Forest cake or apple strudel.

For those who wish to stay overnight, there are guest rooms in the main house, in a duplex cottage, in a restored barn, in log cabins and in the carriage house. Factor in the lovely grounds and it all adds up to a superb getaway spot.

The Coach Stop

MIDDLEBURG

The Coach Stop
9 EAST WASHINGTON STREET
MIDDLEBURG, VA 22117
(703) 687-5515

Style	Home-style
Meals	Breakfast, lunch and dinner, seven days a week
Price Range	Moderate
Superlatives	Hamburgers, prime rib, pork loin
Extras	Full bar

*T*his town was originally called Chinn's Crossroads after a Mr. Chinn, who started the local tavern. The village was established in 1787 by Leven Powell, a lieutenant colonel in the Revolutionary War. Middleburg was eventually chosen as the name because of the town's location midway between Winchester and Alexandria. Fox hunting and steeplechasing have grown so popular around here since the turn of the 20th century that Middleburg is sometimes called "the Nation's Horse and Hunt Capital."

Michael Tate, a Middleburg native, started working at The Coach Stop when he was 15. He later went to Virginia Tech and majored in aerospace engineering, only to discover after three months on a job that he didn't care for it. His brother Mark majored in biology at Randolph-Macon and worked in sales for about 18 months. The two returned to Middleburg, bought The Coach Stop in 1988 and have never regretted it.

It's a popular, simple restaurant with stools at a counter along the left side, circular booths on the right wall and tables and chairs in the middle. Horse and hunt photos are on all the walls. A single rose on each table adds a touch of class.

In the morning, you can have fresh-squeezed orange juice, homemade sausage, fresh eggs, creamed chipped beef on homemade buttermilk biscuits, eggs Benedict or a "Horseman's Special"—two eggs, a couple slices of bacon, hash browns, toast, juice and coffee or tea.

Hummus is served as an appetizer at lunch and dinner. Cream of peanut soup is a regular item. Among the salads is a chicken salad, tuna salad and pasta salad platter. The vegetarian sandwich and the crab cakes on a toasted bun are two of the locals' favorites for lunch. Willard Scott of NBC's *Today* show has been to The Coach Stop more than once and has stated his opinion that the hamburgers served here are "the best." Side dishes for lunch include pan-fried apples, applesauce, corn pudding, mashed sweet potatoes and steamed rice.

According to Michael, an unusual choice that's surprisingly popular at dinner is the wild rice, orzo and lentils. The grilled portobello mushroom is another light entree. Tournedos of beef, roast turkey, Maryland-style crab cakes, broiled salmon, country ham, honey-dipped fried chicken and grilled center-cut pork chops with apple-currant chutney are some of the regular entrees. Almost any item here with turkey in it is guaranteed to be fresh and good. The chef cooks two fresh turkeys every day.

You can wind up your meal with blackberry, raspberry or strawberry pie. Or with bread pudding.

MIDDLEBURG

Magpie's Cafe

118 WEST WASHINGTON STREET
MIDDLEBURG, VA 20118
(540) 687-6443

Style	Cafe
Meals	Lunch and dinner, seven days a week
Price Range	Inexpensive/Moderate
Superlatives	Burgers, fresh fish, apple crisp
Extras	Full bar

*M*argaret MacMahon moved to Middleburg in the 1970s and holds a retail degree from Marymount College. She worked in a few restaurants before buying this yellow-and-white residence in 1984 and transforming it into a casual eatery on the east end of town.

Magpie's is really a cafe on the outside and a tavern

Magpie's Cafe

on the inside. Outside, it's a place to sit, relax, eat and watch the traffic go by. Inside, there's a bar to the left and tables straight ahead. It's dark and rustic. A small room to the right with lots of windows and a black-and-white-checked tile floor seats around 12. Another bar and more space are on the second floor.

The menu, which changes frequently, is handwritten on blackboards, which are propped up at the tables. Sandwiches and entrees are offered all day. The cold sandwiches might include chicken salad and tuna salad. Burgers and ham and Swiss might be among the hot sandwiches.

The lunch specials are things like chili dogs, chicken pasta salad, fish and chips and roast beef and Swiss.

Fresh fish, steaks and pasta dishes are popular at dinner. The evening specials include such items as grilled swordfish and cheese tortellini.

Children are welcome here. Their food is served on Frisbees.

And everyone—adults and kids alike—should save room for the homemade apple crisp à la mode.

Red Fox Inn

2 EAST WASHINGTON STREET
MIDDLEBURG, VA 20118
(800) 223-1728

Style	Fine dining
Meals	Breakfast, Saturday and Sunday; lunch, Monday through Saturday; dinner, seven days a week; Sunday brunch
Price Range	Moderate/Expensive
Superlatives	Peanut soup, crab cakes
Extras	Full bar

George Washington wasn't even born when this place opened as Mr. Chinn's Ordinary in 1728. The route in front went east to Alexandria and west to what was then the frontier town of Winchester. In 1812, the ordinary was remodeled and renamed the

Red Fox Inn

Beveridge House. It served as a Confederate hospital during the Civil War. Renamed the Middleburg Inn in 1887 and the Red Fox Inn half a century later, the property now includes three nearby historic buildings as well as the main structure.

The dining rooms are historically authentic—low ceilings, fieldstone walls, wooden beams, fireplaces, pierced-tin sconces. The tables have cloth napkins and candles.

Breakfast, served only on Saturday and Sunday, includes such items as a crabmeat omelet and sausage gravy and biscuits.

At Sunday brunch, you can get French toast, Belgian waffles and eggs Benedict. One of the favorite choices is "Eggs Chesapeake"—poached eggs with jumbo lump crabmeat and hollandaise sauce on an English muffin, served with home fries.

The lunch appetizers include crab and artichoke casserole. Among the popular sandwiches are a crab cake sandwich, the "Grilled Applewood Smoked Chicken Sandwich" and a grilled steak and onion pita. Fish and chips, grilled beef kabobs and a vegetable frittata are some of the entrees.

Grilled lamb chops, filet mignon, crab cakes and roasted baby chicken are among the evening options. Specials featuring fresh fish, fresh fowl and fresh beef are created every day by the culinary staff.

Patrons may reserve overnight accommodations in any of the four historic buildings. Fresh flowers, plush bathrobes and bedside sweets enhance the romantic atmosphere of the guest rooms.

Ice House Cafe

HERNDON

Ice House Cafe

760 ELDEN STREET / HERNDON, VA 20170
(703) 437-4500

Style	Casual nice
Meals	Lunch, Monday through Friday; dinner, Monday through Saturday
Price Range	Moderate
Superlatives	Fresh seafood, "Tournedos Baltimore"
Extras	Full bar

Located in Herndon, one of the fastest-growing communities in Virginia, the Ice House Cafe is in a 50-year-old building that was originally a law office. The cafe's tavern was a small barbershop before being joined to the larger building.

Established in 1979, the cafe was taken over by Alice Dai's family in 1991. Alice is the manager of operations. This is one family that knows restaurants. It also owns La Bonne Auberge in Great Falls and Santa Fe East in Old Town Alexandria.

The Ice House is a wonderful place with a historic feel. There are old photos on the walls and white linens, green cloth napkins and fresh carnations on the tables. Though there's seating for more than 100 patrons, the atmosphere is intimate. The patio behind the tavern was damaged in the harsh winter of 1995–96 but was redone with a dark green awning and new furniture in 1997. Patrons enjoy live jazz on weekends between 8 P.M. and midnight. And their pleasure is enhanced in knowing there's no cover charge.

Grilled hickory-smoked pork loin and the "Chesapeake Reuben" (with crabmeat, smoked ham, slaw, Swiss cheese and Thousand Island dressing) are two of the popular sandwiches at lunch. The entrees include beef stroganoff, fresh calf's liver and rainbow trout.

The dinner appetizers are an interesting mix of food styles—smoked Norwegian salmon, the "Saigon Spring Roll," a Southwestern flour tortilla pizza, oysters Rockefeller. The daily specials often feature one or two fresh seafood entrees—roasted monkfish topped with crabmeat, for example. The regular entrees include "Duckling à la Oriental," "Pork Loin à la Rome," "Trout à la Siam," Maryland lump crab cakes and "Tournedos Baltimore"—choice beef tenderloin served with Châteaubriand sauce.

The desserts are made in-house. They might include "Raspberry Chambourd Cheesecake" with crème anglaise and the "Chocolate Sheba," a walnut dessert with chocolate mousse and dark rum.

Leesburg Restaurant

9 SOUTH KING STREET
LEESBURG, VA 20176
(703) 777-3292

Style	Home-style
Meals	Breakfast and lunch, seven days a week; dinner, Wednesday through Saturday
Price Range	Inexpensive/Moderate
Superlatives	Peanut soup, meatloaf
Extras	Wine and beer

Originally called George Town for King George II, this community was renamed Leesburg to honor the Lee family. The place is steeped in history. If you've ever wondered where James Monroe was when he drew up the Monroe Doctrine, it was at Oak Hill, his residence in Leesburg. The town served as the temporary national capital during the War of 1812, when the Constitution and the Declaration of Independence were stored nearby. Today, Morven Park, the home of two Virginia governors and the location of the Museum of Hounds, Hunting and Carriages, is open to the public.

The Leesburg Restaurant was founded in 1865. According to Ward Brewer, who runs the restaurant for Danny Taylor, this was one of the first "real" res-

Leesburg Restaurant

taurants in the area—that is, a place where food, not liquor, was the main draw.

Danny is a certified public accountant. The previous owner approached him one day for advice on selling the restaurant. I don't know how much advice he got, but it's clear that the man didn't have to spend much time or effort selling his property, because Danny bought it. That was on November 1, 1995.

It's a small-town folksy kind of place, with stools, wooden booths and tables in a couple of rooms. Ward knows most of the customers by name. "We've got regulars and some in trouble," he joked, referring to the courthouse just down the street. "If we see someone in here with a man in a suit, he or she is probably in some sort of trouble."

The breakfast special includes two eggs, juice, bacon or sausage, home fries, toast and coffee or tea. Or you can order eggs Benedict, chipped beef, sausage gravy or a breakfast sandwich. But the most popular morning meals are the combination platters—hot cakes and eggs; French toast, eggs and bacon;

eggs with ham, hash browns and toast.

The peanut soup can be a lunch or dinner starter. And if you come on Thursday, you can get the restaurant's popular meatloaf.

The sandwiches served at lunch include a tuna melt, smoked turkey and cheese, burgers, steak and cheese, a Reuben and a BLT. The platters—among them hot roast beef with gravy and liver and onions—come with two side orders.

The dinner entrees include fried chicken, fillet of flounder, crab cakes, country ham steak and New York strip steak. These come with two side orders, a tossed salad and hot rolls.

Drop in if you're ever in Leesburg. You're sure to become one of the many people with whom Ward shares a smile and a laugh.

Lightfoot

13 NORTH KING STREET / LEESBURG, VA 20176
(703) 771-2233

Style	Casual nice
Meals	Lunch and dinner, Tuesday through Sunday
Price Range	Moderate
Superlatives	"Blue Ridge Spinach Salad," "Mocha Ya Ya"
Extras	Full bar

At the time of this writing, Lightfoot, a Leesburg favorite, was in the process of moving into a larger space around the corner on North King Street. It's a certainty that the atmosphere will be just as friendly and the food just as good as in the old spot.

Though she'd planned a career in food service, Ingrid Gustavson had no intention of operating a restaurant. After graduating from the Culinary Institute of America, she started a small catering business. As it grew, her sister Carrie helped deliver, set up and serve on her lunch hours and weekends. The sisters finally decided to try their hand at running a restaurant. They opened in 1993.

You'll find a "Day Menu" and a "Night Menu" at Lightfoot. The items change frequently.

The "Day Menu" features salads and sandwiches. Among the salads, the "Blue Ridge Spinach Salad" takes top billing. The California Caesar has the traditional makings, plus grilled chicken breast, Gulf shrimp and sun-dried tomatoes. The "Chinatown Salad" combines grilled chicken, crispy Chinese noodles, carrots, bean sprouts, water chestnuts, snow peas, scallions, fresh greens and peanut dressing. The "Groovy Meatloaf Sandwich" is meatloaf, tomato, onion, watercress and red Thai curry mayonnaise on a toasted baguette. The grilled eggplant sandwich comes open-faced on homemade herb bread.

The "Night Menu" appetizers might include smoked trout and potato cakes, fried green tomatoes and oysters served with two sauces. The light entrees include such things as "Shrimp Mediterranean Salad" and the "Lightfoot Burger." "Cowboy Marinated Roasted Boneless Half Chicken," salmon, and grilled New York strip steak might be among the regular entrees. One of the pasta entrees is "Carnival Pasta," which

teams fettuccine, grilled chicken, tomato, spinach, garlic, corn, bacon and herbs.

The desserts are generous in size and delicious to eat. The blackberry-apple crisp comes in the kind of dish you might use for cereal in the morning. The Key lime pie has a mound of whipped cream the size of a softball next to it. The house specialty, "Mocha Ya Ya," is a flourless chocolate torte.

Tuscarora Mill

Tuscarora Mill

203 HARRISON STREET SE
LEESBURG, VA 20175
(703) 771-9300

Style	Fine dining
Meals	Lunch and dinner, seven days a week
Price Range	Moderate/Expensive
Superlatives	Atmosphere, salmon, roasted rack of lamb
Extras	Full bar

The Tuscarora Mill became a "must" for this book when it was repeatedly recommended to me by people from Northern Virginia and Maryland.

The gristmill was constructed in 1899. After its days

as a mill were over, the building housed a general store until December 1984. The restaurant opened the following year.

You'll immediately notice the great wooden beams, which were needed to support as much as 300 tons of grain. Old belts and pulleys are still in evidence also. The restaurant boasts a tasteful decorating scheme with whimsical touches. Big globe-style street lamps are mounted on vertical beams. Quilts and tapestries hang high on the walls. Fresh flowers are on each table, and instrumental or classical music plays in the background. It's all inviting, rustic and elegant at the same time.

For starters, you might choose the gazpacho, the sampler of pâtés and terrines, crab and artichoke tortellini or sauteed calamari. The tossed salad has organic greens and a champagne vinaigrette. If you prefer, there's a traditional Caesar salad, a spinach salad, a summer tomato salad, an asparagus and crab salad and an avocado and mango salad.

Heart-healthy entrees include sauteed breast of chicken, rigatoni and grilled Atlantic salmon. Some of the entrees may be ordered as "Small Plates"—a littler portion for a lower price. Grilled filet mignon and roasted rack of lamb are among these. "Southwestern Vegetarian Stir-Fry," spicy beef with penne pasta and beer-battered soft-shell crabs are a few of the regular entrees. You might get roasted eggplant, scalloped potatoes or asparagus with your meal.

And you just might be lucky enough to find cheesecake and chocolate torte among the desserts, all of which are made in-house.

Purcellville Inn and Stonewall Pub

VA 7 / PURCELLVILLE, VA 22132
(540) 338-2075

Style	Fine dining/Pub
Meals	The inn serves lunch on Sunday and dinner Friday through Sunday; the pub serves lunch and dinner seven days a week
Price Range	Inexpensive/Moderate
Superlatives	Waitresses, mussels, "Buffalo Burgers"
Extras	Full bar

*H*ealthy people like to get on their bicycles in Alexandria and pedal 45 miles to Purcellville, dubbed "Everyone's Hometown." The town began taking shape because it was on the road between Leesburg and Winchester. Prosperity ensued when the railroad came in 1874. The bicycle path runs on the old railroad bed.

When you see the golf course on the southern side of Va. 7, slow down and look for the Purcellville Inn. It's located in the middle where you park for the driving range. The two-story beige building is nestled among oak and maple trees.

Built around 1915, this house became an inn in the 1930s and a restaurant a couple of decades later. Attilio Vidali, a native of Rome, Italy, came to the United States in 1978 and worked in Washington, D.C., restaurants for many years. In 1994, he purchased the Purcellville Inn.

The beautiful dining room on the main floor has dark green walls, white trim and draperies with a flowered print on dark green. The fireplace burns real wood. The rustic pub downstairs has mauve and green cloth napkins on dark green tables. There's room here for another 35 people. The patio out back has an eclectic mix of glass, wrought iron, plastic and wooden furniture. The pub menu is in effect on the patio.

The waitresses at the Purcellville Inn are exceptionally cordial, helpful, pleasant and knowledgeable. They'll be happy to recommend an appetizer like stuffed roasted peppers or pasta-wrapped scampi or a soup such as chilled cucumber or wild mushroom. An entree with an Italian twist is the "Caciucco"—a variety of seafoods in a lightly spiced tomato sauce. You can also get a "Veal Chop Milanese" or chicken stuffed with goat cheese and served with sun-dried tomato pesto sauce.

The Stonewall Pub is more casual. It offers burgers, sandwiches, soups, salads, pasta and entrees. Crème caramel is the pub's signature dessert, but Key lime pie, blackberry cobbler, chocolate cake and cheesecake are popular as well.

ROUND HILL

Round Hill Diner
VA 7 AND VA 719 / ROUND HILL, VA 20142
(540) 338-3663

Style	Cafe
Meals	Breakfast and lunch, seven days a week
Price Range	Inexpensive
Superlatives	Blueberry hot cakes, meatloaf

*F*or some reason, Round Hill just sounds like a small town, and indeed it is. The name comes from a local hill that was surveyed in 1725 and that later served as an observation point for both armies during the Civil War. The town was incorporated in 1900.

The Round Hill Diner is located in a little building just to the left of and slightly back from an Amoco station. Looking for a challenge, owner Joan Farris took over the fledgling cafe in 1992. She had worked for the previous owner and decided to venture out when the opportunity presented itself.

The small eatery seats around 40 and serves breakfast whenever it's open, except that hot cakes are not made after 1:30 P.M. Joan says that's because the grill needs time to cool before the place closes. "You can make a hamburger in a skillet then, but the temperature in a skillet is not right for hot cakes," she explained.

The blueberry hot cakes are mighty popular. You can also get bacon, eggs, omelets and other breakfast fare.

Pork barbecue, sandwiches and hamburgers hand-pattied on the premises are offered at lunch. The most popular of the daily specials is the meatloaf, served on Thursdays. Other specials include chicken cordon bleu and hot turkey and hot roast beef sandwiches.

All the soups—like vegetable beef and navy bean—and pies are homemade.

The Round Hill Diner is a small, simple place with old-fashioned country cooking.

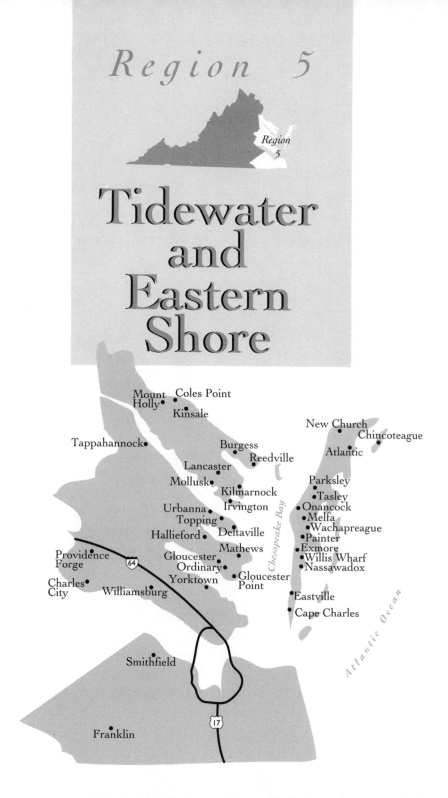

Region 5

Region 5

Tidewater and Eastern Shore

Mount Holly
Coles Point
Kinsale
Tappahannock
Burgess
Reedville
Lancaster
Mollusk
Kilmarnock
Irvington
Urbanna
Topping
Hallieford
Deltaville
Mathews
Providence Forge
Gloucester
Ordinary
Yorktown
Gloucester Point
Charles City
Williamsburg
Smithfield
Franklin

New Church
Chincoteague
Atlantic
Parksley
Tasley
Onancock
Melfa
Wachapreague
Painter
Exmore
Willis Wharf
Nassawadox
Eastville
Cape Charles

Chesapeake Bay

Atlantic Ocean

64

17

"Water, water everywhere" comes to mind in this part of Virginia.
So do the romance of sunsets, the taste of fresh fish and the
aroma of salt air. The land is flat and the small-town
people are sincere, wholesome and hardworking.

Much more farming is done here than you might expect. In some spots,
wheat fields stretch as far as the eye can see. And fishing is big business,
of course. This is also the leading tourist region in the state.
Quaint fishing villages, bed-and-breakfasts in renovated
historic homes, day and evening cruises and clamming and crabbing
adventures are all here to enjoy.

You don't have to go far to get off the beaten path on the Eastern Shore.
Water is never more than a few miles off either side of
U.S. 13, which serves as the beaten path in this area. More than a
dozen barrier islands under the administration of the Nature
Conservancy offer some of the most remote and most rewarding bird-
watching anywhere. And up and down the peninsulas
are little villages and restaurants that will entice you to visit,
if only for a weekend, a day or an hour.

Mount Holly Steamboat Inn

VA 202 / MOUNT HOLLY, VA 22524
(804) 472-3336

Style	Casual nice
Meals	Dinner, seven days a week; Sunday brunch
Price Range	Moderate/Expensive
Superlatives	Soft-shell crabs, Key lime pie
Extras	Full bar

*T*here really isn't a village of Mount Holly. The nearest town is Montross, four miles away. But it wouldn't be fair to say there's nothing here. There's a one-room brick post office. There's a farm-implement dealer occupying two corners of the intersection of Va. 202 and a county road. There's nearby Nomini Baptist Church, whose current brick sanctuary, built in 1858, replaced a meeting house erected in 1790. And until 1996, there was a combination gas station, convenience store and auto-repair place. But it blew up one day—something about fumes inside the building.

Mount Holly House, as Mount Holly Steamboat Inn was originally called, was built in 1876 to serve travelers and merchants on the Nomini Creek steamboat route to and from Washington, D.C. Manfred and Margie Soeffing moved from the Virgin Islands to take over the inn in 1990. Manfred, a native of Germany, once worked as a general contractor. Margie, originally from New York, had worked in a large hotel in the Virgin Islands, but her expertise was in accounting. They learned the innkeeping business as they went along.

As with many historical properties, there's always renovation going on here. The main dining room is bright and contemporary. The entire wall facing the water is glass. The furniture is rich-grained oak.

Dinner may start with mushroom caps stuffed with crab imperial or oysters and ham.

The seafood dinners include "Crab Norfolk," rockfish, stuffed rainbow trout, fried oysters, baked salmon, and soft-shell crabs, which are caught in the water right in front of the inn. On Saturday evenings, an extensive seafood buffet is featured. The house specialties are a deluxe seafood platter (lobster tail, a crab cake, shrimp, a soft-shell crab and fried oysters) and a combination of prime rib and crab legs. All entrees come with salad, dinner rolls, a twice-baked potato and the vegetable of the day.

The most popular dessert here is Key lime pie.

Sunday brunch is an all-you-can-eat buffet that includes poached salmon, spicy shrimp, baked ham, crab salad and many other things. The chef will prepare omelets and eggs to order as you watch.

Sailboats and motorboats are welcome here, though advance notice is required.

Driftwood

VA 612 / COLES POINT, VA 22442
(804) 472-3892

Style	Home-style
Meals	Lunch and dinner, Tuesday through Sunday

Price Range	Inexpensive/Moderate
Superlatives	Steaks, home-cooked vegetables
Extras	Full bar

One of the many small harbors in Westmoreland County, Coles Point sits on the southern side of the Potomac River at the tip of a peninsula and at the end of Va. 612. It's little surprise that two of the annual events at this village at the end of the land are a spring sailboat race and a rockfish tournament.

If you can read nautical flags, you'll see right away that those out front of this restaurant spell *Driftwood*. There's also a good-sized red and white sign on top of the building.

It's a small, square brick building with windows in the front. The carpeting is gray and burgundy, the tablecloths burgundy and the walls in the front dining room gray and white. The little back room has wood paneling. The place is so clean that a repairman once commented that it was the first time he hadn't felt the need to brush off his pants after lying on the floor to fix something.

In 1993, Spencer and Pam Standbridge bought the restaurant from Pam's parents, who'd started it 13 years earlier. It's very popular among locals. Pam says one reason is consistency.

At lunch, Spencer and Pam serve sandwiches, burgers, platters and fried fish, among other things.

At dinner, steaks, seafood and daily specials like lobster tail stuffed with crabmeat are featured.

The vegetables are all fresh and home cooked. People practically stand in line for them. The bread is baked on the premises, and all the desserts are homemade as well.

Driftwood is the type of place that emphasizes value. You pay a fair price for a good meal in impeccably clean surroundings. The friendly people are a free—and highly appreciated—bonus.

COLES POINT

Pilot's Wharf
COLES POINT PLANTATION / VA 612
COLES POINT, VA 22442
(804) 472-4761

Style	Family-style
Meals	Breakfast, Sunday; lunch and dinner, Thursday through Sunday. The restaurant may be open more days in the summer.
Price Range	Moderate/Expensive
Superlatives	Crabmeat, Caribbean entrees
Extras	Full bar

The Coles Point Plantation brochure describes the plantation as "a friendly family resort on the Potomac River near the Chesapeake Bay." It offers 130 boat slips, a full-service boatyard, a campground, fishing, biking and hiking trails, canoe rentals, cabins and the restaurant called the Pilot's Wharf.

To reach the restaurant by land, take Va. 202 off Va. 3, then turn onto Va. 612 and follow it to its end. If you're coming by water, find the Ragged Point Light. In layman's terms, turn right just after the light if you're coming from the north, or go left just before the light if you're coming from the south.

The fresh, bright restaurant has white tablecloths, royal-blue napkins and gray valances with ropes criss-crossing them. Every chair offers a view of the water.

Chef Robert Hayes has a rich background. He's worked in Italian, Cuban and Japanese restaurants—and even in a South Pacific Mexican restaurant with a French twist.

Sandwiches and burgers are the lunch fare. The popular "Spinnaker" is an open-faced steak sandwich on rye with horseradish mayonnaise.

Crab bisque is the house specialty among the appetizers, but you can also start your dinner with such items as spicy shrimp, fried mozzarella sticks and chicken wings. The salads include crab, shrimp, Caesar, crab and tomato and grilled chicken. The combination entrees include steak and shrimp, crab and steak and steak and lobster. Crab imperial, stuffed flounder, lobster tails and shrimp scampi are among the seafood choices. Grouper with sauteed fresh papaya is one of Robert's specialties. Another is swordfish baked and wrapped in banana leaves, served with mango chutney. Prime rib, New York strip steak, liver and onions, grilled chicken and other entrees are also offered.

Chocolate mousse cake, bread pudding with bourbon sauce and mud pie are some of the desserts.

The Mooring

The Mooring
PORT KINSALE MARINA / VA 203
KINSALE, VA 22488
(804) 472-2971

Style	Family-style
Meals	Lunch, Saturday and Sunday; dinner, Wednesday through Sunday. Call for winter schedule.
Price Range	Moderate
Superlatives	Crab cakes, rockfish, "Chocolate Tear"
Extras	Full bar

*E*stablished in 1706, Kinsale is the oldest port town on the Virginia side of the Potomac. It's named for an Irish seaport; the word may ultimately derive from the Gaelic term *Cean Saile*, meaning "head of the salt water." The community's history is preserved in the Kinsale Museum, an 18th-century building that previously served as a pub and a meat market.

The Mooring is located up Va. 203 off Va. 3. For

boaters, it's just one mile from the Potomac on the Yeocomico River.

The restaurant is leased by brothers Scott and Patrick Busby. They'd always hoped to work together, so when the opportunity to run The Mooring presented itself in early 1997, they jumped at it. Patrick is the chef. His wife, Louise, does the bookkeeping and works out front. Scott also helps out in front. Their friend Francis O'Dea, who prepares meals at the White House most of the year, lends a hand in the summer.

The dining areas are bright. There's a porch with red tables and a green floor. Near the bar is a dining room with orange plaid carpet, a stone fireplace and six tables with white linen napkins. The largest and most dramatic room is the large addition, which has glass on three sides and a bar in the center.

Lunch plates run the gamut from burgers, crab cakes and pork barbecue to grilled chicken salad and fried oysters. "The Busby" is a grilled and marinated chicken breast topped with Patrick's mustard sauce, Smithfield ham and melted provolone, served on a sourdough bun.

Seafood is featured at dinner. Jumbo lump crab cakes, grilled rockfish, fried oysters, catfish and a soft crab plate are among the options. Landlubbers might prefer the slow-roasted prime rib, which is accompanied by garlic mashed potatoes. The 14-ounce rib-eye steak is billed as "the finest cut known to man."

For dessert, you can order apple strudel with caramel sauce and ice cream, but seriously consider having the "Chocolate Tear." Shaped like a teardrop, it's a delicate chocolate mousse wrapped in a thin crust of dark chocolate and garnished with strawberry sauce. It's wonderful.

Lowery's

U.S. 17 AND U.S. 360
TAPPAHANNOCK, VA 22560
(804) 443-2800

Style	Family-style
Meals	Breakfast, lunch and dinner, every day except Christmas
Price Range	Inexpensive/Moderate
Superlatives	Local seafood, crab cakes, hot fudge cake
Extras	Wine and beer

*T*he town called Tappahannock lies on the river called the Rappahannock. The two names are variations on an Indian word meaning "on the rise and fall of water." Among the buildings in Tappahannock's 12-block historic district are the Scots Arms Tavern (built around 1680), the Ritchie House (built around 1706) and the Debtor's Prison (built before 1769).

A full parking lot and people waiting in line at a restaurant that seats more than 300 are sure signs that something is being done right. That's certainly the case with Lowery's, which has been feeding the Tappahannock crowd since 1938.

William Lowery III and his brother Robert now manage the restaurant started by their parents. William Lowery IV, affectionately known as "Duby," is the first member of the third generation to help run the business.

The decor is family-friendly. The paper place mats have a travel guide to the area that includes town history, distances to places like Baltimore and Williamsburg, local historic sites and a map of the original town grid.

To say the menu is comprehensive is an understatement. Breakfast options include eggs, corned beef hash, creamed chipped beef, waffles, hot cakes, steak and seafood options like oyster stew and a seafood omelet.

At lunch, the sandwiches range from burgers and barbecue to chicken, fish and rib-eye steak. You can also get an oyster burger or a crab burger. The lunch specials include things like a hot roast beef sandwich with mashed potatoes and gravy and chicken with mashed potatoes.

The dinner menu is several pages long. There are hot appetizers, cold appetizers and specialty appetizers. Listed under "Favorites" are broiled crab cakes, shrimp stuffed with crabmeat, a seafood platter and a half-pound of tenderloin. Such entrees as fried chicken and deviled crabs are listed under "Old Standbys." More than 20 seafood entrees and combinations are on the menu. Char-broiled steaks are available, as is a steak and seafood combination meal. There are also numerous listings for chef's suggestions, hot sandwiches, children's meals, salads and cold plates. If this isn't enough of a choice, there are specials on little pieces of paper clipped inside your menu.

More than a dozen desserts are offered—pies, hot fudge cake, peach cobbler, dessert of the day. If you don't have room right after your meal, you're welcome to buy a whole pie and take it home.

After you've been here, you'll understand why the parking lot is full and why so many people eat at Lowery's.

Horn Harbor House
HORN HARBOR HOUSE ROAD (VA 810)
BURGESS, VA 22432
(804) 453-3351

Style	Family-style
Meals	Dinner, Wednesday through Monday during summer and Friday through Sunday from March to Memorial Day and from Labor Day to Thanksgiving
Price Range	Moderate/Expensive
Superlative	Seafood bisque, seafood au gratin
Extras	Full bar

This is a cozy family restaurant tucked into a cove on the Great Wicomico River. If you're coming by road, follow the signs starting at the turn from U.S. 360 onto Va. 200 next to the bank in Burgess. In about a mile, you'll turn again at a Horn Harbor sign; continue to the last sign. By water, the restaurant is five miles from the Great Wicomico Light.

Buddy and Kathy Becker bought the property, which includes a campground and a small marina, in 1970 and opened the restaurant the following year. They're native Virginians, she from Orange and he from Richmond.

A couple of large fishtanks are right inside the entrance. The largest resident is about eight inches long. Kathy reaches in and pets it, which the fish seems to enjoy. The restaurant's interior is gray and brown. Windows overlook a narrow porch and the water beyond. The walls are decorated with an eclectic collection of birds, lanterns, buoys and old signs. "Lots of the things are stuff people have brought in," explained Kathy. The marlin, for example, was caught in the Bahamas. When the person who had it mounted actually received it, he found it was too large to put in his house. So he gave it to Horn Harbor House.

The restaurant can seat a couple hundred folks. Buddy and Kathy need that kind of room in the summer. "You can sit in the middle of the road in winter," according to Buddy. But that doesn't hold true in summer, when the local population increases about eightfold.

Seafood cocktails—shrimp cocktails, crabmeat cocktails, oyster cocktails—are popular appetizers here. You can also get oysters and clams on the half shell or steamed. The soups include seafood bisque and clam chowder. The bisque is one of Buddy's own recipes.

Sandwiches, pizza and spaghetti are offered. But the popular entrees, of course, are things like spiced steamed shrimp, regular steamed shrimp, stuffed shrimp, fried or broiled seafood platters, catch of the day and crab cakes. For a cool dish on a hot summer night, you might try the cold seafood sampler, which includes a crabmeat cocktail, steamed shrimp, spiced shrimp, clams and oysters. The house specialties are seafood au gratin and crabmeat au gratin. Like all the entrees, they come with a baked potato or french fries, slaw or the vegetable of the day and hush puppies or hot rolls.

You can follow any of this with pie, ice cream or cheesecake.

Elijah's

REEDVILLE
Elijah's
MAIN STREET / REEDVILLE, VA 22539
(804) 453-3621

Style	Casual nice
Meals	Lunch, Friday through Sunday; dinner, Wednesday through Sunday
Price Range	Inexpensive/Moderate
Superlatives	Roasted tenderloin, seafood, bread
Extras	Full bar

Without telephones, faxes and e-mail, word still traveled in the 1860s. When Elijah Reed of Maine heard that Chesapeake Bay was full of menhaden—a fish valued for its oil and used in fertilizer—he packed his ship, sailed south and opened a factory, which burned in 1873. The following year, he bought land on Windmill Point, later renamed Reed's Point. In

1888, his son, the postmaster, named the town Reedville in honor of his father. This charming waterfront town is noted for its "Millionaire's Row." Fishing magnates built fabulous homes here at the turn of the century. In fact, Reedville was known for a time as the richest town per capita in the country.

It took two tons of sand to sandblast the old walls and beams of Elijah's, a former mercantile store and later the first cannery in Virginia. "It was like a sand volleyball court inside," stated owner and chef Taylor Slaughter. "We shoveled it out the side windows and built the porch on top."

For Taylor, it was a labor of love. You see, his restaurant is named for Elijah Reed, who was his great-great-grandfather. And one of the owners of the old cannery—Blundon & Hinton, Inc.—was another of his great-great-grandfathers.

Taylor opened Elijah's in May 1996. He has more than history in his favor—namely, a degree in marketing and finance and a diploma from the Baltimore Culinary Institute.

The interior is mostly old wood accented with antique light fixtures. Labeled cans from the old cannery rest on shelves above the bar. Fresh flowers are on each table.

Taylor feels strongly about cooking with fresh herbs. In fact, he has three herb gardens from which to pick. His herbs add pizazz even to his chicken noodle soup.

Some of the favorites at lunch are the fried oyster sandwich, the grilled turkey sandwich with Brie and homemade chutney and the baked Virginia ham sandwich, all of which come with homemade potato chips.

Pasta dishes and grilled entrees are also offered.

Some of the evening appetizers are steamed mussels, chicken tenders and artichoke hearts with garlic sauce. Seafood bisque is a regular item. This is seafood country, so it's only natural to find baked salmon, broiled scallops and fried shrimp and oysters among the entrees. The "Fisherman's Penne" has sauteed tomato, onion, chives, basil, oregano and the seafood of the day, served over pasta. Among the casual dinners are beef stir-fry, chicken stir-fry, Cajun catfish, a steak sandwich and chicken pie. Specials include roasted tenderloin, trout stuffed with crabmeat and fried soft-shell crabs with tomato sauce.

The desserts are homemade. If you don't have room, I suggest you ask for one boxed and enjoy it later.

Conrad's Upper Deck

1947 ROCKY NECK ROAD / MOLLUSK, VA 22503
(804) 462-7400

Style	Family-style
Meals	Dinner, Friday and Saturday from March through November
Price Range	Inexpensive/Moderate
Superlatives	View, seafood
Extras	Full bar

*I*solated at the end of a back road on the Rappahannock River and Greenvale Creek, Conrad's Upper Deck is no secret to Lancaster County residents and regular visitors to the Northern Neck. They flock here by car, van, motor home, pickup and powerboat, parking in the oyster-shell lot or tying up at the bulkhead. Conrad's is easy to find from River Road (Va. 354) at Mollusk. Just turn onto Rocky Neck Road and drive two miles to the end.

The place is a special treat, since it's open only two nights, and then only for part of the year. It seats 110 in two dining rooms and is especially popular for birthdays. Make sure you bring cash, since Conrad's does not accept credit cards.

The restaurant sits atop E. J. Conrad & Sons, a wholesale seafood operation that has been in business since 1935. Milton Conrad bought the business from his father in 1972 and opened the restaurant in the early 1980s.

Conrad's features an all-you-can-eat buffet of steamed shrimp, fried scallops, oysters, clams, crab balls, baked fish, ribs, fried chicken, corn on the cob, vegetables and hush puppies. The piping-hot clam chowder is excellent.

You can also order off the menu. The menu selections are generous and include two vegetables or a trip to the salad bar. Some popular entrees are the seafood platter, fried flounder stuffed with crabmeat, two pounds of snow crab legs, and the "Pick Three"— your choice of three from among oysters, fish, popcorn shrimp, scallops, clams strips and crab balls. Beef and chicken entrees are also on the menu, as is a selection of foods for children under six—burgers, fries, chicken tenders.

Local patrons claim never to have room for dessert. Still, you'll sometimes catch them succumbing to a slice of Gale Conrad's homemade German chocolate pie.

Lancaster Tavern
8373 MARY BALL ROAD / LANCASTER, VA 22503
(804) 462-5941

Style	Family-style
Meals	Lunch, Thursday through Sunday; dinner, Thursday through Saturday
Price Range	Inexpensive
Superlatives	Old-style family dining in a colonial atmosphere

*E*xcept for the small, painted sign over the front door—*Lancaster Tavern 1790*—the weathered, brown clapboard building could be mistaken for the private home it used to be. It's across from the Mary Ball Museum on Mary Ball Road (Va. 3), the main thoroughfare through Lancaster.

The former tavern has been operated as a restaurant for more than 15 years, first by Ann Carter and now by her daughter, Linda Grigsby. Ann still helps out.

Most of the 200-year-old building is said to be original, down to the pine-plank floors. Up to 20 guests can be seated at four tables in assorted mahogany and pine chairs. Other furnishings include an 1810 dresser, a vintage piano, a copy of the famous Gilbert Stuart portrait of George Washington and an old Singer sewing machine that serves as the cash drawer. A local woman sometimes plays the harp on Sunday.

The Lancaster Tavern features home cooking served family-style. There's no menu. You just sit down and the ladies start bringing out the "cuisine du jour." It's all you can eat for one fixed price. Chicken and dumplings are served every Thursday. On other nights, it's anybody's guess—perhaps homemade vegetable soup, roast beef, sliced turkey, peas, broccoli, glazed carrots, boiled potatoes, green beans, corn, beets and applesauce. Everything comes with coffee or tea and dinner rolls. Dessert might be spice cake with raisins or white cake with chocolate icing—or something else entirely.

Don't worry about leaving the Lancaster Tavern hungry. The platters and bowls keep on coming until you say stop. Then the ladies bring out dessert.

Chesapeake Cafe

KILMARNOCK

Chesapeake Cafe

652 NORTH MAIN STREET (VA 3)
KILMARNOCK, VA 22482
(804) 435-3250

Style	Casual nice
Meals	Breakfast, lunch and dinner, Monday through Saturday
Price Range	Inexpensive/Moderate
Superlatives	"Oyster and Crawfish Pie," bread pudding
Extras	Full bar

*T*here's no mistaking that this town's name is Scottish. It's said that in the fourth century, an Irish missionary named Marnoc established a church, or *kil*,

in Scotland—thus Kilmarnock. How the name made its way to this part of Virginia is even less certain.

Traveling north on Va. 3 from downtown, you may think you've missed the Chesapeake Cafe, but look for the stained cedar building with the brown-and-white-striped awning on your right.

The plain exterior doesn't do justice to the fine interior. It's understated, classy and exceptionally neat and clean. Fine prints adorn the walls. The dining areas are nicely partitioned on different levels; it's a step or two up or down from one to another. Located in the back is the Angler's Cove Lounge, where there's a sign that reads, "If you are grouchy, irritable or mean, there is a 10 percent charge for putting up with you."

In the morning, you can get eggs prepared the way you want them, omelets, eggs Benedict, steak, corned beef hash, buttermilk pancakes, French toast, pastries, biscuits, cereal, cottage fries, grits and other items.

You can eat your lunch on the premises or carry it

out. Crab soup, French onion soup and a soup du jour are offered, as are several salads and a cold-plate sampler. The sandwiches come on multigrain bread, French bread, toast or a croissant. Grilled items like burgers and Philly cheese steaks come with french fries.

You can begin your evening meal with an appetizer, soup, a dinner salad or a large salad. There are several choices in each category. Seafood is the specialty here, as you'll note from the menu. A seafood platter, yellowfin tuna and baked Atlantic salmon are among the entrees. Several chef's specials—like the Chesapeake Cafe's signature "Oyster and Crawfish Pie," "Curry Crab Napoleon" and pasta dishes—are offered each night. The latter might be mussels and pesto or another interesting variation. A few light dinners and sandwiches are offered, as are ribs, pork chops, filet mignon and marinated chicken breast.

The desserts change daily. The bread pudding is a popular favorite.

The Crab Shack

PAINTER POINT ROAD / KILMARNOCK, VA 22482
(804) 435-2700

Style	Cafe
Meals	Lunch and dinner, Tuesday through Sunday
Price Range	Moderate
Superlatives	Setting, crab soup
Extras	Full bar

*T*hough this is one of the neatest places in the state,

I knew nothing of it until I saw the sign on Va. 200 north of Kilmarnock. You turn onto Bluff Point Road and go 3.2 miles, then turn right on Painter Point Road and follow it about another mile to where it ends. For those coming by water, The Crab Shack is on Indian Creek at red marker number eight. It has a deepwater dock and a bulkhead with gas and diesel fuel.

It's cute, colorful and clean, and the view over Indian Creek is spectacular. The wooden patio on the shore has an outdoor bar and four tables with umbrellas. It's surrounded by attractive ornamental grasses and perennials. As for the building itself, it's a shack in name only. The bar sports a grass overhang, like those Caribbean places. The tablecloths are a bright print of little fish and seashells. Each table has fresh flowers in a small Perrier bottle. Two sides of the little building are glass.

Of course, crab is the mainstay here. There's crab soup, crab dip, crab nachos, crab salad, a crab sandwich, crab ravioli, crab cakes and crab clusters. The steamed mussels, clams and shrimp—popular at lunch—come with corn on the cob and new potatoes.

The dinner starters might include barbecued shrimp and crab dip with French bread. Several salads are offered. The seafood entrees are the most popular, of course, but there are a few choices for landlubbers as well.

The desserts include Key lime pie, "Chocolate Mousse Gâteau," homemade ice cream and other sweet specialties.

Speaking of sweet, this is a sweet place with happy people and a very calming atmosphere.

Lee's

Lee's

34 MAIN STREET / KILMARNOCK, VA 22482
(804) 435-1255

Style	Home-style
Meals	Breakfast, lunch and dinner, Monday through Saturday
Price Range	Inexpensive
Superlatives	Fried shrimp, fried chicken, homemade pies

*T*his is a classic family business. Brothers Bill and Jerry Lee operate it with brother-in-law Steve Smith. The brothers' father, Foster Lee, bought it in the 1940s from his father, who opened it in 1939.

It's clean and simple. The booth benches, drapes and carpets are bluish green. There's pine paneling on the bottom half of the walls and white stucco on the top. A wonderful sailing mural—purportedly painted by an Indian fellow for a six-pack of beer—fills one wall.

Two of the breakfast specials—appropriately dubbed "Special No. 1" and "Special No. 2"—are, respectively, a ham omelet and a cheese omelet, either of which comes with juice, grits, toast and cof-

fee. Eggs, pancakes, breakfast meats, cereal, oatmeal, biscuits with hot apple butter and juices are also available.

Sandwiches, burgers, tuna salad, chicken salad, crab cakes, oyster cakes and chicken croquettes are among the offerings at lunch.

Dinner comes with two vegetables and rolls. You'll note that the word *vegetables* is in quotes on the menu, presumably because the list includes macaroni and cheese and applesauce as well as pickled beets, stewed tomatoes, slaw, mashed potatoes and other things. Most of the entrees are seafood dishes—crab cakes, oysters, fried scallops, broiled scallops and trout. Hamburgers, pepper steak, beef liver and chopped beef are also available. The fried chicken and fried shrimp are the most popular choices among the locals.

And the homemade pies are good enough reason for coming in all by themselves. Coconut cream pie, pineapple cream pie, sweet potato pie and apple pie are some of the favorites.

Royal Stewart Dining Room

TIDES LODGE RESORT AND COUNTRY CLUB
VA 709 / IRVINGTON, VA 22480
(800) 248-4337

Style	Resort
Meals	Breakfast and dinner, seven days a week
Price Range	Moderate
Superlatives	Prime rib, rack of lamb, veal chops
Extras	Full bar

Entrance to The Tides Lodge, location of the Royal Stewart Dining Room

*I*rvington is a neat, tidy town of well-kept homes, shops and yards. One of its historic sites is Christ Church, completed in 1735 and unchanged since. The old church has a three-tiered pulpit and high-backed pews.

If you fail to catch the Scottish theme when you read this restaurant's brochure (which has a plaid border) or when you turn onto St. Andrews Lane, you'll feel it the minute you step into the Royal Stewart Dining Room. The carpet is red plaid, and the waitresses wear red plaid kilts and sashes.

Large, round wrought-iron chandeliers, tan walls, cream linens and pewter salt and pepper shakers contribute to an air of casual elegance. A solarium-style dining area on one side overlooks the manicured grounds and the water beyond.

E. A. Stephens, Jr., the owner, was seven years old when his parents built the Tides Inn a few miles from here. They lived on the other side of town (which, once you've been to Irvington, you'll realize is a whole mile or so away). Thus, Stephens grew up in the hospitality business. He's the man responsible for building the Tides Lodge and its Royal Stewart Dining Room in 1969.

It will be a long time before Stephens runs out of food ideas. He collects menus. In fact, he boasts cabinets full of them. When it's time for a change, he just peruses his vast collection for possibilities.

A breakfast buffet is strategically stationed so you'll walk by it when being seated. If you choose to go à la carte, you can order eggs as you like them, egg alternative if you need it, pancakes, Belgian waffles, bacon, sausage, home fries, fresh fruit and pastries.

At dinner, the appetizers include mixed smoked seafood on lettuce, an artichoke fritter with curry sauce and a baked blue crab puff. Cheese soup and corn chowder with Smithfield ham are among the soups. There are two dinner menus — one for weekdays and one for weekends. The main difference is prime rib, which is offered on weekends. According to Stephens, a railroad chef taught the staff how to make it right. And he raves about his favorite, the rack of lamb. "The veal chop is also excellent," he says. There are more than half a dozen other entrees.

Pastries or a sundae can finish your dinner. But the focus here is on flavored coffees — French vanilla, orange brandy, chocolate raspberry, hazelnut, cinnamon and others.

Other eating options at the Tides Lodge include the Binnacle Restaurant (which overlooks the water and the marina), the Inn View Cafe, an ice cream parlor and a sandwich bar.

The Tides Lodge is a four-diamond resort, and tasteful attire is requested. Slacks and dress shirts are appropriate in the Royal Stewart. Jackets are not required at dinner but are commonly worn, with or without a tie.

The Inn

The Inn

250 VIRGINIA STREET / URBANNA, VA 23175
(888) 758-4852

Style	Casual nice
Meals	Breakfast, Saturday and Sunday; lunch and dinner, seven days a week
Price Range	Inexpensive/Moderate
Superlatives	Fresh seafood, chef's specials
Extras	Full bar

A small harbor community, Urbanna is one of only four remaining towns of the 19 ordered built by the House of Burgesses in 1680. It has long been an active port for shipping tobacco, trading fish and welcoming cruisers. Today, the town is noted for its annual Oyster Festival.

If you had three guesses to try to determine what The Inn used to be, it's not likely you'd get the right answer. Now a cozy, contemporary dining establishment with guest rooms in a rear building, the facility was a Coca-Cola bottling plant in the early 1960s.

Robert Harwell and Lora Rudisill came to Urbanna by water a few times on their 31-foot boat, the *Southern Exposure*. Seeking an opportunity to work together, the pair purchased the inn in the summer of 1996 and opened in October after major renovations.

The three dining rooms have white linens, black chairs and small oil candles. An outdoor brick patio is screened by wisteria vines and has a bar. There's another bar in one of the dining rooms and a raw bar in the back of the building.

The Inn serves breakfast on Saturday and Sunday mornings. Its signature breakfast dish is the "Urbanna Egg Blossom," which has eggs, spinach, shrimp and mixed cheeses in a pastry that looks like a flower blossom. Items like French toast and eggs Benedict are also offered.

The raw bar is a popular spot at lunchtime. The appetizers served at lunch include "Catfish Bites" and "Captain's Wings." Soups and salads are offered, as are sandwiches and seafood platters. Steamed shrimp, oysters, clams and crab legs are popular items.

You can begin your dinner with an appetizer like warm Brie, oysters on the half shell or "Urbanna Pot Pie"—smoked ham, mushrooms and sweet oysters in phyllo. The "Virginia Street Salad" teams mixed greens and melted Brie with kiwi, toasted almonds and vinaigrette. All entrees are accompanied by a salad, homemade bread, fresh vegetables and potatoes or rice. Surf and turf, broiled scallops, poached salmon and fried oysters are some of the entrees. Among the popular choices are the chef's specials, which may include pork and beef dishes as well as seafood entrees. The chicken and beef options include chicken Marsala and filet mignon. There are also pasta entrees each evening.

The homemade desserts change with the availability of fresh berries and fruit.

Virginia Street Cafe

VIRGINIA AND PEARL STREETS
URBANNA, VA 23175
(804) 758-3798

Style	Home-style
Meals	Breakfast, lunch and dinner, seven days a week
Price Range	Inexpensive/Moderate
Superlatives	Clam chowder, raisin bread pudding
Extras	Full bar

*O*nce a five-and-dime store, the space where the Virginia Street Cafe is located had to be completely renovated before the cafe's opening in 1989.

Like many restaurant owners, J. J. Wade says the place feels like a second home—sometimes even a first home. The Virginia Street Cafe is one large room with pine partitions about four feet high and several inches wide with real plants in them. The walls are cream,

and the chairs have striped seats and cane backs. The maple floor is the original.

Eggs, omelets, hot cakes and French toast are on the breakfast menu. The eight "Club Breakfasts" are complete meals that include juice and coffee.

From barbecue and chicken fillet to filet mignon and a combo club, you'll find most any sandwich you could want on the lunch menu. The soft-shell crab sandwich is available only in season, but the crab cake sandwich and the oyster sandwich are offered most of the year. Among the subs are a meatloaf sub, a rib-eye sub and a Polish sausage sub. The lunch platters—hot turkey sandwich, deviled crab, fried trout and others—come with some combination of mashed potatoes, french fries, hush puppies, potato salad and slaw.

A popular item at dinner is the clam chowder, made from a house recipe that has neither milk nor tomatoes in it. Oyster stew and chili are also available. The seafood entrees include salmon, trout, crab cakes,

Virginia Street Cafe

shrimp, scallops, oysters and clam strips. Beef liver and onions, meatloaf, New York strip steak, prime rib, chicken livers, pork chops, ham steaks, fried chicken and baby back ribs are also offered.

J. J.'s raisin bread pudding is made from scratch and is the most popular dessert she offers. She prepares strawberry shortcake and a variety of other berry desserts in season.

Eckhard's

VA 3 / TOPPING, VA 23169
(804) 758-4060

Style	German
Meals	Lunch, Sunday; dinner, Wednesday through Sunday
Price Range	Moderate
Superlatives	"Oysters Florentine," Jäger schnitzel
Extras	Full bar

*M*any people spend decades looking forward to retirement, only to discover it's not quite busy enough to suit them. Such was the case with Eckhard Thalwitz. He and his wife, Bruni, started The Bavarian Chef north of Charlottesville in 1973, then started The Little Chef up the road. They retired more than 10 years later and moved to the eastern part of the state. On the way home from what Eckhard calls "a boring trip to Florida" in 1995, they saw a For Sale sign on a building they'd often thought should be something other than a convenience store. They wrote down the phone number, continued home, made a

phone call, put in an offer even though two others were already in the works—and promptly became unretired.

If you're driving north, Eckhard's is on the right side of the road on a curve just before the bridge to Irvington and Kilmarnock. The interior has been renovated with a pleasing mix of navy blue, pink, white and cream. The tables have double linens in pink and white and a fresh pink carnation. The carpet is navy blue with pink roses.

"Oysters Florentine," fried calamari and smoked trout are some of the appetizers. The soups include lobster and shrimp bisque, wild mushroom and a Hungarian goulash soup.

German food is the specialty here. Eckhard trained

Eckhard's

in some of the finest hotels of Europe before moving to the United States in 1961. Jäger schnitzel is a popular dish of veal medallions topped with mushrooms, bacon and crème fraîche. The bratwurst sampler features three types of sausage, sauerkraut and mashed potatoes. Paprika goulash, sauerbraten, Wiener schnitzel and Mandel schnitzel are some of the other entrees.

American options include char-broiled filet mignon, roasted lamb shank, salmon au gratin and mountain trout.

Although Black Forest cake isn't on the menu, it's often available. German apple torte, bread pudding with bourbon sauce and a "Bavarian Nut Ice Cream Ball" are among the other sweets.

DELTAVILLE

Galley

U.S. 33 / DELTAVILLE, VA 23043
(804) 776-6040

Style	Family-style
Meals	Lunch and dinner, seven days a week
Price Range	Inexpensive/Moderate
Superlatives	Barbecue, crab cakes
Extras	Full bar

*N*amed for its position in the delta of the Rappahannock River, this little town was originally called Unionville for two churches that united here. However, during the days of secession, local residents did not want to be affiliated in any way with the Union, so they renamed their community Deltaville.

The Galley opened in this wooden building in 1992. Judging by the number of cars outside and the cheerfulness of the folks inside, I surmised right away that this is a popular spot to get a bite to eat. In fact, I underestimated the number of patrons when I looked at the cars in the parking lot, not knowing that the Galley provides shuttle service to people docking at local marinas.

You step into a small bar area at the entrance. To the left is the dining room, which has barnboard and cream walls with watercolor paintings on them. Little oil lamps are on the tables.

The lunch specials include the catch of the day and country-fried steak. The Galley serves the sandwiches you'd expect (ham and cheese, tuna salad, chicken salad) and some you probably wouldn't, like a trout sandwich and grilled tuna steak on a bun. Appetizers, soups, salads and side orders are also available.

At dinner, the seafood entrees are served oven-roasted, seared or beer-battered, and there are lots of choices. The lobster tail comes at market price, as does surf and turf and the catch of the day. There's also a nice selection of pasta dishes, chicken, barbecue, beef and ribs.

All the desserts are homemade.

If you're on the go, you'll be happy to learn that the entire menu is available for takeout. The Galley's barbecue sauce, billed as "World Famous," is also for sale.

Red Sky

U.S. 33 AND COUNTY ROAD 1102
DELTAVILLE, VA 23043
(804) 776-6913

Style	Casual nice
Meals	Dinner, Tuesday through Sunday in summer and Wednesday through Saturday in winter
Price Range	Moderate
Superlatives	Quesadillas, oysters Rockefeller
Extras	Full bar

*I*n a twist on the traditional saying, "Red sky at night, sailor's delight," Chris Rhodes likes to proclaim, "Red Sky at night, diner's delight." He and his wife, Michelle, opened this restaurant in July 1993.

Inside, you'll find bright red linens, little white lights and oil lamps. Gentle rock music plays in the background.

Red Sky has a good reputation both near and far. The menu changes daily, and there are always nightly specials.

The quesadillas are popular appetizers. Other choices might be sauteed escargots, oysters Rockefeller and French puff pastry stuffed with Chesapeake Bay blue crab. The soups might be cream of potato and "Southwestern-Style Seafood Ambrosia." Sometimes, a Greek salad is offered. Or you might get to select a Caesar or a pan-seared tuna Caesar.

Chef Walter Wilkes uses innovative combinations to create interesting nightly specials. One possibility is "Grilled Tuna Veracruz" over linguine, topped with a savory sauce of tomato, peppers and onions. Another is baked monkfish in a puff pastry with Canadian bacon, cheese and a Cajun Bearnaise sauce. Other entrees include herb-roasted pork tenderloin and baked flounder stuffed with crab imperial. A combination of catfish and crayfish tails in a lobster cream sauce is among the sauteed dishes, as is chicken piccata in a Chardonnay and butter sauce.

The homemade desserts change frequently. Bread pudding, "Coconut Rum Flan" and strawberry shortcake are some of the choices.

If you're in the area at lunch, consider stopping at Chris Rhodes's other eating spot, the Steamboat Grill at Piankatank River Golf Club in Hartfield. Though Chesapeake Bay seafood is featured there, the cuisine is broad enough to satisfy landlubbers as well.

Sandpiper Reef at Misti Cove

VA 632 (GODFREY BAY ROAD)
HALLIEFORD, VA 23068
(804) 725-3331

Style	Casual nice
Meals	Lunch, Sunday; dinner, Thursday through Saturday
Price Range	Moderate
Superlatives	Salmon, prime rib
Extras	Full bar

*W*hen you arrive at the end of Va. 632, you'll be in a small community that looks and feels like a summer camp. The building that houses Sandpiper Reef at Misti Cove—a low, gray structure with cream trim and a big screened porch—is reminiscent of a dining hall. Actually, this place was once a church camp for girls.

The restaurant's exterior gives little hint of what's inside. It's all dressed up with pink and white linens, comfortable chairs and candles on the tables. Piano music plays in the background.

Paul and Jesse Christie bought the business in 1991. Paul is a former automobile dealer. Their motto is simply, "Good food and good service." And they deliver on both counts.

You can lead off your dinner with seafood bisque, potato wedges, a house salad, crab balls, stuffed mushrooms or beer-battered onion rings.

Among the seafood entrees are broiled flounder, a seafood platter, stuffed shrimp, fillet of salmon and fresh crab cakes. There's a vegetarian entree each day. The "Reef and Beef Kabob" is composed of shrimp, scallops, beef tenderloin and grilled vegetables. Delmonico steak, filet mignon, pork chops, chicken and barbecued ribs are among the other options. Prime rib is served on Friday and Saturday nights. If you're in a more casual mood, you can get chopped sirloin, a burger, a crab cake sandwich or a grilled chicken sandwich. The casual meals come with french fries and slaw. The sandwiches are served on homemade rolls.

This isn't a place to hurry, so leave time and room for one of the fine homemade desserts—Key lime pie, chocolate silk pie, rum cake, bread pudding,

"Piankatank Pecan Fudge Pie," cheesecake, ice cream or sherbet.

To find Sandpiper Reef at Misti Cove, begin at the intersection of U.S. 33, U.S. 17 and Va. 198 in the town of Glenns. Follow Va. 198 west to Va. 626 (Hallieford Road). Turn left and go a quarter-mile to Va. 632. Turn left and follow the signs to the restaurant. If you're coming by water, note that the restaurant is on the Piankatank River directly across from Fishing Bay. Also note that the water is just two feet deep at high tide, so a dinghy landing will be in order at the dock.

Tobin's

MAIN STREET / MATHEWS, VA 23109
(804) 725-7900

Style	Home-style
Meals	Lunch and dinner, seven days a week. Tobin's serves Sunday breakfast during the summer only.
Price Range	Inexpensive/Moderate
Superlatives	Seafood platters, ice cream pies
Extras	Full bar

*T*his small town sponsors some innovative events. The first Ugly Pickup Truck Contest was held in the summer of 1996, followed by a town tailgate party on the courthouse green. Once a shipbuilding center, Mathews was responsible for a third of all the ships constructed in Virginia between 1790 and 1820. The largest vessel made here, the *Orozimbo*, weighed 588

Tobin's

tons and sailed every sea in the world before being lost in the Atlantic in 1883.

Located on Main Street at the corner of Brickbat Road, Tobin's has served the public since the late 1950s. The cinder-block walls are painted cream. A few watercolor prints hang on the walls. Ten booths line the left wall, and there's space for about 56 people at the tables. Adults get dark green paper place mats, while children have doodle place mats with spaces to play tick-tack-toe, to solve a maze and to play other games.

Burgers, turkey sandwiches, ham sandwiches, roast beef sandwiches, Reubens, clubs, tuna salad sandwiches and chicken salad sandwiches are offered at lunch. Hot lunches include a shrimp basket, roast beef and gravy and a small Delmonico steak, all served with two vegetables and hot rolls. The children's lunch menu has chicken nuggets, clam strips, a hot dog, grilled cheese and peanut butter and jelly, all served with french fries.

The evening appetizers are mozzarella sticks, breaded mushrooms, breaded zucchini slices and a

sampler platter of all three with two dipping sauces. Clam chowder and shrimp cocktails are also offered. The lowest-priced entree is spaghetti with marinara sauce, and the highest is the fried seafood platter. In between are small and large Delmonico steaks, pork chops, ham steaks, fried chicken, pasta dishes, lots of fried seafood and steamed shrimp in half-pound and pound servings.

Tobin's bread pudding is homemade, the recipe handed down from the original owners. The berry and cream pies are also homemade. But ice cream pies are the most popular desserts here.

GLOUCESTER
The Blue Fin
U.S. 17 BUSINESS / GLOUCESTER, VA 23061
(804) 693-9390

Style	Family-style
Meals	Lunch and dinner, Wednesday through Monday
Price Range	Inexpensive/Moderate
Superlatives	Crab cakes, lemon meringue and coconut meringue pies
Extras	Full bar

Gloucester, named for Henry, duke of Gloucester, is the birthplace of some well-known people—Walter Reed, Pocahontas, John Buckner and Thomas Calhoun Walker among them. Buckner was the man who brought the first printing press to Virginia. Walker was the state's first black collector of customs.

The Blue Fin

Barbara Horsley may be less famous than such people, but there's no denying she's a better restaurateur. After closing her building-supply business, Barbara joined her daughter, Jennifer Northstein, as a waitress at a local restaurant. Barbara often thought, "If only I could buy this place," referring to a building at the junction of U.S. 17 Business and Va. 3. Well, the building finally went up for sale, and she did buy it. With limited experience as a waitress but a solid business track record and lots of confidence, Barbara spruced up the former pool hall and sandwich shop and opened The Blue Fin in November 1987.

It's mostly gray and slate blue. There's a carved seabird in each of the octagonal porthole windows. Oil lamps on each table keep things bright. The tables can seat at least 60 people. There are nine booths as well.

For lunch, you can get crab salad, shrimp salad, chicken salad or tuna salad. The seafood choices— fresh, never frozen—include a sampler plate, a shrimp

basket and fried rainbow trout. There are a lot of crab cakes in this part of the state, and The Blue Fin's are definitely some of the best. In fact, they're Barbara's specialty. Sandwiches come with french fries or onion rings.

Among the dinner entrees are crab cakes, stuffed flounder, seafood kabobs and clam strips. Combination platters are also offered. On the landlubber section of the menu, there's Delmonico steak in two sizes, surf and turf, New York strip steak, filet mignon, hamburger steak, calf's liver with onions and gravy, Hawaiian-style chicken and fried chicken.

If you've paced your meal to include dessert, try the lemon meringue pie or the coconut meringue pie. Barbara makes them herself—just one more skill of this multitalented woman.

GLOUCESTER

Kelsick Gardens

6604 MAIN STREET / GLOUCESTER, VA 23061
(804) 693-6500

Style	Cafe
Meals	Lunch and early dinner, Monday through Saturday
Price Range	Inexpensive
Superlatives	Chicken salad, gingersnaps
Extras	Wine and beer

Gloucester native Beth Haskell went to Virginia Tech for a while and studied in the old College of Home Economics. Before finishing, she got married,

Kelsick Gardens

"ran a catering business, then ran kids for 15 years," as she puts it.

She always wanted her own business, but not a full-service restaurant. "This seemed to be what Gloucester needed and what I could do," she said of her gourmet shop and cafe, which she launched late in 1992.

The flowers and the tables with dark green umbrellas on the front patio are eye-catching. Inside, the place is a lot larger than most gourmet shops with an eatery. There are seats for at least 27. The paint and wallpaper are pastel orange. The watercolor paintings on the walls are for sale. Instrumental music plays in the background. It's all quite fresh and inviting.

The same menu items are available all day—sandwiches, salads, soups and combinations. The homemade soups might be baked potato and bean. The daily special might be a country ham salad sandwich or a Cajun catfish fillet with wild mushroom and herb couscous. Heart-healthy entrees like a "lite" quiche Lorraine are also offered.

This is a good place for children who like peanut butter and jelly. It comes on white bread without the crusts and with raisins on the side.

Every person eating here or taking something to go gets a menu. You print your name at the top, check a box for "To go" or "Here," circle what you want, write in the dessert, hand it in and have a seat.

A word about dessert. The homemade gingersnaps are a signature item here. There's also "Bumbleberry Pie"—a Canadian favorite that includes blackberries, raspberries, apples and rhubarb. Tough choice.

The gourmet shop offers a nice selection of wine, baskets, crackers, teas, teapots, napkins, spices and specialty foods.

Kelsick Gardens holds special dinners that pair food courses and appropriate wines. And it hasn't forgotten beer drinkers. Some of the special dinners feature microbrewery beers instead of wine.

GLOUCESTER
The Merry Toad
6553 MAIN STREET / GLOUCESTER, VA 23061
(804) 694-8043

Style	Pub
Meals	Lunch, Tuesday through Saturday; dinner, Monday through Saturday
Price Range	Inexpensive/Moderate
Superlatives	Seafood dishes, homemade desserts
Extras	Full bar

*T*om and Erika Swartzwelder abandoned life in the

The Merry Toad

was growing up, he had a family friend—sort of a great-aunt figure—whose name was Mary. Her nickname, for reasons unknown to him, was "Toad," and he grew up calling her "Mary Toad." She has since passed away, and Tom chose to honor her memory by using a slight twist on her nickname for his restaurant's name. He thinks she'd like it.

The Merry Toad's seafood chowder is creamy and full of seafood. The raw bar features steamed clams and oysters on the half shell. The "Oyster Po' Boy Sandwich," served on a hoagie roll, comes with "Toad Sauce." But don't worry. It's just a theme name—there aren't any toad parts in the sauce. Other sandwiches include soft-shell crab with Cajun mayonnaise, roast pork with sweet and sour mayonnaise and "Daffodil Chicken Salad" with a light curry mayonnaise. The "Cheddar Grill"—billed as "too good to be called grilled cheese"—has sharp cheddar, tomato and crispy bacon.

You can start your dinner with an appetizer of "Coconut Fried Shrimp," baked oysters or "Toad Bread"—a spinach, artichoke and garlic bread, served hot. You have lots of entree choices—oyster-stuffed filet mignon, "Toadally Crab Cakes," pasta primavera with shrimp and scallops and "Chesapeake Bay Cioppino," which is billed as a "toadal twist" on this classic fisherman's stew.

Erika makes the desserts. The "Chocolate Turtle Tart" is her signature sweet.

fast lane for small-town living. Tom was a trial lawyer and Erika a stockbroker when they decided to make a major change. They moved from Atlanta to Gloucester and opened a nice restaurant named Capers.

The restaurant developed an excellent reputation and was written up favorably in newspapers and magazines. But after three years, Tom and Erika got bored with it. "When that happens," Tom said, "your attitude is transmitted to the staff, and something has to change."

What changed was the restaurant. They painted the inside chartreuse with purple trim and introduced a pub theme, a new menu and a new name. When Tom

Seawell's Ordinary

Seawell's Ordinary

U.S. 17 / ORDINARY, VA 23131
(804) 642-3635

Style	Casual nice
Meals	Lunch, Monday through Saturday; dinner, seven days a week; Sunday brunch
Price Range	Moderate/Expensive
Superlatives	Chicken with Brie and raspberry sauce, grilled shrimp with andouille sausage
Extras	Full bar

*T*he wee town of Ordinary has so few buildings that you could count them on your fingers and be only a couple of digits short. In fact, it has fewer buildings than there are words in these two sentences.

Some say the town was named for Seawell's Ordinary. If you look up *ordinary* in the dictionary, you'll find it listed as an adjective first; it means customary, usual, familiar. As a noun, it means "a person, object or situation that is common." Places that serve food

and drink to travelers have always been common. Seawell's Ordinary opened in 1757, four and a half decades after the original part of the building was constructed as a private residence. Thomas Jefferson's early maps show it as Sewell's Publick House. Joseph Seawell had a horse-racing track on his farm, so his "public house"—or restaurant—was a busy place for eating, drinking and gambling.

The ordinary apparently closed in 1871. It served as a home until 1948, when it was opened as a restaurant again. Nine years later, the building was moved 100 feet back to make way for the expansion of U.S. 17. In 1990, realtor Eleanor Evans sold the property to her husband. It has since become a family operation, with son David now at the helm.

The interior is characteristic of buildings this age. It has lots of wood, small-pane windows and little oil lamps. The dining room on the right has burgundy walls. The room on the left has the bar. The tables have white linen tablecloths and green napkins.

The two most popular lunch items are the pork barbecue and the shrimp and crab salad. The homemade barbecue sauce is vinaigrette-based, not tomato-based. The shrimp and crab salad comes on an English muffin with provolone cheese melted over the top.

At dinner, you can enjoy a seafood soup du jour or a regular soup du jour. The appetizers include a baked phyllo strudel and fried won tons. The "Ordinary Salad," which isn't ordinary at all, has mixed greens, melted Brie, toasted almonds, kiwi and homemade sesame vinaigrette dressing. Veal, chicken, filet mignon, pasta dishes and a low-calorie vegetarian choice of penne pasta with broccoli and sweet peppers are offered, but with the water so close, entrees from the sea predominate. The cornmeal-crusted trout is served with hazelnut butter. The "Oysters Volcano" come with a white wine and cream sauce, diced tomatoes, capers and pesto sour cream. Grilled salmon, a broiled seafood platter, baked scallops au gratin and surf and turf are also offered.

Chocolate pâté is the signature dessert here. It's made with imported chocolate and premium rum, then formed into a loaf, sliced and served on a bed of raspberry sauce.

If your out-of-state plates, your Brownie camera and your bold shirt don't identify you as a tourist in these parts, your pronunciation of Seawell's might. It's not *See-well*, as the spelling suggests. It's *Sool*—rhymes with pool. If you say it right, surely no one will notice the other things.

River's Inn

River's Inn

8109 YACHT HAVEN DRIVE
GLOUCESTER POINT, VA 23062
(804) 642-9942

Style	Casual nice
Meals	Lunch and dinner, seven days a week. The restaurant is closed Christmas and New Year's Day.
Price Range	Moderate
Superlatives	Baked oysters, "Chesapeake Blue Plate," "Hazelnut Mousse"
Extras	Full bar

Gloucester Point, located at the York River and Chesapeake Bay, is about 15 miles from the town of Gloucester. It was originally called Tindall's Point for an early mapmaker. Gloucester Point was once considered a candidate for Virginia's colonial capital. But by a vote of 21 to 18, the capital stayed at Jamestown.

The River's Inn is worth finding, so pay close attention. At the first traffic light north of the bridge from Yorktown, turn right on Lafayette Heights Road. At the first stop sign, go left on Greate Road. Turn right on Terrapin Cove Road, then right on Yacht Haven Drive. There are some signs and little green arrows as you find your way.

You'll wind up at an excellent restaurant and a very pretty marina. There's a deck outside that seats more than 100 and has a different menu from the restaurant. Inside, windows along two sides look out onto the marina. Though there's room inside for about 100 people, the River's Inn has an intimate atmosphere.

Mahogany barstools wind around a semicircular bar and along a wall next to it. There are fresh flowers on the tables.

Tom Austin opened the River's Inn in May 1996. You'd never guess that the place was a machine shop in its previous existence.

The most popular appetizer at lunch is "Baked Oysters River's Inn"—oysters on the half shell topped with crabmeat, country ham, cream, seasoned crackers and a dill hollandaise sauce. There's also oyster stew, steamed littleneck clams with artichoke hearts and sauteed escargots. The Caesar salad is a comprehensive choice that includes grilled potatoes and toasted brioche; it's your option to add fried oysters or grilled duck breast. Sandwiches and entrees are also offered at lunch.

The "Chesapeake Blue Plate" is popular at dinner. It comes with she-crab soup, Caesar salad and an entree that combines a crab cake, crab imperial in a puff pastry and fried oysters with Virginia ham. The herb-roasted rack of lamb with sausage is also a favorite. Everything else sounds wonderful, too. Shrimp, lobster, a variety of other seafood dishes, veal, chicken, duck and filet mignon are among the options.

The "Hazelnut Mousse," the Key lime pie and the cheesecake are all excellent desserts. And if you think pound cake is boring, try the River's Inn's version. It's grilled and served with butter pecan ice cream, chocolate sauce and whipped cream.

Nick's Seafood Pavilion

WATER STREET / YORKTOWN, VA 23690
(757) 887-5269

Style	Family-style
Meals	Lunch and dinner, seven days a week. Nick's is closed on Christmas.
Price Range	Moderate/Expensive
Superlatives	Seafood shish kabobs, lobster with rice, baklava
Extras	Full bar

*E*stablished in 1691, this small town was the site of the last major conflict of the Revolutionary War and the surrender of Lord Cornwallis to George Washington. The Yorktown Victory Center provides a comprehensive presentation on the American Revolution—exhibits, interpreters, even a living-history program with reenactments of events of the period. You can also enjoy the town's history by driving on its narrow streets among its many clapboard buildings, but walking is the order of the day. People stop, read, photograph, enjoy the York River and—above all—celebrate our nation's precious freedom.

Nick's Seafood Pavilion, a statue-laden building under the Yorktown Bridge, is a veritable institution here. The restaurant was opened in June 1944 by the late Nick Mathews and his wife, Mary. She still sits behind the counter giving out lollipops, postcards, greetings and thank-yous.

It's a large place with ornate lamps, a couple of

gigantic chandeliers and some big plants. Fancy mirrors hang on the walls. Pink and aqua are the dominant colors.

It's hard to imagine there's a seafood item that's not on the menu at Nick's. You can order flounder, rainbow trout, red salmon, shrimp, scallops, rockfish, mackerel, snapper, bluefish, cod, crab legs, lobster and more. Nick's specialties are Alaskan king crab legs, seafood au gratin, broiled scallops and seafood shish kabobs.

If you'd like something other than fish, don't despair. There are plenty of other entrees. Familiar items like T-bone steaks, prime rib, pork chops, broiled chicken, Cornish hens, spaghetti and veal cutlets are offered. Things like pheasant, sweetbreads, veal scallopini, chicken cacciatore, broiled chicken livers and broiled quail are also available. A couple of items that call for a bit of explanation are "Lamb Neframia à la Greque" and "Prime Beef Shish Kabob Oriental." The lamb dish is a casserole with browned lamb chops, potatoes and butter, topped with tomato paste. The beef dish is pieces of tenderloin steak with green peppers, onions and tomatoes.

There's a homemade dessert to please everyone here—everything from napoleons and rum pie to baklava, baked Alaska and rice pudding.

Backfin

1193 JAMESTOWN ROAD
WILLIAMSBURG, VA 23185
(757) 220-2249

Style	Family-style
Meals	Lunch and dinner, Monday through Saturday
Price Range	Inexpensive/Moderate
Superlatives	Crab cakes, cornbread
Extras	Full bar

Williamsburg is the home of the College of William and Mary, chartered in 1693. The town began to develop when the colonial capital was moved here from Jamestown in 1699. Virginia's capital was relocated to Richmond 80 years later. Williamsburg's historical preservation movement started in 1926. Since then, the town has become a haven for tourists with an interest in history. It's equally noted for its shopping, entertainments and dining.

The restaurant called Backfin was recommended by several locals. If you're traveling on Jamestown Road from the Colonial Williamsburg area, look for a Texaco station just before an intersection; drive behind the service station. Housed in a former convenience store, this restaurant provides food as good as that at higher-priced places, where you sometimes pay dearly for atmosphere.

Backfin has two dining rooms separated by a partition. There are booths against the wall and tables in the middle.

Clam strips, oysters, shrimp, scallops, catfish, flounder and other fried or broiled seafood items are popular at lunch. Crab cakes are a house specialty. French fries, hush puppies and slaw are the usual sides.

Shrimp, clams, oysters on the half shell, crab balls and crab legs are among the dinner appetizers. The cornbread is wonderful here. Personally, I've often shied away from cornbread because it tends to be dry and crumbly, but Backfin's version is the best I've ever had. Combination platters are available at dinner. Lobster tail is the most expensive thing on the menu. But you don't have to eat seafood, of course. You can get a New York strip steak, fried chicken or pit-cooked barbecue.

If you're not quite full after this, try the chocolate mousse pie or the cheesecake. There's no Key lime pie in Virginia that's as good as what you get in Florida, but Backfin's comes awfully close.

Old Chickahominy House

Old Chickahominy House

1211 JAMESTOWN ROAD
WILLIAMSBURG, VA 23185
(757) 229-4689

Style	Home-style
Meals	Breakfast and lunch, seven days a week
Price Range	Inexpensive
Superlatives	Chicken and dumplings, Brunswick stew, hot biscuits
Extras	Wine and beer

*T*here's no feature of a historic house more welcoming than a front porch with rocking chairs resting quietly and an American flag waving in a slight breeze.

If there's a wait to be seated at the Old Chickahominy House—and it's likely there will be—you can sit on the porch and rock. But I opted for wandering through the part of the building that houses an antique and gift shop. American and English antiques

Backfin

adorn display cases, and gifts, housewares and toiletries fill a couple of rooms and some nooks and crannies. Most of the antiques are on the main level across the hall from the dining rooms. The Christmas shop on the lower level offers greeting cards, cookbooks, fine lotions, china, Virginia gifts and jewelry. You can even buy a T-shirt with the restaurant's menu on the back.

When you do get called into the 18th-century-style dining room, you'll soon discover that everything here is homemade.

You'll see the name of "Miss Melinda" in a few places on the menu. She started the business in 1955. For the past decade or so, it's been run by her daughter-in-law, Maxine Henderson.

The "Plantation Breakfast" includes Virginia ham, bacon or sausage with two eggs, grits, hot biscuits and coffee or tea. You can also order "Miss Melinda's Pancakes" or creamed ham on toast.

At lunch, "Miss Melinda's Special" consists of a cup of Brunswick stew, Virginia ham on hot biscuits, fruit salad, homemade pie and coffee or tea. If you'd like more of the Brunswick stew, you can buy it by the quart to go. The Old Chickahominy House is famous for its chicken and dumplings and its chicken soup as well. Hamburgers are also offered.

The Old Chickahominy House ships fully cooked boneless Edwards hams, Wigwam bone-in hams and an uncooked, country-style, pepper-coated Virginia ham. It will also ship most gifts, but not antiques or framed pictures.

The Trellis Cafe, Restaurant & Grill

WILLIAMSBURG

The Trellis Cafe, Restaurant & Grill

403 DUKE OF GLOUCESTER STREET
WILLIAMSBURG, VA 23185
(757) 229-8610

Style	Casual nice
Meals	Lunch and dinner, seven days a week. The Trellis is closed on Sunday during January. Reservations are strongly recommended.
Price Range	Moderate/Expensive
Superlatives	Chocolate desserts
Extras	Full bar

*T*his restaurant was recommended to me so many times via e-mail, note and spoken word that it wasn't possible to go through Williamsburg without stopping.

An attractive place in Merchant's Square, it has patio dining out front. Inside are multiple rooms with exposed-brick walls. The various dining areas create an intimate atmosphere, and you might be surprised to learn that the restaurant can seat more than 200 people. Fresh flowers and elegant plates with The Trellis's name on them lend a classy touch.

All the food is prepared under the watchful eye of executive chef and cookbook author Marcel Desaulniers. He and John Curtis opened the restaurant in 1980.

The menu changes seasonally to take advantage of foods at their freshest. There aren't many restaurants where you'll find white trumpet mushrooms, Jerusalem artichokes, celery root and chestnuts. Quail, wild boar, lobster, antelope, pheasant and Texas venison are some of the special game items available at certain times of the year. Freshly baked bread and seasonal vegetables or wild rice come with every meal. Stable menu items include pork medallions, sliced calf's liver, beef tenderloin, catfish and pan-seared salmon.

Besides having a reputation that extends at least statewide, The Trellis is famous for its "Desserts to Die For," a phrase that's found at the top of the dessert menu as well as on the title page of one of Desaulniers's cookbooks. The two best-known desserts are "Chocolate Temptation" and "Death by Chocolate." Other desserts sound as elegant as they look—"Diamonds on Ice" and "White Chocolate Balloon," for example. On the lighter side, you can always order strawberries with whipped cream. If you haven't left room for dessert, make sure you exercise your final option: dessert to go.

Other cookbooks by Desaulniers include *An Alphabet of Sweets*, *The Trellis Cookbook* and *The Burger Meisters*. Though there's no space on the premises to display books and gifts, you can ask your waitress about the T-shirts, mugs, calendars, pepper grinders, baseball caps and whimsical wooden sculptures available for purchase.

Coach House Tavern

CHARLES CITY

Coach House Tavern

BERKELEY PLANTATION / VA 5
CHARLES CITY, VA 23030
(800) 291-6003

Style	Casual nice
Meals	Lunch, seven days a week; dinner, Friday and Saturday. Reservations are required for dinner.
Price Range	Moderate/Expensive
Superlatives	Crab, pound cake
Extras	Full bar

*E*stablished in 1616, history-rich Charles City County is sandwiched between the James River and the Chickahominy River. The first free black community in America was established here during the 1600s. Thomas Jefferson married Martha Skelton in Charles City County. President John Tyler was born here. Robert E. Lee spent many boyhood years here.

Charles City County is also the home of Berkeley Plantation, whose centerpiece is a three-story Georgian brick house built in 1726 by Benjamin Harrison IV and his wife, Anne. Their son Benjamin signed the Declaration of Independence and served as governor of Virginia from 1782 to 1784. William Henry Harrison, the third son of Benjamin Harrison V, was the ninth president of the United States. William Henry Harrison's grandson—yet another Benjamin Harrison—was our 23rd president.

The house at Berkeley Plantation and the 10-acre grounds overlooking the James River were opened to the public in 1938. Owner Malcolm Jamieson and his wife still live in the house, which is open daily. There is an admission fee, but you need not purchase a ticket to eat at the Coach House Tavern, a rustic old building of uncertain origin near the main house.

Sandra Capps opened a tiny cafe with just a few tables in 1987 and has expanded a few times since. Steve and Elisa Danz became partners with Sandra in 1996. Steve does much of the cooking and manages operations. Elisa is the wine buyer.

The restaurant seats 150 and can serve an additional 200 in an outdoor tent. The slate floor in the entry and the aged beams attest to the building's longevity. There are fresh flowers on the tables. Instrumental music plays in the background.

At lunch, there's French onion soup, a soup du jour, garden salad and country-style chicken salad. A Monte Cristo, a vegetarian sandwich and a "Coach House Club" are among the sandwiches offered. Lunch entrees include grilled tuna, pan-seared salmon and sliced beef tenderloin.

Dinner is a comprehensive event. You'll get an appetizer, a soup, a salad, sorbet, an entree, dessert and a beverage. You might start with smoked salmon or venison summer sausage, followed by "Chicken Corn Chowder," then a salad. Sorbet is delivered before your entree choice, which might be crab cakes, venison medallions or veal chops with a creamy basil sauce.

The pound cakes served at the Coach House have won numerous awards. They come in delectable flavors such as champagne poppy seed and bourbon walnut.

CHARLES CITY

Indian Fields Tavern

VA 5 / CHARLES CITY, VA 23030
(804) 829-5004

Style	Casual nice
Meals	Lunch and dinner, seven days a week. Reservations are recommended.
Price Range	Moderate/Expensive
Superlatives	Free-range chicken, "Steak Lyon's Den," "Sally Lunn Bread Pudding"
Extras	Full bar

*T*his plantation was established sometime between

Indian Fields Tavern

1897 and 1903. When the fields were prepared for planting, Indian artifacts were unearthed—thus the name Indian Fields.

Indian Fields Tavern was renovated and opened by Archer Ruffin and David Napier. Ruffin became sole owner two years after the June 1987 opening. David Napier went on to start other restaurants, one of which—David's White House in Providence Forge—is covered in this book.

The building is nestled in the shade of pecan, weeping willow, oak and beech trees. The beds of perennials are beautiful. It's a tranquil spot surrounded by fields and sky. Depending on the time of year, you'll find wheat, soybeans or corn at various stages of growth. Inside, the cream-colored dining room with dark green trim seats about 30. Another dining room has maroon walls. There are also tables on two screened porches. Fresh flowers and classical music enhance a peaceful atmosphere.

A couple of popular lunch entrees are the chicken salad and the grilled Smithfield ham sandwich, which comes open-faced on delicious, homemade Sally Lunn bread. Sally Lunn was a French lady who lived in Bath, England. The recipe for her famous bread came to America with the colonists. The bread's popularity is due in part to the fact that it requires no kneading. Other offerings at lunch include a quiche of the day, the catch of the day, crab cakes and a mixed grill of sausage and duck breast.

Dinner starts with appetizers like a tartlet of duck bacon and "Jalapeño Crab Cheesecake." Salads and a soup du jour are offered. One of the entrees is free-range chicken, cured and smoked on the premises. "Crab Cakes Harrison" come grilled and served over Smithfield ham with hollandaise sauce. Lamb, roast pork, shrimp, grilled filet mignon and a special vegetarian entree are also available.

The signature dessert is "Sally Lunn Bread Pudding." Other desserts include layer cakes, a variety of cheesecakes and an interesting rice custard from an old family recipe.

David's White House

PROVIDENCE FORGE

David's White House

VA 155 / PROVIDENCE FORGE, VA 23140
(804) 966-9700

Style	Casual nice
Meals	Lunch, Tuesday through Saturday; dinner, Tuesday through Sunday; Sunday brunch
Price Range	Inexpensive/Moderate
Superlatives	Crabmeat, "Hunter's Sausage," "Chicken Foxboro"
Extras	Full bar

Settled around 1770 by Presbyterian minister Charles Smith and his congregation, Providence Forge was named for the blacksmith shop started by the pastor and a couple of partners. The forge was destroyed during the Revolutionary War; Smith's house was occupied but not damaged. When the house was later slated for destruction, a local lady bought it and had it disassembled and moved to Williamsburg, where it stands today as Providence Hall.

Heading south on Va. 155 from Exit 214 off I-64, you'll come upon David's White House after a little less than four miles. It's a white house with black shutters, a green and white awning and a porch that spans the front.

Owner David Napier has a casual, easy manner about him—which perhaps comes from living on a boat for the past 13 years. He's also a visionary. When he found this house—a former mill, then a doctor's office with a room for operations—it was broken into apartments and about to fall down. He bought it, lived part-time in an apartment upstairs and started what he'd done a few years earlier at Indian Fields Tavern in Charles City (also covered in this book). He cleaned, gutted, scraped, painted, created a kitchen, refinished, decorated.

David's White House began serving classic Southern cuisine in 1994. One dining room has peach and white double linens and green carpeting. Another has green and white linens and flowered carpeting. There are a couple of smaller dining areas on the second floor.

For lunch, you can get a tossed salad, a spinach salad, a Caesar salad or one of the entree salads—seafood salad, chicken salad with fresh fruit, grilled chicken Caesar salad or "Ragsdale Salad," which is blackened prime rib over fresh greens. The sandwiches number more than a dozen. The lunch entrees include a vegetable-stuffed popover, eggplant Parmesan, baked Virginia ham and a fried catfish platter.

Two favorite dinner appetizers are "Hunter's Sausage" and "Oysters Weyanoke." The latter is also available as an entree. The menu contains more of a balance among meat, fowl and seafood than many places near the ocean. "Chicken Foxboro" is a pecan-crusted chicken breast sauteed with white wine, Dijon and peaches. Barbecued ribs, ham, pork chops, salmon in pastry, rib-eye steak, grilled quail and crab cakes are also offered. Those who like variety should try the "White House Sampler," which includes "Oysters Weyanoke," a fillet of beef and barbecued baby back ribs.

As David's brochure puts it, the White House indeed offers "a gracious and tranquil atmosphere suited to fine dining in plantation style."

C. W. Cowling's

SMITHFIELD PLAZA / VA 10
SMITHFIELD, VA 23430
(757) 357-0044

Style	Family-style
Meals	Lunch and dinner, seven days a week
Price Range	Inexpensive/Moderate
Superlatives	Friendly service, casual atmosphere
Extras	Full bar

*N*amed for Arthur Smith IV, Smithfield is best known for its hams. It was Captain Mallory Todd, a native of Bermuda, who made a business of curing and shipping hams from Smithfield. These amber-col-

ored hams from peanut-fed hogs are now famous worldwide. Only hams dry-cured within the corporate limits of Smithfield can bear the town's name. Smithfield's historic district is listed on the National Register of Historic Places and is a Virginia Historic Landmark. Among its many sites are 10 buildings that predate the Revolutionary War.

If you're looking for a good place to eat in Smithfield, don't let the strip-mall location of C. W. Cowling's deter you. There's a whole different aura inside the restaurant, which opened in June 1988. It has a simple country feel. Photos of barns and local country scenes were taken by a sister-in-law of one of the owners.

The owners, Charlie and Susan Driver Webb, created the name from Charlie's initials (C. W.) and the name of a prominent local family to whom Susan is related (the Cowlings).

This is a good place to bring a pile of friends, because the menu is broad enough to please everyone. At lunch, there are more than a half-dozen salads and twice as many sandwiches. The cheddar melts come on two English muffins topped with either chicken salad, ham, seafood or vegetables. There are also hamburgers, chili cheese dogs, chicken fajitas, Cajun dishes and pasta dishes.

At dinner, you can get sirloin steak, chicken, catfish, shrimp, scallops, flounder or a seafood platter. Ribs are available in the standard full rack or half rack.

You can finish your meal with fried apple pie, hot fudge cake or a sundae served in a crunchy cinnamon shell. As with the rest of the menu, there are enough sweets for everyone in your party to find something satisfying.

Smithfield Station

Smithfield Station

415 SOUTH CHURCH STREET
SMITHFIELD, VA 23430
(804) 874-7700

Style	Casual nice
Meals	Breakfast, Saturday and Sunday; lunch and dinner, seven days a week
Price Range	Moderate
Superlatives	Oysters Rockefeller, Smithfield ham
Extras	Full bar

Though there's waterfront dining at Smithfield Station, patrons don't look over any great expanse of water. On the patio and inside the dining rooms, the view extends over a narrow marina and the Pagan River, which provides access to the Chesapeake Bay.

The main dining room is flooded with natural light, thanks to windows that reach to the ceiling. The pine interior is accented with dark green and mauve fabrics.

Breakfast on Saturdays is à la carte. On Sundays, there's a breakfast buffet.

At lunch, you can choose from a variety of chowders and soups. Some of the tempting appetizers are fresh oysters, steamed shrimp and clams, served steamed or on the half shell. The menu touts "a couple of really special things we do." One is oysters Rockefeller—fresh oysters baked with spinach, Pernod and Parmesan cheese. The other is called an "Onion Block"—deep-fried seasoned onions in a tidy little cube. There are close to a dozen salads and cold plates. You won't be surprised to learn that the sandwiches include a crab cake sandwich and a Smithfield ham sandwich. If you're in the mood for a light meal, you have 10 or so items from which to choose, among them a five-ounce cut of filet mignon. The "Chicken Isle of Wight" is stuffed with ham, Swiss cheese and roasted peanuts. There's also a fresh quiche every day.

At dinner, you'll find an even balance of chicken, pork, pasta, beef and seafood entrees. For the person who doesn't want just one thing, there are combination plates. One of these is a medley of boneless chicken breast, shrimp and beef tenderloin served on sliced Smithfield ham.

Smithfield Station operates a raw bar from June to September.

The 17-room inn above the restaurant and in the lighthouse down the boardwalk is always open. Package deals are available. Boats up to 70 feet in length can be accommodated in the marina. Power and water hookups are available at most slips.

This is one place where I'd like to return—to eat and to stay.

Main Street Eatery

119 NORTH MAIN STREET
FRANKLIN, VA 23851
(757) 562-1001

Style	Casual nice
Meals	Lunch and dinner, Monday through Saturday
Price Range	Moderate
Superlatives	Crab cakes, Caesar salad
Extras	Full bar

*T*his town was first called Southampton, after the earl of Southampton. But since it was easily confused with the community of Southampton Court House, its name was changed to honor Benjamin Franklin. It was incorporated as a town in 1876 and as a city in 1960. During the Civil War, Union gunboats shelled Franklin and its railroad station. In 1881, fire destroyed more than three dozen buildings here. Today, Franklin's biggest industries are paper and peanuts.

There's no sign of the former hardware store, undertaker's establishment or department store at the bright restaurant called the Main Street Eatery. The cream ceiling and walls reflect natural light from the huge front and side windows. There are two dining levels downstairs and another dining room on the second floor, making space for more than 200. A blue neon coffee cup on the back wall imparts an art deco touch. The whole place has a California feel.

Popular items at lunch include the Main Street Eatery's signature Caesar salad, a blackened grilled tuna sub and a chicken sub. Ranch chicken is also a top seller.

Two menus are given out at dinner: a Main Street Eatery menu and a Southampton Room menu.

The first one includes appetizers like cheese sticks, deep-fried calamari rings and a designer potato. Entrees include grilled tuna steak, rib-eye steak, pork stir-fry, fajitas, shrimp, crab cakes and a barbecue platter.

The other, fancier menu's appetizers might be a grilled tuna and pineapple brochette and blackened salmon with Caribbean salsa. One of the entrees might be "Oysters Virginia Beach," served in a spicy cream sauce on a bed of wild rice. Another might be "Chicken Chesapeake," which is a whole chicken breast stuffed with crabmeat and topped with a silky cheddar sauce. There are steaks and pork entrees, too.

Another classy touch is the recent introduction of a "Wine and Dine" series of dinners, in which five-course dinners are designed to complement specific wines.

Rebecca's

7 STRAWBERRY STREET
CAPE CHARLES, VA 23310
(757) 331-3879

Style	Home-style
Meals	Lunch, seven days a week; dinner, Wednesday through Monday
Price Range	Inexpensive/Moderate
Superlatives	She-crab soup, homemade cobbler
Extras	Wine and beer

Although you might expect a town named Cape Charles to be located at the southern tip of the Eastern Shore, it's actually about 15 miles north of the tip. Established in 1884 as a railroad terminus, Cape Charles is the headquarters of the Eastern Shore Railroad. Its historic district is listed on the Virginia Landmarks Register and was placed on the National Register of Historic Places in 1991.

If you happen to get hungry while you're exploring downtown Cape Charles and the beaches, Rebecca's is the place to go for down-home cooking at down-home prices. You'll find it tucked in a storefront on a side street just off Main Street. Constructed around 1930, the building has seen service as a grocery store, an arcade, a dance hall and a Sears catalog store.

Owned by Eddie and Susan Bell, this is a family restaurant with an emphasis on seafood. Eddie is an Eastern Shore native whose old livelihood died with the oysters more than a decade ago. His brother, Tim, helps at the restaurant during the summers.

Eddie and Susan have had Rebecca's since 1988. It's tough to run a restaurant here year-round. Eddie has seen lots of them come and go—and come again and go again. He says that local folks who once depended on oysters for a living can no longer afford to eat out at high prices. Tim agrees. "No one is here for the atmosphere," he says. "They're here for the food."

Soups and stews head the lunch menu. The sandwiches include a clam fritter sandwich, an oyster fritter sandwich and a crab cake sandwich. Burgers, grilled ham and cheese, a chicken fillet sandwich, a hot roast beef sandwich and a BLT are also offered. The basket of chicken tenders is popular, as is the shrimp special.

At dinner, you can order lots of seafood, as you might expect. Crab cakes come two to an order and clam fritters three to an order. Steamed shrimp can be purchased by the half-pound or the pound. Seafood platters are served broiled or fried.

For the sweet tooth, there are homemade pies and cobblers.

And if you're wondering who Rebecca is, she's Eddie and Susan's daughter. Her elementary-school artwork adorns the walls, alongside the nautical seascapes and prints.

Sting-Ray's
U.S. 13 / CAPE CHARLES, VA 23313
(757) 331-2505

Style	Family-style
Meals	Breakfast, lunch and dinner, seven days a week
Price Range	Inexpensive/Moderate
Superlatives	Chili, navy bean soup
Extras	Wine and beer

*I*f you're in the mood for breakfast, lunch or dinner after leaving the northern end of the Chesapeake Bay Bridge-Tunnel, don't let the gas pumps at the Cape Charles Exxon station put you off. Cape Center, as the complex is called, is on the eastern side of the highway a few miles north of the bridge-tunnel. It's a one-stop convenience place where you can fuel up, walk the dog, picnic under pines and stock up on most anything from ice and candy to souvenirs and lottery tickets. Tucked in the back of the big, red, barnlike building is Sting-Ray's, where there's fast food by day and elegant dining by night.

Sting-Ray's boasts fiery chili and navy bean soup that includes hunks of ham. As the old saw goes, "Eat here and get gas."

Owner Ray Haynie makes all the chili and has competed in various chili cookoffs around the state. He's never won, but he's finished in the top four. Haynie grows his own jalapeño peppers. He also owns the pottery shop next door. When he visits Laredo, Texas, on pottery-buying trips, he stocks up on ancho and casabel peppers, too. "They'll knock you down," he

laughs. Haynie's chili packs what you might call a delayed heat reaction.

For spicing up your home life, the store offers a variety of hot sauces with names like "Insanity Sauce," "Capital Punishment" and "Cafe Fear Hot Sauce," which has what's described as a "near-death rating."

By day, the restaurant deals in fast food for tourists—soups, sandwiches, burgers, subs, chicken and such. But in late afternoon, the tables are cloaked in white and the gourmet menu emerges—seafood, crab imperial, certified Angus beef, rack of ribs, stuffed flounder.

According to a framed newspaper article on the wall, Sting-Ray's is a roadside filling station, a rest stop and a fast-food restaurant rolled into one. By night, the locals know it as "Chez Exxon."

Eastville Manor
6058 WILLOW OAK ROAD (VA 631)
EASTVILLE, VA 23347
(757) 678-7378

Style	Fine dining
Meals	Lunch, Tuesday through Friday; dinner, Tuesday through Saturday in summer and Wednesday through Saturday the rest of the year. Reservations are recommended. The restaurant is closed during January.
Price Range	Moderate
Superlatives	Five-course wine dinners
Extras	Wine and beer

Eastville Manor

The county seat of Northampton County since the early 1700s, Eastville has the oldest continuous court records in the nation, dating back to 1632. Constructed around 1731, Eastville's colonial courthouse now serves as a clerk's office. Eastville is the easternmost county seat in Virginia—thus the name.

Eastville Manor, located east of U.S. 13 on Va. 631, is one of the newest culinary delights on the Eastern Shore. As I drove on crushed stone past flower beds and lawns to the big, white mansion, the words *subdued elegance* came to mind. I felt underdressed until Melody Scalley reassured me that all would be fine.

Melody and husband, William, came here from Washington, D.C., because they wanted to open a small, fine-dining restaurant in the country. The Victorian mansion dates to 1886. It took Melody and William a year to renovate the first floor and open the kitchen and the dining room. The renovation continues to this day.

Melody grows flowers for the tables and herbs and vegetables for the kitchen. William, who once ran a catering business on Capitol Hill, has been a chef for more than 20 years. He changes the menu frequently.

At lunch, you can count on fresh fish from the grill, sandwiches, burgers, a quiche of the day and fresh fruit.

The dinner entrees might include medallions of duck breast, grilled tuna with basil-marinated tomatoes and crab cakes in a Dijon and chive sauce. A vegetable and rice or potatoes come with the entrees.

Once a month—most often on the third Thursday of the month—the Eastville Manor offers a special five-course wine dinner that includes four or five wines that complement the cuisine.

Big Bill's Captain's Deck

U.S. 13 / NASSAWADOX, VA 23413
(757) 442-7060

Style	Home-style
Meals	Breakfast, lunch and dinner, seven days a week
Price Range	Inexpensive/Moderate
Superlatives	Belgian waffles, "Neptune's Special"
Extras	Full bar

Located about a third of the way up the Eastern Shore, the community of Nassawadox developed around a sawmill. Today, you can visit the Nassawadox Sawmill Museum.

The signs outside this restaurant say Captain's Deck Restaurant, but the menu says Big Bill's Captain's Deck. Either way, many local residents recommend the place, particularly if you're in the mood for breakfast, which is served any time of the day.

Big Bill Downing is a gregarious former hospital administrator. His restaurant is surely popular for breakfast, judging by the number of cars, pickups and panel trucks I saw in the parking lot the morning I visited.

The bright, spacious dining room can seat about 170. The space is surrounded by large picture windows and hanging plants. A shelf going around the room is stacked with baseball caps—hundreds of them—advertising all sorts of teams and companies. Downing, who has had the restaurant for more than 15 years, started with perhaps 25 caps, and customers keep bringing in more. You'll also note the restaurant's nautical theme, which extends to the restrooms, where orange life rings on the doors are labeled "Gulls" and "Buoys."

The breakfast menu is extensive—and colorful. For example, one item reads, "Express: Two eggs, bacon, home fries, toast or biscuit and you're outta here." Seafood, Mexican dishes, scrapple and omelets are also offered at breakfast. The variety might explain the popularity.

Lunch specialties include breaded veal cutlets, hamburgers, fried oysters and hot roast beef.

Seafood entrees are popular at dinner. Char-broiled steaks, liver and onions, pizza and chicken round out the evening menu.

For dessert, you can get pie, cake, pudding or "Fruit Cob"—short for cobbler.

During the summer, Big Bill's features live music on Saturday nights.

Little Italy Ristorante

Little Italy Ristorante

10227 ROGERS DRIVE
NASSAWADOX, VA 23413
(757) 442-7831

Style	Italian
Meals	Lunch and dinner, Monday through Saturday
Price Range	Inexpensive/Moderate
Superlatives	Pasta dishes, tiramisu
Extras	Full bar

When folks on the Eastern Shore crave a break from seafood, seafood and more seafood, many of them turn to the Little Italy Ristorante, a white-brick storefront just east of U.S. 13 in Nassawadox.

Shortly after noon on the weekday I visited, the parking lot across Rogers Drive was crowded with cars and pickups. A parade of takeout customers came and went. Inside, the dining room was nearly full and the aroma of Italian cooking permeated the air.

On the wall right inside the door are two United States maps and a world map. Customers can put a pin on their hometown, state or country. Hundreds have done so. The pleasant dining room can seat about 40. It's decorated with plastic grapevines clinging to trellises and posters of Italian scenes clinging to the walls. Italian music plays in the background.

"We do have seafood, Italian-style!" contends owner and chef Franco Nocera. He and his wife, Cathy, have operated Little Italy since 1992. As a concession to their Eastern Shore customers, they offer shrimp Parmesan, shrimp scampi over pasta and seafood Alfredo.

There are several pizzas on the lunch menu, as well as cold subs and hot subs.

For dinner, you might try baked ziti, stuffed shells, tortellini Alfredo or one of the spaghetti dishes. There are also meat, chicken and veal entrees, as well as half a dozen vegetable entrees.

The tiramisu is a specialty dessert.

If you're on the go, just come on in and take your order right out. For special occasions, you can get party trays of all the cold cuts, subs and Italian casseroles offered at Little Italy.

E. L. Willis & Co.

WILLIS WHARF

E. L. Willis & Co.

4456 WILLIS WHARF ROAD
WILLIS WHARF, VA 23486
(757) 442-4225

Style	Casual nice
Meals	Lunch, Monday through Saturday; dinner, Friday and Saturday. Reservations are recommended on weekends.
Price Range	Inexpensive/Moderate
Superlatives	Seafood sandwiches, "Bayside Seafood Combo"
Extras	Full bar

*I*t's not too difficult to guess that a man named Willis once had a wharf here. He was Edward Willis, and he purchased land for his wharf in 1854. Today, Willis Wharf remains a real waterfront fishing village.

The old mercantile building that houses the dining establishment called E. L. Willis & Co. has served as a store or a restaurant since 1850. In both its setting and its cuisine, E. L. Willis & Co. offers a taste of the past. It's very quaint. Very Eastern Shore. To find it, you must venture off U.S. 13 at Exmore and go east on Va. 603 to Willis Wharf.

You can relax on the screened porch overlooking the marsh and watch the fishing vessels snaking through the narrow channel to the Atlantic Ocean. It's a pleasant diversion during lunch or dinner. Make sure you bring cash, as E. L. Willis & Co. does not accept credit cards.

Owner Pam Widgen, an Eastern Shore native, has owned and run the place since the early 1990s. She doesn't advertise and so depends on loyal local business, referrals from lodging places and travelers who seek her out—or who just get lucky while exploring the back roads.

The dining room is decorated with Pam's vintage kitchen utensils and laundry implements, like washboards and hand-cranked ringers. You'll also note the collection of old oyster cans and the assortment of nostalgic commercial signs.

Pam makes all her own soups. But her specialty is fresh seafood. Among the offerings at lunch are crab cake sandwiches, clam fritter sandwiches and fish fillet sandwiches. Liverwurst sandwiches, ham sandwiches and turkey sandwiches are served as well. Her platters come with two vegetables.

The dinner entrees include a small loaf of Pam's home-baked bread. The "Bayside Seafood Combo" combines fish, a crab cake, a clam fritter, scallops and clam strips. Catfish, scallops, flounder and prime rib are among the other choices.

Her homemade desserts change all the time. From the looks of what I saw, I'd recommend any one of them.

The Trawler

EXMORE

The Trawler
U.S. 13 / EXMORE, VA 23350
(757) 442-2092

Style	Family-style
Meals	Lunch and dinner, seven days a week
Price Range	Moderate
Superlatives	She-crab soup, sweet potato biscuits
Extras	Full bar

*T*here are two schools of thought on the naming of Exmore. It was purportedly the 11th rail stop south of the Maryland border. Thus, the northbound crew had 10—or *X*, in Roman numerals—more stops before reaching the state line. Others say the place was named for the village of Exmore in England.

You'll easily spot The Trawler's big roadside sign with the fishing-boat logo on the eastern side of U.S. 13 near Exmore. It's an Eastern Shore landmark of sorts.

The Trawler opened in 1980. Carl and Judi Beck bought it a few years later and opened a dinner theater. Productions run 12 days each month from June through November.

About 250 patrons can be seated at the pine tables and booths. The spacious dining area has vaulted ceilings, exposed beams and plank walls. A stained-glass room divider taken from a Chesapeake Bay skipjack dominates the room. Decoys, carvings of shorebirds, seascapes, clam rakes and other fishing and boating artifacts enhance the nautical aura.

From oyster sandwiches, soft-shell crab sandwiches, grilled tuna sandwiches and catfish sandwiches to combinations and platters of crabmeat, shrimp, scallops and stuffed flounder, seafood dominates the extensive lunch menu. The signature items are sweet potato biscuits and she-crab soup so thick that your spoon can hardly touch bottom.

If it's dinnertime and you're not in the mood for seafood, you can order steak, prime rib, chicken cordon bleu or just plain grilled chicken. All dinner entrees include a cup of clam chowder, a trip to the salad bar, hush puppies, sweet potato biscuits and your choice of potato, pasta or rice pilaf.

The desserts include pecan pie, apple pie, "Peanut Butter Blast," "Chocolate Nemesis" and others. Just don't ask for the recipes. Both *Bon Appétit* magazine and *Gourmet* magazine have requested recipes from The Trawler to publish in their pages. They didn't get them.

The Fish House

U.S. 13 / PAINTER, VA 23420
(757) 442-3474

Style	Family-style
Meals	Lunch and dinner, seven days a week
Price Range	Inexpensive/Moderate
Superlatives	Eastern Shore recipes
Extras	Wine and beer

*T*he very small town of Painter—which consists of a traffic light, a couple of convenience stores with gas pumps and a brick post office—is located pretty close to the center of the Eastern Shore.

Fresh seafood and the Eastern Shore are synonymous, but Danny Doughty, owner of The Fish House, has taken it a step farther. "Our fish are still alive when they come through the back door," he says.

Doughty also owns and operates Ches-Atlantic Seafood, a wholesale packing house located behind the restaurant. He selects his fish from the more than 50 commercial vessels that unload their catch every day. This cuts out the middleman, according to Doughty, a fourth-generation seafood businessman. He ships fish all over the eastern seaboard. Among his customers is the famous Fulton Fish Market in New York City. But first, The Fish House takes its pick of flounder, gray trout, striped bass, croaker, bluefish, tuna, clams, crabs and other seafood.

The Fish House

The atmosphere inside the restaurant is ultracasual, the decor a collection of farm and nautical memorabilia. The menu is equally casual. When I asked about the baked tomatoes, I was told they were mixed in a bowl "about the size of the one Aunt Bessie gave me for Christmas last year." The tomatoes are then baked in a pan "something like that one I got from the flea market in Gilford."

Doughty and his crew have taken some of their food to the Virginia State Fair, where they won the Director's Choice Award in 1996 for "quality, presentation, hospitality and appearance." The most popular soup here is the oyster stew, but The Fish House is also known for its she-crab soup and Eastern Shore clam chowder, which has a clear broth. Cook Bessie Edwards, who's worked here forever, makes the desserts. Her sweet potato pie and sweet potato biscuits are particularly special.

The Fish House's buffet—offered on Friday, Saturday and Sunday—is popular with the locals.

PAINTER

Formy's Pit Barbecue

U.S. 13 / PAINTER, VA 23420
(757) 442-2426

Style	Family-style
Meals	Lunch and dinner, seven days a week
Price Range	Inexpensive
Superlatives	Pit-cooked pork

Ah, the aroma of pit-cooked barbeque! That's the first thing you notice as you enter Formy's.

You can't miss the place—just look for the long, white building and the big sign with the pig on it.

"We sell no swine before its time," says the menu. Owner Jim Formyduval explains that the pork is cooked in his own secret sauce for 24 hours over a fire of oak and hickory.

All barbecue is good, says the modest Formyduval, a North Carolina native—some is different, that's all. He does concede that people seem to like his version. He's never had a complaint, at any rate.

The place caters mostly to the traffic on U.S. 13. Formyduval opened his Eastern Shore restaurant in a former day-care center early in 1997 because there was no place for barbecue in the area. About 40 customers can be seated in the casual dining room.

You don't have to order barbecue, of course—though you'll probably want to. There's chicken, ribs, shrimp, fish, hamburgers and hot dogs. Everything comes with hush puppies and two vegetables. Fresh turnip greens are available in season.

You don't even have to eat you food here. Everything—including the chocolate cake and the caramel cake—can be packaged for takeout.

There's another Formy's south of the Chesapeake Bay Bridge-Tunnel in Virginia Beach.

Island House
Restaurant

WACHAPREAGUE

Island House
Restaurant

17 ATLANTIC AVENUE
WACHAPREAGUE, VA 23480
(757) 787-4242

Style	Casual nice
Meals	Lunch and dinner, seven days a week. The Island House is closed from Christmas to the end of January.
Price Range	Moderate
Superlatives	View, seafood, homemade desserts
Extras	Full bar

Wachapreague, dubbed "the Flounder Fishing Capital of the World," is the site of some serious fishing. There are spring and fall flounder tournaments, a ladies' tuna tournament and marlin tournaments. The town boasts four marinas, lots of charter fleets and about 200 permanent residents.

The Island House Restaurant overlooks the broad marshes between the Eastern Shore and the Atlantic Ocean. To find it, follow the signs from U.S. 13 onto Va. 180 into Wachapreague.

The first building on this site was a combination hotel and restaurant constructed in the early 1900s and washed away by a major storm in 1933. Z. R. Lewis and his son Randy built the first Island House in 1978. It was destroyed by fire 14 years later. Not to be deterred, the Lewises built another restaurant, this one modeled after the Parramore Island Lifesaving Station, complete down to the lookout tower. On the first floor are the main dining room and a banquet room. A dining room with expansive water views is on the second floor.

The Island House's crab cakes—"long a favorite of Jimmy Buffett," according to the menu—are delicious. Randy is a friend of the popular singer and cooks for him and his crew when they are within commuting distance.

The restaurant offers light fare (soups and salads), a raw bar, early-bird specials (chicken, tuna, shrimp and a crab cake platter), local seafood and combinations.

The desserts are homemade. I can testify that the cheesecake is absolutely wonderful.

Paradise Cove

MELFA
Paradise Cove
U.S. 13 / MELFA, VA 23410
(757) 789-9671

Style	Home-style
Meals	Breakfast, lunch and dinner, seven days a week
Price Range	Inexpensive/Moderate
Superlatives	Sausage gravy and biscuits
Extras	Full bar

*M*elfa was the last name of an official who supervised the construction of the railroad down the Eastern Shore. This area saw action during the War of 1812. On May 30, 1814, a British admiral landed at nearby Pungoteague Creek with about 500 marines and fought a battle with American militia; the British were forced to withdraw to Tangier Island. Today, world-renowned bronze sculptors William and David Turner have a gallery near Melfa.

When Jean and Nick Petrides arrived here from Long Island in 1992, they had no idea of buying a 50-year-old restaurant. They'd come to purchase a bed-and-breakfast advertised in a New York newspaper, but it had sold by the time they arrived. Jean and Nick decided to linger because the Eastern Shore reminded them of the Long Island of the early 1960s. But when their real-estate agent suggested they buy a restaurant, they initially said no way.

They obviously changed their minds, as they now work seven days a week at Paradise Cove. The dining rooms have a lived-in, utilitarian air. Nick's artwork hangs on the walls. A talented artist, he takes care of the lounge, which is separate from the restaurant. Jean cooks the Italian dishes. She's backed up in the kitchen by three local women who prepare the seafood and other things.

The regular customers love the sausage gravy and biscuits. Eggs, omelets and pancakes are also offered at breakfast.

At lunch, you can get soups, salads, sandwiches, burgers and platters.

Prime rib au jus is a popular choice at dinner, as are pork chops and the various seafood entrees. Chicken parmigiana, shrimp scampi and linguine with clam sauce are among Jean's Italian selections.

You can follow any of this with a piece of cheesecake, a piece of fruit pie or a slice of cake.

Tammy & Johnny's

Tammy & Johnny's

U.S. 13 / MELFA, VA 23410
(757) 787-1122

Style	Home-style
Meals	Lunch and dinner, seven days a week
Price Range	Inexpensive
Superlatives	Fried chicken

*I*n this land of fresh and abundant seafood, subtly crisp and succulent fried chicken is a good find. However, I didn't give Tammy & Johnny's a second look as I raced up U.S. 13 north of Melfa. The red brick and orange building on the western side of the road looks like the usual fast-food restaurant. But it turns out it's a locally owned landmark. On the word of more than one loyal patron, I decided to give it a try.

"It's fresh. People can trust our chicken," states John R. "Ronnie" Edward, who owns the restaurant with his wife, Shirley. "We use 100 percent cotton-seed oil and change it every day."

Ronnie and Shirley built the place in 1967 and have added onto it over the years. He's an Eastern Shore native who put in lots of years with a telephone company. Tammy and Johnny are their children. Actually, they're not children now. They're both 30-somethings who work at the family business, as do nearly two dozen other employees.

The chicken is wonderful, the flavor locked inside. The trick has to do with marinating it for 24 hours in a secret concoction and frying it for just the right time at just the right temperature—380 degrees. That's 30 degrees hotter than usual. How they do that without burning it is another family secret.

Tammy & Johnny's also offers shrimp, soft-shell crab sandwiches, burgers and french fries.

The restaurant's following is so strong that business thrives even when the Chesapeake Bay Bridge-Tunnel is out of commission. About 50 people can be seated in the immaculate dining room at booths and utilitarian fast-food tables. The takeout counter is almost always busy. And for fresh-air buffs, there are seven picnic tables under the shade of holly trees.

Armando's

10 NORTH STREET
ONANCOCK, VA 23417
(757) 787-8044

Style	Casual nice
Meals	Dinner, Tuesday through Sunday
Price Range	Inexpensive/Moderate
Superlatives	Artistic cuisine, specialty beverages
Extras	Full bar

*F*ounded in 1680, the picturesque village of Onancock covers just under one square mile. It is home to Hopkins and Brothers (one of the oldest general stores in the country), Kerr Place (a gorgeous brick building dating from 1799) and several lovely 19th-century homes.

Venturing into Armando's for the first time, your startled reaction might be, "Can I afford this?"

I'll answer with a slightly different question: "Can you afford to miss this?" Armando's is more than a unique dining experience. It's the work of an artist.

Armando's last name is Suarez, but on the menu, it's simply *Armando*, with a little heart for the *o*. The menu explains how this native of Argentina ventured to New York City in 1970 and dabbled in everything from hair styling to jewelry and leather design before ending up in the little town of Onancock. In 1988, he opened a gourmet pizza and croissant sandwich shop in an abandoned grocery store as part of Onancock's downtown revitalization. Fascinated with the design of the building, which dates from around 1940, he remodeled extensively, exposing old brick and preserving an old skylight. He converted the parking lot into a patio courtyard. Bored with just pizza and sandwiches, Armando expanded to a full menu of original creations in 1991.

The wide range of beverages served here — cappuccino, espresso, international coffees, special teas, imported beers, a fine array of wines — is unusual among Eastern Shore eateries.

The extensive menu makes pleasurable reading while you sip Perrier or Irish coffee and let Armando

Armando's

prepare your meal from scratch. The veal piccata, for example, is described as "an artistic expression of pure genius: scallop of veal gently sauteed with garlic and those incredible shiitake mushrooms in a velvet sauce of lemon, butter and citrus zest. What makes it so ingenious? The elegant simplicity of it all."

Shrimp Danielle, crab crepes and lobster ravioli are some of the entrees, along with a variety of chicken and veal dishes.

Armando says moving to this small town on the Eastern Shore is the best move he's ever made. The many diners who fill the place inside and out just might agree.

Market Street Inn

Market Street Inn

47 MARKET STREET
ONANCOCK, VA 23417
(757) 787-7626

Style	Home-style
Meals	Breakfast, lunch and dinner, Monday through Saturday
Price Range	Inexpensive/Moderate
Superlatives	Crab cakes
Extras	Wine and beer

*T*he menu at the Market Street Inn contains this lighthearted warning: "We do not tolerate whiners, so don't!"

Gordon and Tina Blalock moved from Richmond to Onancock because they liked the pace of living on the Eastern Shore and thought it would be a great place to raise a family. The Market Street Inn was the third restaurant in its downtown building when they bought it more than a dozen years ago.

The restaurant is pretty well hidden, so Gordon and Tina depend on local business, word of mouth and a little advertising. Local motels also send customers their way. One group of regulars consists of men, mostly retired, who gather in midmorning and midafternoon. They sit at their special table near the kitchen door under a mantle and an antique clock.

The large dining room is divided by a long planter with silk plants and hanging baskets. The decor is a combination of nautical and Early American.

At breakfast, you'll find such things as pigs in a blanket and "Apple Shenandoah Pancakes" with whipped cream.

Lunch features big salads, burgers and sandwiches.

At dinner, there are salads, a few sandwiches, several seafood entrees, some beef entrees and lemon pepper chicken.

As is the case with most small businesses, the employees must wear many hats here. The daytime dishwasher, Marie Bothers, also makes most of the desserts. She's great at both. The dishes are squeaky clean, and the desserts can be pronounced wonderful. My delicious, lighter-than-air chocolate mousse almost levitated from the plate. And the blueberry pie comes warm with a crust that effortlessly surrenders at the touch of a fork.

Flounder's
U.S. 13 / TASLEY, VA 23441
(757) 787-2233

Style	Casual nice
Meals	Lunch and dinner, Tuesday through Saturday. Reservations are recommended.
Price Range	Moderate
Superlatives	Homemade desserts
Extras	Wine and beer

On the Eastern Shore, with Chesapeake Bay to the west and the Atlantic Ocean to the east, all the seafood is as fresh as the dawn. You can discover that for yourself at Flounder's, a cozy cottage on the side of the road near the tiny town of Tasley.

The restaurant is just off the eastern side of U.S. 13 north of Va. 650, but it can be hard to spot among a cluster of dilapidated buildings that used to be antique shops. Once a two-room tenant's shack, Flounder's was moved from a nearby plantation with its original windows and pine floors intact. The brick part—which includes the kitchen and the fireplace—was added later.

"I was pretty well born with a knife in my hand," said waterman Darryl Hurley, whom I found filleting flounder, trout, drum and rockfish out back of the restaurant just before 30 guests were to arrive for dinner.

Darryl's wife, Linda, is in charge. Her mother, Virginia, makes all the desserts. Both ladies share the cooking responsibilities with chef Greg Lewis. Son Darryl, though just of elementary-school age, knows his way around the herb garden.

They named the restaurant Flounder's because it's close to Wachapreague, which is billed as "the Flounder Fishing Capital of the World." It's quaint and cozy, to say the least. The main dining room has only four tables. Another room has two tables. Down a brick path lined with herb and flower beds is a deck with umbrella tables.

It's all very sweet, and the seafood just doesn't get any fresher.

The Owl Motel and Restaurant
U.S. 13 / PARKSLEY, VA 23421
(757) 665-5191

Style	Home-style
Meals	Breakfast, lunch and dinner, seven days a week
Price Range	Inexpensive
Superlatives	"Chocolate Rum Pie"
Extras	Wine and beer

Though Parksley qualifies as a small town, it's not as small as some in the area. It has around 40 businesses and several hundred residents. Parksley came into being as a railroad town in 1885. Today, it's the location of the Eastern Shore Railway Museum and several well-preserved Victorian homes with turrets, expansive porches and gingerbread trim.

Back in 1937, when the late John Roach, Sr., built

a country store and service station in Parksley, and during World War II, when he constructed 10 tourist cabins, and in 1947, when he opened a small restaurant, lots of owls lived in the pine woods along the highway.

Today, the woods behind this motel and restaurant may still be home to a few owls. But owls are more plentiful inside the motel office, gift shop and restaurant. There are carvings and pictures of owls. Owls peer from shelves, counters, clocks and lamps. They look out from behind doors. A framed piece of needlework hanging on one wall poses the question, "Whooo wouldn't enjoy a meal at The Owl?"

The Owl is a monument to the early days of automobile travel. The old white cabins still stand. A traditional white-block motel building was later constructed closer to the highway.

The focal point inside the restaurant, where local civic groups often meet, is a big brick fireplace you could crawl into. The fireplace has a raised hearth. A giant brass kettle hangs inside it.

John Roach, Jr., and his wife, Donna, are carrying on the family business. They use only fresh local produce and specialize in home-baked breads and desserts. In 1997, when the restaurant celebrated its 50th anniversary, John and Donna rolled back prices to their 1947 levels. Coffee sold for a nickel, for example. By today's standards, The Owl's regular prices are still modest.

The menu changes frequently. You might find a fried shrimp special, surf and turf, fried chicken, country ham and crab cakes.

Many of the dessert recipes were developed by John's mother. Donna, too, is a natural dessert chef— her parents own a bakery in Onancock. The homemade desserts include "Virginia Peanut Pie," "Lemon Angel Pie," cherry cobbler, bread pudding and the very good, very popular "Chocolate Rum Pie."

Wright's Seafood Restaurant and Crab Galley

ATLANTIC

Wright's Seafood Restaurant and Crab Galley

WRIGHT ROAD / ATLANTIC, VA 23303
(757) 824-4012

Style	Casual nice
Meals	Dinner, seven days a week from Memorial Day to Labor Day
Price Range	Moderate/Expensive
Superlatives	Water view, stuffed flounder, seafood platters
Extras	Full bar

The small town of Atlantic is located a few miles south of Chincoteague Island on the ocean side of U.S. 13, the main highway down the Eastern Shore. Most of the farmers in this rural area raise chickens, so you'll see quite a few chicken houses.

In fact, what is now Wright's Seafood Restaurant and Crab Galley started as a sandwich shop in an old poultry-processing plant. That was nearly three decades ago, when the place had two tables. Now, it has two kitchens, three dining rooms that can seat a total of 350 patrons and a banquet room that extends over the water on pilings.

The only things that haven't changed are the panoramic view and the location. From U.S. 13, take Va. 175 toward Chincoteague, then turn south on Atlantic Road. After about half a mile, turn left on Wright Road (Va. 766), which is a winding road flanked by fields. Suddenly, you'll come upon a long, low building with yellow vinyl siding. You're here.

Like most of the restaurants profiled in this book, Wright's—where the owners claim that "everything is always just right"—is a family business. Carol and Lewis Wright and their daughter Theresa McCready manage the daily operations. Lewis runs one kitchen and Theresa is in charge of the other.

In the "Crab Galley" dining area, neatness doesn't count. In another room, white tablecloths and napkins lend a semiformal air. In yet another room, you'll find old Liberty ship hatch covers embedded with sand, shells and starfish, a fascination for children and adults alike.

The menu served in the "Crab Galley" features à la carte items and several all-you-can-eat choices. The main menu has more than two dozen fresh seafood entrees, along with prime rib, steaks, baby back ribs, chicken and pork chops.

If you're a thirsty traveler, you'll particularly appreciate Wright's iced tea, which will be delivered to your table in a carafe. It's great for those in need of instant refills.

Garden and the Sea Inn

4188 NELSON ROAD
NEW CHURCH, VA 23415
(757) 824-0672

Style	Fine dining
Meals	Dinner, Thursday through Sunday from March through Thanksgiving. Dinner is also served one other weeknight by reservation only; call for information. Reservations are recommended for Saturday dining.
Price Range	Expensive
Superlatives	Shrimp, scallops, oysters
Extras	Wine and beer

New Church is the first community south of the Maryland state line. It was established in the early 1700s when the Reverend Francis Makemie organized the institution that gave the town its name—a new church.

The Garden and the Sea Inn is an oasis of country tranquility just a block west of busy U.S. 13. While

Garden and the Sea Inn

coats and ties are not required, one feels compelled to dress up a little—a shirt with a collar, at least.

The inn and restaurant, located in a Victorian gingerbread house of coral, green and beige, has been owned by Tom and Sara Baker since 1994. Tom trained at the Culinary Institute of America and has worked at some of the finest restaurants in Virginia. Sara runs the inn, which includes six guest rooms between the main house and another building on the landscaped property.

Gourmet meals are served either in the main dining room, on the enclosed porch or under umbrellas on the garden patio.

The menu changes all the time. One fixed-price dinner offered recently included entrees of smoked mountain trout and breast of chicken with orange marmalade and almonds. Another recent fixed-price dinner combined chilled cucumber soup, a salad of lettuce, apple slices, pecans and poppy seed dressing and an entree of grilled boneless lamb rib-eye. A la carte items are also offered.

Guests come from far and wide to savor Tom Baker's culinary art with or without fine wine—and with or without a tie.

CHINCOTEAGUE

AJ's on the Creek

6585 MADDOX BOULEVARD
CHINCOTEAGUE, VA 23336
(757) 336-5888

Style	Casual nice
Meals	Lunch and dinner, Monday through Saturday
Price Range	Moderate/Expensive
Superlatives	Chowder, fresh seafood, steaks
Extras	Full bar

Chincoteague Island measures seven miles by one and a half miles. Although the first white man arrived here in the 1670s, the 1800 census reported a population of only 60. The little town of Chincoteague was the first in Virginia to have a public school; the superintendent was paid $50 per year in the early days. Today, Chincoteague is noted for its fresh fish, its craftsmen and its wild ponies. Each year, ponies from neighboring Assateague Island are brought here to be auctioned. The pony swim takes place in July.

Commercialism has left its mark on Chincoteague. The island is awash with places for tourists and an-

AJ's

glers to dine. But ask Eastern Shore locals where they go, and most will say AJ's.

The main dining room seats around 100. It's light, bright and airy—upscale yet relaxed. Colorful prints and carvings of egrets, herons and shorebirds accent the room.

Sisters Lisa and April Stillson bought the place in 1985 when it was a fast-food joint called McDuffy's. They named it for their other partner, Anthony John Stillson, who also happens to be their father.

April is in charge of the kitchen. She taught herself to cook by watching cooking shows on television, and the results are remarkable.

At lunch, you can get seafood chowder, burgers, sandwiches, clam strips and platters. The crab cake sandwich and the fried shrimp basket are excellent.

Two of the popular appetizers at dinner are fried artichoke hearts and "Texas Toothpicks." The raw bar menu includes clams, oysters and salmon. The house specialties are the catch of the day and flounder smothered in seafood. April's seafood lasagna, crab Alfredo and mussels marinara give the local sea bounty an Italian touch. Several pasta dishes and several veal dishes—veal and shrimp, veal Marsala, veal piccata, veal Oscar—are offered, as are steaks, lamb chops and surf and turf.

"We were young and foolish," says Lisa of the sisters' decision to buy the restaurant when they were in their mid-20s. But they've done well. Perhaps their personal-service motto—"Every customer is the most important one"—has had something to do with their success.

CHINCOTEAGUE

Chincoteague Inn
100 MAIN STREET / CHINCOTEAGUE, VA 23336
(757) 336-6110

Style	Casual nice
Meals	Lunch and dinner, seven days a week from March through October
Price Range	Moderate/Expensive
Superlatives	View, outdoor bar
Extras	Full bar

*T*he Chincoteague Inn, overlooking Chincoteague Channel, is just what you'd expect of a vintage waterfront restaurant on an island that's a mecca for fishermen. It's very salty (in the nautical sense) and very, very casual.

The inn has weathered cedar siding and a weathered wraparound deck with an anchor chain for the

Chincoteague Inn

prime rib au jus as "supreme." His seafood specialty is the "Bay Platter," which combines baked fish fillet, baked scallops and shrimp on a stick. And some patrons will tell you that the inn's crab imperial is the very best of all.

Pony Pines

railing. From the open-air bar, you can watch a fleet of charter fishing boats. Old Key West and Ernest Hemingway—and maybe Jimmy Buffett—spring to mind. Part of the building is around 100 years old. One of the first commercial structures on the island, it started as a dock before a small restaurant was added.

Paul and Jane Tatum have owned it now for around 20 years. Even though the Tatums reduced the size of the dock by adding the outdoor bar, fishermen still bring their catch to sell to the inn. Inside the restaurant, the atmosphere ranges from the salty to the delightful. The lounge is dark, and the main dining room is as bright as all outdoors.

The entrees run the gamut from scallops, crab cakes, oysters, flounder and lobster to seafood Florentine, lobster tail with Delmonico steak and soft-shell crabs fixed a number of ways. The Chincoteague Inn is most definitely a seafood place. What else would you expect here? Still, chef Walt Van Hart, Sr., ranks his

CHINCOTEAGUE

Pony Pines

7305 EASTSIDE DRIVE
CHINCOTEAGUE, VA 23336
(757) 336-9746

Style	Home-style
Meals	Lunch and dinner, seven days a week
Price Range	Inexpensive/Moderate
Superlatives	History, "Fisherman's Delight"
Extras	Full bar

"*A* Chincoteague landmark since 1930" boasts the menu for Pony Pines. The restaurant and lounge overlook Assateague Channel and Assateague Island. According to local folks, this is one of the places visitors should go on the island.

The building sits in a grove of pine trees across the channel from where the ponies live. It started as a small bar and has grown into a restaurant that can seat about 170 patrons in two dining rooms. The Judge family has been operating it for more than three decades.

Both of the pleasant dining rooms have rather typical seaside decor. Large windows face the street and the water beyond. The dimly lit lounge offers big-screen television and nightly entertainment.

On the day I visited, the waitress arrived at my table with a small, round loaf of wonderful, warm bread with a buttery crust. I then made my selection from the soups, salads, burgers and sandwiches on the lunch menu. The "Chincoteague Bay Chicken Sandwich" comes with crabmeat.

Dinner features a salad bar, a wide choice of seafood selections and the broiled "Fisherman's Delight"—a bountiful combination of flounder stuffed with crab imperial, shrimp stuffed with crab imperial, crab cakes, scallops and clams.

If you're one to seek out local landmarks, don't miss Pony Pines.

Index of Towns

Index of Restaurants